Managing for Accountability

Preserving the Public Trust
in Public and Nonprofit
Organizations

Kevin P. Kearns

Jossey-Bass Publishers • San Francisco

Substantial discounts on bulk quantities of Jossey-Bass books are available to corporations, professional associations, and other organizations. For details and discount information, contact the special sales department at Jossey-Bass Inc., Publishers (415) 433–1740; Fax (800) 605–2665.

For sales outside the United States, please contact your local Simon & Schuster International Office.

The set of questions in Chapter Six guiding decision makers at the final phase of strategy development is adapted with permission from Bryson, J. M. *Strategic Planning for Public and Nonprofit Organizations: A Guide to Strengthening and Sustaining Organizational Achievement*. San Francisco: Jossey-Bass, 1988, p. 173.

 Manufactured in the United States of America on Lyons Falls Pathfinder Tradebook. This paper is acid-free and 100 percent totally chlorine-free.

Library of Congress Cataloging-in-Publication Data

Kearns, Kevin P., date.
    Managing for accountability : preserving the public trust in public and nonprofit organizations / Kevin P. Kearns.
       p. cm.—(Jossey-Bass public administration series) (Jossey-Bass nonprofit sector series)
    Includes bibliographical references (p.) and index.
    ISBN 0-7879-0228-4
    1. Public administration. 2. Nonprofit organizations—Management. 3. Strategic planning. 4. Public interest. 5. Responsibility. I. Title. II. Series. III. Series: Jossey-Bass nonprofit sector series.
JF1411.K39 1996
350—dc20
                                          95-53710

FIRST EDITION
HB Printing   10 9 8 7 6 5 4 3 2 1

A joint publication in
The Jossey-Bass
Nonprofit Sector Series and
The Jossey-Bass
Public Administration Series

Contents

To Lorna, Maura, and Ned
with love and gratitude

Preface

The headlines in newspapers and magazines around the country are easy to find and impossible to ignore:

Leader Used N.A.A.C.P. Money to Settle Sex Harassment Case
—*New York Times,* July 29, 1994

This story described an out-of-court agreement in which the executive director of the N.A.A.C.P. allegedly committed himself and the organization to a financial settlement with a former employee. Several board members said they were outraged and that they had no knowledge of the case or the settlement.

Animal Charity in the Doghouse
—*Chronicle of Philanthropy,* March 8, 1994

Here, critics said the American Society for the Prevention of Cruelty to Animals (ASPCA) strayed from its mission and is not getting maximum benefit from its $20 million in annual revenues. Specific concerns focused on the self-elected board, overtime pay for staff, and construction and design flaws in the ASPCA's new headquarters building.

West Virginia Town Caught in Its Own Speed Trap
—*Pittsburgh Post-Gazette,* February 20, 1994

The paper reported that thousands of traffic tickets were written by police officers in the tiny town of Osage, West Virginia, but no one knows where the money went. The state police investigated but the city's records and its governing body were in disarray.

The first of these cases was a major controversy involving a nonprofit organization that captured national headlines and widespread public attention, fueling debates about the credibility of the non-profit sector. The second case also involved a nonprofit organization, but with far less of the high-level corporate intrigue and human drama that major newspapers find so appealing. And the third case was a municipal government scandal, hardly noticed beyond the confines of a tiny mining town nestled in the mountains of West Virginia.

But, while these three cases differ in context and scale, they have one very important thing in common: they all involve fundamental questions of *accountability*. Did the organization, its employees, and its leaders fulfill their obligation to serve the public interest and preserve the public trust? Who should be held accountable for these transgressions? What exactly were the obligations and responsibilities of the people involved in these cases? To whom and for what were they accountable?

Beneath these and countless other headlines there is a story of intense public scrutiny of governmental and nonprofit organizations and growing concerns about citizen confidence in these institutions. In some cases, naturally, it is a story of greed, arrogance, and careless neglect (if not willful violation) of laws, regulations, or administrative procedures. In other instances, it is a story of insufficient oversight by the organization's governing body, whether composed of elected government officials or volunteer members of a nonprofit board of directors. Oftentimes, however, it is a story of otherwise competent, honest, and well-intentioned professionals who suddenly found themselves or their organizations in the glaring light of public scrutiny. Not because they broke a law. Not because they violated implicit ethical norms or moral imperatives. But rather because they were asked, quite literally, to account for their own or their organization's actions. Citizens are asking: "Did you perform in accordance with your implied contract with us as expressed in your mandate, your mission, and your espoused values?" Often this question is asked not by citizens themselves but by their elected representatives, by investigative reporters, or by the growing number of watchdog groups who have taken it upon themselves to monitor the activities and services of government and nonprofit organizations.

While major scandals and controversies capture headlines, the day-to-day process of serving the public trust quietly and consistently takes place in thousands of government and nonprofit agencies across the country as they manage finances, serve clients, and monitor outcomes. This book can be a resource for governmental and nonprofit organizations in serving the public interest and preserving the public trust. The central argument of the book is that accountability must be seen as a strategic resource as well as a legal and moral imperative.

Purpose

No one who believes in the inherent value of public service enjoys watching elected officials, career bureaucrats, or nonprofit executives come under fire in the popular media. And only a hopeless cynic (or perhaps a sadist) would take perverse pleasure in seeing the credibility and morale of a once-proud organization wither in the face of an accountability controversy or scandal. It is especially disturbing, even tragic, when the people involved in these controversies are not evil, arrogant, or corrupt. And it is puzzling when an organization that is managed strategically and effectively in all other respects somehow loses sight of its mandate and core mission—to preserve the public trust.

Perhaps there was a time, long ago, when citizens, the news media, and even oversight agencies would accept the idealism and good intentions of public servants as a measure of their accountability. If ever there was such a time, it is long past. Today, the people who work in government and nonprofit organizations cannot say: "Leave us alone. We are well-intentioned people doing thankless work under difficult circumstances." Now they must open their doors, literally and figuratively, to public scrutiny.

Evidence abounds of an urgent credibility crisis in government and nonprofit organizations (Estes, Binney, and Bergthold, 1989). There is anecdotal evidence contained in headlines like the ones quoted earlier that appear with increasing frequency. There are opinion polls and scholarly studies showing that people have become more cynical toward and distrustful of their public institutions (Kanter and Mirvis, 1989). And there seems to be a vigorous market for books exposing the abuses of governmental and nonprofit organizations.

Simply stated, citizens are fed up with all kinds of institutions, and their wrath is not directed solely at public servants. They are angry about a health care system that does not meet their needs, despite having the most advanced technology and the most skilled professionals in the world. They distrust industrial organizations that they perceive as profit-maximizing behemoths. Since the turbulent sixties, they have vigorously criticized the policies and management practices of government agencies at federal, state, and local levels. And, more recently, they have questioned the credibility of the nonprofit sector—perhaps the last bastion of public service idealism.

We can wring our hands and bemoan the unfairness of it all, but this is not likely to be very helpful—except, perhaps, as a therapeutic catharsis. We can continue to respond with damage control or crisis management approaches to accountability controversies as they arise, but this is like closing the barn door after the horse has escaped. Finally, and most desirably, we can adopt a strategic management approach to accountability, driven by reasoned strategies and tactics designed to respond proactively as well as reactively to the increasingly stringent expectations of our constituents.

This book is designed to help public and nonprofit organizations keep the notion of accountability at the forefront of their strategic planning and management systems.

Need

Books on accountability in public and nonprofit organizations fall into several broad categories. There are books addressed to specific but relatively narrow aspects of accountability such as financial management, internal control, program monitoring and evaluation, and compliance with legal and regulatory standards (Anthony, 1988; Bookman, 1992; Gross, 1991; Hopkins, 1992, 1993). Also, there are books that propose elegant theories and concepts of accountability from the perspective of moral philosophy, applied ethics, and political theory (Burke, 1986; Cooper, 1990; Bowman, 1991; Gortner, 1991; Thompson, 1987). Finally, there are books that take a confrontational approach by exposing the sins of certain organizations alleged to have violated the public trust (Bennett, 1989; Sennot, 1992; Gaul and Borowski, 1993b; Glaser, 1993).

This book is based on pragmatic principles rather than passionate ideology. Certainly, I have passion for the ideals of accountability in public institutions, but my primary objective is to offer constructive advice rather than inspirational exhortations or elegant theories. My experience in government and nonprofit organizations tells me that they are staffed, for the most part, by competent people who themselves are committed to the ideals of accountability. Therefore a book that merely extols the virtues of accountability, while inspirational for some, leaves most saying, "Yes, of course, but *how?*"

Thus this book fills the need for a pragmatic approach to the topic of accountability that is also broad and flexible enough to be applied in many different types of organizations. This is accomplished by linking the notion of accountability to the methods of strategic management.

Scope and Treatment

Strategic management has deep roots in military planning and has long been used in the corporate sector to increase profitability, market share, and technological competitiveness. In the past two decades, the strategic approach has found its way into public and nonprofit organizations as a way to enhance cost-effectiveness and service quality.

In this book, I take some generic strategic management templates and apply them to the topic of accountability. For example, rather than scanning competitive environments (in the strategic management jargon) for a broad array of threats and opportunities, this book introduces the notion of an *accountability environment* that contains specific types of strategic threats and opportunities for public service organizations. But this approach is more than just an exercise in manipulating terms by bending them to fit the topic of accountability. Rather, it leads to a fundamentally new conceptual framework for defining accountability, clarifying issues and choices, and developing strategies and tactics.

In the process, we will see that managing the accountability environment in these turbulent times involves much more than merely complying with legal and regulatory mandates, which itself is no small task. Rather, being accountable sometimes involves negotiating with and appropriately responding to the demands of clients, special interest groups, and other powerful stakeholders. Other times, accountability is defined in terms of discretionary judgments, calculated risks, and entrepreneurial ventures. Finally, accountability is sometimes defined in terms of administrative advocacy, when government and nonprofit professionals must interpret and communicate the needs of citizens to higher authorities who have the power and resources to meet those needs.

For the most part, I have intentionally refrained from offering specific procedural recommendations or management philosophies for enhancing accountability. For example, I have tried to avoid making strong normative statements, pro or con, about specific financial management and control systems or any other discreet mechanism that might be considered an accountability instrument or tool. This is not a cookbook of easy-to-follow recipes guaranteed to keep you out of court or out of the headlines. Still, while this is not a cookbook, it is road map of sorts—it presents a conceptual framework and a corresponding set of strategic management methods that decision makers can use to interpret their accountability environments and to assess the strengths and vulnerabilities of their organizations.

The reader will quickly notice that the general approach of the book is to pose probing questions, not to offer universal solutions or quick fixes. My own view, which is shared by many others (for example, Mintzberg, 1994a, 1994b), is that strategic planning systems are most valuable when they help decision makers ask the right questions about their organizations and the world around them. I know of no strategic planning or management framework that is actually capable of developing and implementing strategies. Only decision makers and managers can do that.

The approach presented here can be directly applied by leaders and managers who want to incorporate the notion of accountability into their strategic management systems. Certainly it is fair to ask: *Why should a busy manager, elected official, or nonprofit board member take the time to read this book?*

First, I have tried very hard, with the encouragement and able assistance of my editors, to cut through the academic terminology and theories with an approach that is reasonably straightforward, practical, and logically organized in a sequence of recommended steps. Naturally, the book draws heavily upon the extensive literature and research on this topic. But I have tried to boil this down to the essence needed by managers and leaders to make the difficult choices confronting them, and I have refrained from lengthy reviews and theoretical critiques of the literature.

Second, I have tried to strike a middle ground in terms of the preexisting knowledge the reader will need to understand and use the methods presented here. For example, the reader who has substantial experience with strategic management methods will immediately feel comfortable with the philosophy and concepts presented here; those who have somewhat less experience will find a helpful overview of strategic management in Chapter Three. Also, the Special Resource Section presents a step-by-step summary of the major components of the approach in the form of worksheets designed to be used by managers, employees, and governing boards.

Third, I have incorporated examples and cases that are timely and interesting without being overwhelming in scope or complexity. Naturally, some of these deal with accountability crises like those that have occurred in the executive suites of the United Way of America, the Foundation for New Era Philanthropy, and Orange County, California. Others, however, describe the admirable efforts of large and small organizations to enhance their accountability to the public trust.

Finally, the book presents approaches and techniques that are applicable in organizations with diverse missions and varying levels of resources and expertise. These include the vast array of government jurisdictions and agencies at the federal, state, and local level. In the private nonprofit sector, I am primarily addressing professionals and board members in organizations that serve a public purpose. Salamon (1992, p. 13) refers to these as "public serving" nonprofits to distinguish them from "member serving" organizations such as recreational and social clubs. The book will be useful to organizations that have encountered and struggled through an accountability controversy or crisis. Others will find it useful as a tool for maintaining or enhancing their outstanding record of performance in serving the public trust.

Audience

While practitioners are a primary audience, the book also is addressed to students and scholars interested in public and nonprofit management. Indeed, I hesitate to classify students as a secondary audience because I believe so strongly that future professionals need to be well versed in these issues and prepared for the accountability environments that await them as they launch their professional careers.

Toward this end, the book may be used as a primary or supplemental textbook in university courses on public and nonprofit management, strategic planning, governance, professional ethics, and other related topics. It will be especially useful for students and faculty who need an instructional aid that takes a practical approach to the topic of accountability, perhaps as a complement to theoretical readings and exercises.

University instructors may be especially interested to know that I developed the conceptual framework presented in Chapter Four for use in a capstone seminar on accountability that I taught several years ago. My students responded enthusiastically to the framework, and their responses have been so positive that I was inspired to do additional work on this framework—refining it in relation to existing literature, testing and applying it as a diagnostic tool for actual accountability controversies, and sharing it with top-level executives from whom I have received valuable feedback and advice.

Overview of the Contents

Part One, consisting of the first two chapters, presents the accountability environment facing public and nonprofit organizations. Here, I examine some of the historic and contemporary trends that have contributed to the current climate of intense public scrutiny and challenge. It is an environment in which public and nonprofit organizations are judged by more rigorous, and sometimes subjective, standards of behavior and performance. Traditional definitions of accountability are too narrow and restrictive to be useful in this dynamic environment. A strategic approach to accountability is needed to respond effectively to the challenges and opportunities in this environment.

Part Two, consisting of Chapters Three through Six, presents tools for managing accountability. Based on principles of strategic management, I present a template that can be used to scan the accountability environment for specific types of challenges and opportunities. I also suggest a way to assess the organization's strengths and weaknesses with respect to maintaining its account-ability. The development of accountability strategies cannot take place in a vacuum. Nor should these strategies reflect only regula-tory or legal mandates. Rather, they should seek to improve the fit between the organization and its multifaceted and dynamic accountability environment.

Part Three, consisting of the last three chapters, illustrates tac-tical and strategic approaches to accountability challenges. The emphasis is on relating theory to practice with illustrations and case histories. The book concludes with a discussion of the role leaders should play in creating an organizational environment in which accountability becomes a strategic priority, as well as a legal and moral imperative.

The Special Resource Section provides a distilled summary of the key questions decision makers should ask about their account-ability environment and their organization's strengths and liabilities.

Thus, there is a flow to the topics presented in this book. It starts by interpreting the accountability environment of public and nonprofit organizations. It then turns to a set of tools and methods for diagnosing accountability issues. Finally, it explores ways to build accountability into organizational strategies, routines, and cultures.

The challenge of managing public and nonprofit organizations has never been greater. The expectations and needs of the general public are increasing while resources are shrinking, or at best hold-ing constant. In this dynamic environment, accountability—once defined primarily in legalistic terms—has evolved to include a wide range of performance standards for serving the public trust. With advances in information technology, lapses of accountability are reported practically in real time. And private nonprofit organiza-tions are being subjected to the same type of scrutiny once reserved for government organizations.

It would, of course, be a statement of supreme arrogance to suggest that this book had all the answers to these challenges. I do hope, however, that this book poses some of the questions that public and nonprofit professionals will find useful in devising their own strategies and tactics for enhancing the accountability of their organizations.

Pittsburgh, Pennsylvania   KEVIN P. KEARNS
October 1995

Acknowledgments

It is a rare and exhilarating experience when a professor's teaching activities and research agenda dovetail directly. The seeds of this project were sown in a graduate seminar on nonprofit accountability I taught at the University of Pittsburgh Graduate School of Public and International Affairs in 1993. As I prepared for one of the class sessions, I found myself searching for a conceptual framework that could convey to my students the various dimensions and meanings of accountability, especially in relation to strategic management. What resulted from that exercise was a primitive version of the framework presented in Chapter Four of this book.

My students, in typical fashion, responded with constructive comments and questions that helped me refine the framework. Thus I am deeply indebted to the students in that seminar for their encouragement, support, and substantive assistance: Elizabeth Barak, Bethany Blakey, H. Edward Born, Amy Butcher, David Coplan, Kati Csoman, Catherine DeLoughry, Thistle Elias, Ann Fraser, Karol Gilchrist, David Ginn, Samuel Gunde, Carol Henry, Pamela Johnson, David Lam, Cynthia Leeson, Kauchik Mukerjee, Mindee Reuben, Molly Shor, Mark Smith, Jody Stein, Renee Vogt, and William Wasielewski.

Other students too numerous to mention have shown patience and encouragement as I developed and shared these ideas with them. I am especially grateful to my teaching assistants, Paula Bilinsky and Susan Wade, who provided valued support, logistically and intellectually, in the completion of this project. Expert clerical support was provided by my associates Sheila Kelly and Mary Ann Gebet.

I owe an intellectual debt to Barbara Romzek and Melvin Dubnick. In 1987, they published an extraordinary article in *Public Administration Review,* in which they developed an integrating framework for accountability and applied it as a diagnostic tool to explain events leading up to the tragic explosion of the space shuttle *Challenger* in 1986. I read that article when it first appeared and then again in preparation for the seminar mentioned above. Their discussion of how an organization can drift away from its comparative advantages was the inspiration for my own reflections on the linkage between accountability and strategic management. While the framework I propose here differs from theirs, it is influenced by their seminal work.

Developmental work on the ideas presented here appeared in a 1994 article I wrote for *Public Administration Review*. I am grateful for the encouragement of editors David Rosenbloom and, again, Melvin Dubnick as well as the constructive advice of the anonymous reviewers of that paper. Also, the case of the Orange County bankruptcy (an abbreviated version of Chapter Seven in this book) first appeared in a 1995 paper I published in *Public Budgeting and Finance*. Editors Irene Rubin and Richard Zody responded enthusiastically to that paper. Also, I thank the anonymous reviewers of that paper for their thoughtful suggestions. Several colleagues at the University of Pittsburgh, especially Davis Bobrow, Lawrence Howard, John Mendeloff, Guy Peters, Mark Peterson, and Iris Young provided extremely useful feedback on these papers.

I want to extend special thanks to several people who have graciously provided forums where I could share and test these ideas with governing boards, top-level executives, and middle managers in public and nonprofit organizations. Harry Faulk and Debora Corsini at Carnegie Mellon University have for many years invited me to make presentations to the Senior Executive Seminar, the Nonprofit Institute, and the College Management Program. These have been invaluable experiences that have had profound impact on my thinking, my teaching, and my research activities. In addition, Dr. Faulk was a mentor in the early years of my career and, by his example, continues to exert a strong influence on my philosophy and my work.

I am also grateful to Ginger Tippie, who has invited me on several occasions to share my work at conferences sponsored by the American Association of Homes and Services for the Aging.

Near the end of this project I was invited by Dennis Young and Kenneth Kovach to participate in a think tank program for nonprofit leaders at the Mandel Center for Nonprofit Organizations,

Case Western Reserve University. This program, attended by twenty executive directors of major nonprofit associations, focused exclusively on the topic of accountability. I was enormously impressed by the quality of the dialogue among these executives. Their views and feedback influenced the final editing and preparation of this book. I am especially grateful for the comments offered by Connie Rivera, chief operating officer of the Alzheimer's Disease and Related Disorders Association; Paul Wood, president of the National Council on Alcoholism and Drug Dependence; and William Varnell, president and chief executive officer of the Visiting Nurse Associations of America.

Professor Anthony Cahill, my friend and colleague at the University of Southern Maine, provided not only useful feedback on some of the ideas presented here, but also invited me to share them at the 1995 conference of the National Association of Schools of Public Affairs and Administration. This conference focused on curriculum assessment and design with special reference to improving the linkage between professional public administrators and citizens. It was a very informative experience and I am grateful for the opportunity to have participated.

I want to thank the United Way of Allegheny County, especially chief professional officer William Meyer and vice presidents Victor Papale and Scott Frost, for giving me the opportunity to participate in their efforts to enhance the accountability of their member agencies and the United Way itself. This organization has invested an enormous amount of time, energy, and expertise in the development of a very rigorous process for program evaluations and management reviews among United Way agencies in Allegheny County. Their devotion to the ideals of accountability and their willingness to commit resources to this effort has been an inspiration for my own work. They have taught me a great deal about this topic.

Pamela Meadowcroft, director of research at Pressley Ridge Schools, provided most of the information used for the case study presented in Chapter Eight. Her personal and professional commitment to accountability and outcome measurement is extraordinary. I am most appreciative of the many hours she invested in helping me to prepare that case.

I also want to thank the entire staff at Jossey-Bass. I especially appreciate the efforts of senior editor Alan Shrader, assistant editor

Susan Williams, and production editor Xenia Lisanevich, all of whom provided invaluable assistance and substantive advice throughout this project. These are professionals who know their craft very well indeed. It has been a pleasure and a privilege to work with them.

I was particularly impressed by the work of the three anonymous reviewers of the draft manuscript. I have learned over and over again that the process of anonymous peer review is, itself, a remarkably effective accountability mechanism. In this case, the three reviewers approached their assignment with diligence, insight, and expertise. While the reader must ultimately judge the quality of this final document, I can say unequivocally that it is a far better product than the draft manuscript that was sent to the reviewers.

I owe a special debt of gratitude to Professor Davis Bobrow at the Graduate School of Public and International Affairs, University of Pittsburgh. When he was dean at that school, he offered me the opportunity to leave the central administration of the University, at least temporarily, and return to the classroom and the laboratory of public management research. His offer came at a critical juncture in my career—when I would either become more deeply ensconced in university administration or design for myself a new itinerary of teaching, research, and curriculum development. I will always be grateful for his faith in my abilities and for his encouragement every step of the way. Also, I am grateful to interim dean Martin Staniland for his encouragement and flexibility in releasing me from some of my own administrative duties while I put the finishing touches on the book. It has been a pleasure and an honor to serve as his associate dean.

Several friends and associates deserve special mention. Bernard (Ray) Meehan supplied me with a steady stream of news clippings and showed constant interest in this project. Tony O'Connor, William Coles, Robert Foster, Michael Marks, Jack Bucsko, William Kelman, and George Snyder have introduced me to dimensions of personal accountability that cannot be found in any textbook. My parents, Bernard and Dolores Kearns, and my five siblings, Tom, Jerry, Molly, Kathy, and Denny have through the years provided a strong network of support and love.

And finally, Lorna Kearns and our two young children, Maura Helene and Edward Callery, provide everything that is truly important in my life. Lorna has been unwavering in her love and support. My life has been immeasurably enriched by her companionship. As Maura begins to explore the world around her, she provides us with a constant source of joy and wonderment. I love her more than I can say. Our son, Ned, was born shortly after I began this project, and in a very literal way he and this book began to take shape simultaneously. His 4:00 A.M. feedings became a catalyst for early morning writing and editing sessions, and I only hope the reader cannot detect which chapters were written in those wee hours. Words simply cannot convey my gratitude for having these three wonderful people at the very center of my life.

Despite the assistance of everyone mentioned here, I remain solely responsible for any errors or omissions in the final product.

—K.P.K.

The Author

KEVIN P. KEARNS is associate professor and associate dean in the Graduate School of Public and International Affairs, University of Pittsburgh. He is also director of the certificate program in nonprofit management at that school. Kearns received a B.S. degree (1977) from the University of Dayton. He received his M.P.A. degree (1980) in public administration and his Ph.D. degree (1985) in public policy research and analysis, both from the University of Pittsburgh.

Kearns has held numerous positions of academic management and leadership, including: director of research, Intergovernmental Cooperation Project, Allegheny Conference on Community Development; director of executive programs, H. John Heinz III School of Public Policy and Management, Carnegie Mellon University; assistant dean for strategic planning, Graduate School of Public and International Affairs, University of Pittsburgh; and assistant to the president, University of Pittsburgh.

His research on strategic management has focused on adoption and diffusion of innovations among municipal governments; identification and clarification of strategic issues in nonprofit organizations; applications of total quality management in nonprofit organizations; identifying attributes of effective board members in nonprofit organizations; and, most recently, accountability in government and nonprofit organizations. He has published articles in leading journals such as *Public Administration Review, Public Budgeting and Finance, Nonprofit Management and Leadership, Knowledge and Policy,* and *Knowledge: Creation, Diffusion, Utilization.* He is coauthor, with Thomas Saaty, of *Analytical Planning: The Organization of Systems* (1985).

Kearns teaches courses on strategic management, nonprofit management, public administration, and administrative theory. He has won many awards for the quality of his teaching, including the

Teacher of the Year award in the Graduate School of Public and International Affairs in 1993 and 1995 and the dean's commendation for outstanding teaching on seven occasions. He has conducted more than one hundred seminars for top-level executives in government and nonprofit organizations. He has also lectured and provided curriculum development consulting at Hasanuddin University, Indonesia.

Kearns serves on the boards of several nonprofit organizations in the Pittsburgh area and is extensively involved with many others as a volunteer adviser and strategic planning consultant. Also, he has served on the boards of two private corporations.

Managing for Accountability

The Accountability Environment of Public and Nonprofit Organizations

Part One of this book examines the concept of accountability from several different perspectives.

Chapter One discusses how accountability has been interpreted in the public and nonprofit sectors respectively. There are important differences in terms of historical precedents and evolutionary meanings. For example, government employees and elected officials are accustomed to living under public scrutiny. Nonprofits, on the other hand, have (until recently) lived a relatively charmed existence in an unregulated environment. Simply stated, most citizens do not know very much about nonprofit organizations. But as one accountability crisis after another spills across the headlines, citizens and oversight agencies have turned a critical eye toward the nonprofit sector as well. Thus, both government and nonprofit organizations face similar challenges in the current environment.

After presenting several brief cases, Chapter Two reviews some formal definitions of accountability in public and nonprofit organizations. The traditional and somewhat narrow definition of accountability contains several components: a higher authority in a formal chain of command; an explicit mandate and performance criterion; and, a clearly defined mechanism for reporting (literally accounting for) the actions and performance of organizations or individuals. But often these precise conditions do not exist. Still, public and nonprofit organizations are asked to account for their behavior to a host of external stakeholders (clients, advocacy groups, the media) whose formal authority may be questionable. Also, performance criteria used by these stakeholders often are vague, idiosyncratic, and constantly in flux. Thus, Chapter Two concludes with a strategic definition of accountability that is more fluid but also more pragmatic than the narrow traditional definitions.

Chapter One

Accountability Concepts and Controversies

Historical Precedents and Contemporary Trends

Government officials, whether elected or appointed, are accustomed to living in a fishbowl. Their formal training for government service (often in schools of public administration, law, or political science) introduces them to the theory of accountability. Then they get on-the-job training by working with a vast number of oversight agencies in the intergovernmental chain of command and, more generally, by being continuously exposed to public scrutiny and criticism.

Those who work in the private nonprofit sector, on the other hand, have been relatively free of governmental oversight and, until recently, largely insulated from public scrutiny. Now, in the wake of several high-profile scandals, nonprofit professionals and trustees are being held to more exacting standards of accountability, professionalism, and performance.

In both the public and nonprofit sectors, trends toward customer satisfaction, quality management, and cost-effectiveness are having profound impacts on how accountability is defined and measured.

This chapter opens with a brief discussion of a recent controversy in the nonprofit sector, the bankruptcy of the Foundation for New Era Philanthropy. This case illustrates the related but technically distinct concepts of accountability, professional ethics, responsibility, and obligation. While I will not belabor these distinctions in the remainder of the book, it is appropriate to comment upon them at the outset.

We then turn to a comparison of the public and nonprofit sectors and how the concept of accountability has evolved and been interpreted by professionals and the general public. While there are important differences between government and nonprofit organizations, both face similar challenges today.

This chapter focuses on historical and contemporary trends and sets the stage for exploring formal definitions of accountability in Chapter Two.

Foundation For New Era Philanthropy

On May 15, 1995, the nonprofit world and the financial markets were rocked by news that the Foundation for New Era Philanthropy had sought protection under Chapter 11 of the U.S. bankruptcy code. Several hundred nonprofit organizations and highly respected philanthropists had invested millions of dollars in New Era's fund based on promises by its founder and chief executive, John G. Bennett, Jr. He said a group of anonymous donors who had contracted with New Era to find worthy charities for them to support on the condition that their names not be divulged would provide matching funds. Interest earnings on funds held would pay New Era's operating expenses.

Investigators allege, however, that New Era's investment pool was an elaborate ruse, a variant of the so-called Ponzi (or pyramid) scheme in which the invested principal of some participants is used to pay enormous dividends for a few others, thereby attracting more and more investors to the bait. In such a scheme, dividend payments are made just frequently enough to maintain the credibility of the ploy, but it unravels and eventually collapses of its own weight when additional investors cannot be found to support the continuous payout of larger and larger dividends.

In this case, the collapse was swift and shocking. On Thursday, May 11, Prudential Securities filed suit against New Era and Bennett for $44.9 million in unpaid loans. On Tuesday, May 16, the *Wall Street Journal* ran a story questioning the viability of the New Era fund, reporting that Bennett had informed his staff that the anonymous donors did not exist. (Stecklow, 1995). Later that same day, New Era filed for protection under Chapter 11 of the U.S. bankruptcy code (*Chronicle of Philanthropy*, 1995). On May 17, the Commonwealth Court of Pennsylvania froze New Era's assets, and the next day the Securities and Exchange Commission sued New Era and Bennett for fraud. Finally, on May 19, the U.S. Bankruptcy Court ordered New Era to liquidate all assets and to settle with creditors under Chapter 7 of the bankruptcy code.

The New Era scandal was stunning and indeed almost incomprehensible in its own right. But in broader perspective, it added fuel to a firestorm of controversy about accountability in the entire nonprofit sector. The timing for this particular debacle could not have been worse for the credibility of nonprofit organizations in the eyes of the public. It came on the heels of the conviction of William Aramony, former president of the United Way of America, and amid growing sentiment in Congress and in state legislatures to get tough on nonprofit organizations with more rigorous regulatory constraints, oversight mechanisms, and enforcement procedures. A survey commissioned by the *Chronicle of Philanthropy* suggested, not surprisingly, that the New Era scandal has damaged the credibility of the entire nonprofit sector among wealthy philanthropists (Moore, Rocque, and Williams, 1995).

To whom were Bennett, his staff, and the trustees of New Era formally accountable? What were the accountability standards or expectations in this case and how were these standards enforced? Beyond compliance with the letter of the law, what were Bennett's professional obligations and responsibilities?

These questions extend beyond Bennett's activities. What about the investors in the fund? To whom were they accountable and what were their professional obligations and responsibilities as investors? In hindsight, it seems remarkable that they would accept Bennett's claim about the existence of anonymous donors. Did they not have an obligation and responsibility, on behalf of their constituents, to exercise due diligence in the investment of institutional assets? Should they not have pressed Bennett for full and complete disclosure of the fund's structure before entrusting their assets to his care? How could these well-established institutions and respected individuals have been duped by such a transparent scheme? Several investors reported afterward that they were swayed by Bennett's track record and credibility in the philanthropic community, his modest lifestyle, and his genuine passion for the ideals of the institutions he recruited into the scheme. He displayed none of the external trappings of a huckster and he seemed deeply committed to helping investors achieve their charitable goals (Stecklow, 1995). Still, we must ask the question: Do accountability and credibility ultimately boil down to subjective impressions, hunches, and a gut feeling about someone's character and performance?

Finally, we need to ask some questions about the accountability infrastructure in this case—the legal and regulatory framework within which the Foundation for New Era Philanthropy operated. Was this infrastructure sufficient to provide proper oversight in this case? Who was charged with monitoring New Era's activities? What level of oversight was provided by the trustees of New Era? Did they exercise their fiduciary responsibilities and their obligations in stewardship of the organization's mission, policies, and the assets of investors? What are the limits on their responsibilities?

And what about the responsibilities and obligations of government oversight agencies? In the span of only four years (1989–1993), contributions to the New Era fund skyrocketed from $306,000 to over $41 million (Moore, Rocque, and Williams, 1995). Should such rapid and dramatic growth have raised some red flags in the Internal Revenue Service (IRS) long before Prudential Securities filed the suit that eventually brought New Era down? The Pennsylvania Attorney General said that his office received many inquiries from nonprofit groups regarding the legitimacy of the New Era matching funds program in the two years preceding the debacle. On each occasion, New Era complied by providing information that was responsive to the request (Williams, 1995).

Some Important Distinctions

Is the New Era scandal a case of institutional and personal accountability? Of course it is. But there are many pure theoreticians who would be inclined to split hairs in this case by arguing that it is only partially a case of accountability in the strict and formal definition of that term. Rather, they might argue persuasively that the most important issues in this case deal with problems of professional responsibility, obligation, and ethics. These issues clearly are related to the concept of accountability, but are technically distinct notions.

While I will not dwell on these fine-tuned distinctions, I acknowledge that they can help us sort through the maze of issues embedded in the New Era scandal and, as we move ahead toward later chapters, we should know that scholars have appropriately drawn some important distinctions among these terms and concepts.

Accountability, Responsibility, and Obligation

In its most narrow interpretation, *accountability* involves answering to a higher authority in the bureaucratic or interorganizational chain of command. This formal definition of accountability draws a very clear distinction between two fundamental questions: *To whom (in the hierarchical chain of command) are public and nonprofit organizations accountable?* and *For what (activities and performance standards) are these organizations responsible?*

Strictly speaking, only the first question pertains to accountability per se. It deals primarily with mechanisms of supervision, oversight, and reporting to a higher authority in a hierarchical chain of command. Therefore, in a formal and somewhat narrow sense, Bennett, like any nonprofit executive, was primarily accountable to his board of trustees in the supervisory chain of command. The trustees, in turn, were accountable to those who invested in the fund. Also, both Bennett and the trustees were formally accountable to the higher authority represented by regulators in the IRS, the Pennsylvania Attorney General's Office, and other oversight agencies such as the Securities and Exchange Commission.

Thus a very clear issue of accountability might be whether the trustees of the Foundation for New Era Philanthropy implemented appropriately rigorous reporting procedures or a system of internal checks and balances to ensure that Bennett did not operate with complete autonomy and secrecy. Another issue related to the strict definition of accountability is whether New Era filed accurate, truthful, and timely reports with the IRS regarding the mission, finances, and operating structure of the fund. Did New Era literally account for the policies and activities of the fund as required by law? Apparently the IRS was satisfied with New Era's reports and, as noted above, the Pennsylvania Attorney General's office found Bennett and his staff to be responsive to their earlier requests for information and documentation. We must then ask whether the IRS compliance reports and other accountability mechanisms themselves were sufficiently rigorous to bring the alleged irregularities to the surface or whether the oversight agencies had sufficient resources and expertise to ask the right questions and carefully pursue the answers.

It has been said that we cannot legislate morality, and the New Era scandal may be a case in point. Someone who is intelligent and determined can generally find a way around even the most rigorous regulatory framework and enforcement mechanisms. Thus, this book does not make detailed proposals for or endorsements of new and more rigorous regulatory initiatives. Clearly, regulations and oversight are an important component. But this book approaches the topic of accountability at the level of organizational planning, arguing that it must be fully incorporated into the strategic planning of public and nonprofit institutions.

The technical questions regarding chains of command, reporting, and compliance are only part of the story. True, they are important and revealing in their own right, but they do not touch on some of the deeper issues related to the concept of accountability—issues that exist outside the formal bureaucratic infrastructure.

Questions of professional responsibility and obligation open a Pandora's box of issues related to, but technically distinct from, the concept of accountability per se. Here we enter the murky domain of performance criteria and public expectations that are not necessarily monitored through a formal chain of accountability. Should the investors in the New Era fund have taken responsibility for ensuring that the anonymous donors did indeed exist before entrusting their funds to New Era's care? How could they have received these assurances as long as there is an accepted practice in philanthropic circles of ensuring anonymity for donors who request it? If this practice is deemed to be a threat to accountability, who should take responsibility for changing it? Where do obligation and responsibility rest?

Cooper (1990, pp. 59–61) addresses this question by making a distinction between the notions of accountability and obligation. He says that *accountability* is responsibility (and answerability) *to* someone—a superior, an oversight agency, and so on. *Obligation*, on the other hand, is responsibility *for* something—a specified level of performance or an intangible objective like "the public interest."

He notes that within any hierarchical system, there is an ordered relationship among the key actors and stakeholders. Thus, in terms of accountability, public and nonprofit professionals are responsible first to their superiors in the administrative chain of command; second to superiors (elected officials or volunteer trustees) in the governance chain of command; and finally to citizens in the democratic chain of command. But in terms of obligation for serving the public interest and preserving the public trust, Cooper says that the hierarchy of responsibility is in the reverse order of priority: first to citizens or beneficiaries; second to superiors (elected officials or volunteer trustees) in the governance structure; and finally to superiors in the administrative chain of command.

Thus, the notions of accountability, responsibility, and obligation are technically distinct and generally are treated as such in the scholarly literature. This book embraces a broader conception of accountability—one that is perhaps messier than the precise operational definitions, but probably more consistent with the popular usage of the term. In this popular view, accountability includes much more than just the formal processes and channels for reporting to a higher authority. Instead, the term accountability generally refers to a wide spectrum of public expectations dealing with organizational performance, responsiveness, and even morality of government and nonprofit organizations. These expectations often include implicit performance criteria—related to obligations and responsibilities—that are subjectively interpreted and sometimes even contradictory. And in this broader conception of accountability, the range of people and institutions to whom public and nonprofit organizations must account includes not only higher authorities in the institutional chain of command but also the general public, the news media, peer agencies, donors, and many other stakeholders.

As a member of the scholarly community, I have some misgivings about blurring formal distinctions between terms like accountability and obligation that have been so carefully articulated by my colleagues. But as a pragmatist, I sense that the broader conception of accountability is more meaningful to professionals, trustees, elected officials, and others who wrestle with these problems on a daily basis. Thus, with apologies to the purists, I will use the term accountability throughout this book to refer to the broader notions described here.

Accountability and Ethics

The terms *accountability* and *ethics* often are used interchangeably when, in fact, they too are not synonymous. True, both concepts involve the means by which an organization or an individual chooses a course of action and subsequently defends it. Also, both accountability and ethics are related to the concepts of obligation and responsibility discussed earlier.

But ethics is primarily concerned with the responsibility—personal or organizational—for making decisions according to an accepted (or defensible) moral code for distinguishing right from wrong. Accountability, on the other hand, involves the responsibility to answer to a higher authority for whom ethical standards (if they are considered at all) may be only one of many performance criteria. Indeed, it is easy to find examples of intricate accountability systems for perpetuating inherently unethical, immoral, or unjust systems (see Lorentzen, 1990). Nazi Germany, for example, had a sophisticated and rigorously enforced system of internal accountability—as demonstrated vividly at the Nuremberg trials, where many defendants testified that they were simply "following orders." Some people involved in the Watergate scandal used a similar excuse.

There is a hierarchy of ethics, each level with its own set of responsibilities and moral standards (Madsen and Shafritz, 1992, p. 12–13; Rubin, 1990). First, there is *personal morality,* in which an individual's core values shape perceptions of right and wrong. Refusal to serve in the military for religious reasons is an example of personal morality. Second, the notion of *professional ethics* dictates that decisions be made according to standards promulgated and enforced by a given profession. Codes of ethics for various professional associations are a prime example. Next, there is *organizational ethics,* resulting from the formal rules and informal norms that shape the behavior and ethical reasoning of organization members. An organizational policy prohibiting conflicts of interest among staff members is an example of organizational ethics. Finally, there is the domain of *social ethics,* in which members are obliged to behave in certain ways to advance the general welfare of the group. Many of our social norms are expressed in the U.S. Constitution, especially the Bill of Rights.

Clearly, an important part of accountability in preserving the public trust is that government and nonprofit officials will make ethical choices in accordance with personal, professional, organizational, and societal norms. Therefore, being able to defend or account for one's actions according to some ethical framework can be an important part of being accountable at both the personal and the institutional level.

If it is true that Bennett intentionally deceived investors regarding the existence of the anonymous donors, then it is hard to imagine a circumstance in which he could defend (account for) his actions according to any ethical code of conduct. In fact, some people might argue that it is pointless to discuss the questions of technical or procedural accountability in this case—all those questions fade in the face of Bennett's clear violation of organizational, professional, and societal norms of ethical behavior.

Assumptions of the Strategic Approach to Accountability

The strategic approach to accountability presented in this book is based on several important assumptions:

- Accountability, in essence, is the obligation of public and nonprofit organizations to serve a higher authority—the public trust—which is the ultimate source of their mandate, their authority, and their legitimacy.
- While the standards of accountability often are formally codified in laws and regulations, they also are defined by implicit expectations of taxpayers, clients, donors, and other stakeholders.
- Whether the standards of accountability are explicit or implicit, they are dynamic components of any organization's strategic environment.
- Like all other components of the environment, the standards of accountability should be continuously monitored and incorporated into the organization's strategic management process.

The remainder of this chapter explores how the notion of accountability evolved in government and nonprofit organizations respectively. In general, the government perspective on accountability is driven by legal and bureaucratic mechanisms. The nonprofit sector has historically operated in a more loosely regulated and less bureaucratic environment, where accountability has been interpreted in terms of market forces.

Accountability in Government

The general notion of accountability is deeply embedded in the history, traditions, and professional ethos of government service. The accountability environment in government includes explicit political philosophies that constrain government officials in an elaborate system of bureaucratic oversight, a strong academic tradition of research and debate on the theory and practice of accountability, and a professional value system among public administrators and elected officials that is at least relatively congruent. Let us examine each of these components before comparing them with the nonprofit sector, which presents a very different picture.

Explicit Political and Legal Philosophies

To their credit—and our benefit—the Founding Fathers were quite concerned about the notion of accountability and took great pains to ensure that it was one of the philosophical pillars of the young nation. In *Federalist Paper No. 57,* James Madison wrote, "The aim of every political constitution is . . . first to obtain for rulers men who possess most wisdom to discern, and most virtue to pursue, the common good of the society; and in the next place, to take the most effectual precautions for keeping them virtuous whilst they continue to hold their public trust."

According to Madison, a constitution provides the ultimate accountability blueprint for government officials. State constitutions and county and municipal charters also are important tools for ensuring that government officials answer to a higher authority. Many books focus exclusively on the constitutional and legal foundations of public administration (for example, Rosenbloom, 1971; Barry and Whitcomb, 1981; Rosenbloom and Carroll, 1990; Rohr, 1986, 1989), and it is well beyond the scope of this one to provide a comprehensive review. But several key principles demonstrate how deeply rooted the notion of accountability is within the philosophical foundations of our democracy:

- *Republic:* A form of government in which citizens elect, and hold accountable, those who will represent them in political decision making.
- *Supremacy Clause:* A portion of Article VI of the U.S. Constitution asserting that it is the supreme law of the land with precedence over state laws. Thus, the laws of states and localities must ultimately pass muster with the U.S. Constitution in the chain of accountability.
- *Separation of Powers:* The delegation of authority and the assignment of responsibilities among the executive, legislative, and judicial branches of government ensuring that each is held accountable for certain tasks.
- *Checks and Balances:* The allocation of authority among the three branches so that they are a check upon each other, precluding arbitrary or unilateral power by any one of them, and ensuring an accountability sphere among all three.
- *Judicial Review:* The power of the courts to review executive decisions, legislative acts, or the decisions of lower courts to confirm or invalidate them according to constitutional principles.
- *Sunshine Rules and Laws:* Requirements that the general public be notified and allowed to observe many formal business meetings of government agencies and legislative bodies, ensuring opportunity for public oversight and direct accountability.
- *Sunset Laws:* Riders attached to selected legislative initiatives that specify termination dates for certain governmental programs or agencies conditioned on formal evaluations of outcomes and impacts.
- *Referendum:* A procedure in some states and localities for submitting proposed laws, constitutional amendments, and special initiatives like capital projects to the electorate for direct approval.
- *Recall:* A procedure that allows voters to hold elected officials directly accountable for abuse of public trust by voting them out of office between regularly scheduled elections.
- *Freedom of Information:* A federal law enacted in 1966 giving the public access to many types of information held by government agencies. Comparable legislation exists in states and localities.

These are more than abstract philosophical notions. They reflect some of the core values and operating principles on which the nation was founded and subsequently evolved. Every one of these principles was devised to hold government officials accountable to a higher authority through some means of oversight. There is no parallel set of philosophies governing accountability in the private nonprofit sector with anything near the pervasiveness and power of these principles.

Tradition of Scholarly Debate

There is a vast literature in the field of government administration that interprets the notion of serving the public trust with all of its practical and theoretical ramifications. As noted, the *Federalist Papers* provided a philosophical blueprint for the nation, with many recommendations for holding government officials accountable to the public trust. Even the modern scholarly literature on accountability has an extensive track record, dating back to the writings of Woodrow Wilson ([1887] 1987), Leonard White (1926), Max Weber ([1922] 1987), and others. These people laid the intellectual foundation for a professional government bureaucracy, insulated from the political arena, free of patronage and nepotism, and guided by explicit values and standards of accountability.

This literature has seen fierce debates, such as the seminal exchange between Carl Friedrich (1940) and Herman Finer (1941) on whether government accountability is best ensured via external controls (regulations and oversight) or internal controls (professionalism and self-policing). Fifty-five years later, the Friedrich-Finer exchange still stimulates heated arguments in the scholarly community on instruments of administrative control, the concept of representative bureaucracy, and the tension between administrative discretion and accountability (Burke, 1986; Kingsley, 1944; Krislov and Rosenbloom, 1981; Smith, 1971; Staats, 1982; Gruber, 1987). Also, there have been intense debates on Woodrow Wilson's idealized notion of separating politics from administration. Today, most informed observers of government recognize that it is impossible (and not necessarily desirable) to completely insulate appointed officials from the surrounding political environment. Consequently, government managers must be sensitive to issues of both political accountability and administrative accountability.

Strong Professional Ethos

Beyond constitutional principles and scholarly debates, the field of public administration is influenced, at least intellectually, by a professional value system or ethos of accountability. This value system is nurtured and reinforced in academic training grounds for government professionals. Courses on administrative law, professional ethics, political institutions and processes, and intergovernmental relations typically are integral components of academic programs that are springboards for government careers. Even before they take their first job, many aspiring government professionals have become socialized to the general notion of accountability in public service. They understand the constraints on administrative discretion. They know they will be working under the watchful eye of the media. And they understand the intergovernmental maze of oversight agencies and regulations designed to ensure accountability in government bureaucracies. Even if government professionals do not have the opportunity to learn these lessons in school, they are confronted by them very early in their service and throughout their careers (see, for example, Allison, 1988).

Thus, from the day they receive their academic credentials to the day they retire, professionals in government are continuously exposed to the notion that serving the public trust is a cornerstone of their profession. Naturally, for some it is a more compelling principle than for others. And certainly there is ample evidence that the bureaucracy can be easily twisted and manipulated to ensure secrecy and self-protection. But, for all its warts, the bureaucratic framework that characterizes many government institutions still provides a relatively high level of openness and accessibility, especially in comparison with the private nonprofit sector.

Accountability in the Nonprofit Sector

At a recent faculty meeting, one of my colleagues quipped that the life of a graduate student consists of long periods of dreadful boredom punctuated by brief moments of sheer terror. This humorous (and remarkably accurate) observation also describes the history of the nonprofit sector in terms of public scrutiny and government oversight.

Popular interest in the private nonprofit sector has been cyclical, if not sporadic. Years and even decades of relative disinterest or benign neglect of the nonprofit sector have been interrupted by periods of intense public scrutiny and criticism, typically following a highly publicized incident like the New Era scandal that thrust the nonprofit sector into the public eye.

A notable recent controversy involved the national office of the United Way of America and its former president, William Aramony. In 1992, national attention focused on Aramony's $460,000 compensation package and his appropriation of United Way funds for travel and living expenses, and on the appearance of inadequate oversight by the board of trustees (Glaser, 1993). In April 1995, Aramony was convicted of multiple felony counts including fraud, money laundering, and filing false tax returns.

The United Way incident, the Covenant House scandal (Sennot, 1992), and the case of television evangelist Jim Bakker all contained three things that people find irresistibly titillating—money, power, and sex. They were prime targets for extensive coverage on television and in newspapers and tabloids around the country. They also provided the catalyst for a string of books intended by their authors to expose abuses in the private nonprofit sector. *Free Ride: The Tax-Exempt Economy* (Gaul and Borowski, 1993a) is a frontal attack on the very foundation of nonprofit sector. Based on the authors' earlier series of articles in the *Philadelphia Inquirer* (Gaul and Borowski, 1993b), the book describes the proliferation of tax-exempt organizations, alleged abuses by selected organizations, and the inability of the IRS to effectively monitor and regulate the sector. *Unhealthy Charities* (Bennett and DiLorenzo, 1994) focuses on three of the largest health charities in the world—the American Cancer Society, the American Heart Association, and the American Lung Association. The book is critical of the program priorities of these organizations.

Also, there are many scholarly works that have challenged the underlying rationale of tax exemptions for certain types of nonprofit organizations such as hospitals (for example, Herzlinger and Krasker, 1987).

Simmering Controversies in a Laissez-Faire Environment

Dramatic controversies—and the books that follow them—might explain, in part, the current epidemic of accountability fever in the private nonprofit sector. But it would be a mistake to conclude that widespread public concern about nonprofit accountability is a recent or merely temporary phenomenon. In fact, a kind of simmering controversy over the appropriate role of the nonprofit sector and how it should be regulated has existed for more than two hundred years—ever since the emergence of charitable organizations in the United States (for example, see Hall, 1987a, 1987b; Bremner, 1994).

The broad legal parameters governing modern nonprofit organizations can be found as early as the sixteenth century, in the portions of English common law related to charitable trusts. The general stipulations were that the trust should be organized solely to carry out its charitable purposes, that the assets of the trust should be kept productive, and that trustees were prohibited from making improper investments or engaging in self-dealing for personal gain (Fremont-Smith, 1989, p. 76). Today we see these broad principles embodied in the ever-growing, and increasingly sophisticated, register of federal and state laws governing nonprofit organizations.

But the current legal and regulatory framework took many years to evolve. The formal concept of a private charitable corporation was not even firmly established under federal law until the mid 1800s (Hall, 1987a, pp. 4–8), and it was not until the twentieth century that the legal and regulatory environment of nonprofit organizations began to grow in complexity and sophistication. Even today, accountability in the nonprofit sector has been defined almost entirely in terms of fiduciary responsibility, with the IRS as the primary national enforcement mechanism. Thus, the federal tax laws have been the primary mechanism for regulating the nonprofit sector at the national level (Fremont-Smith, 1989; Scrivner, 1990).

There continues to be wide variation among the fifty states regarding their efforts to hold nonprofit organizations accountable to the public trust (Simon, 1987). While most states require some form of registration and annual reporting, many do not have rigorous enforcement or oversight mechanisms.

Periodic Inquisitions

From time to time, there have been national reviews and investigations regarding accountability in the nonprofit sector. In recent years, the strongest advocate for tighter controls at the national level has been Representative J. J. Pickle of Texas. As former Chair of the Oversight Subcommittee of the House Ways and Means Committee, Pickle convened public hearings on several occasions to explore alleged abuses in the nonprofit sector. In 1987, his subcommittee heard testimony from small businesses alleging that exemptions from the federal income tax give certain nonprofit organizations (especially those engaged in commercial activities) an unfair competitive advantage in the commercial marketplace. In 1993–1994, the subcommittee undertook a much larger agenda including proposed limits on executive compensation, limiting the proliferation of nonprofit organizations, improving public access to reports filed annually with the IRS, and giving the IRS authority to issue graduated sanctions (short of revoking tax exemptions) to curb abuses. The subcommittee made recommendations on only some of these issues, primarily those involving public access to information and IRS enforcement powers. It is clear that the subcommittee's broader agenda was driven, at least in part, by media coverage of alleged abuses by certain organizations and several of the recent books that are highly critical of the nonprofit sector.

More recently, Congress has considered legislation to severely constrain the advocacy activities of nonprofit organizations, especially those that receive grants or contracts from the federal government. And incidents like the New Era scandal will no doubt provide additional ammunition to those who insist on much greater governmental oversight of nonprofit activities.

Weak Traditions of Scholarship

In comparison with the government sector, the literature on accountability in the private nonprofit sector is neither substantial nor sophisticated. True, there are many specialized textbooks on financial accountability in nonprofit organizations (Olenick and Olenick, 1991) and written materials dealing with the growing array of legal and regulatory mandates with which nonprofit organizations must comply in order to preserve their tax-exempt status (Bookman, 1992; Hopkins, 1992, 1993). But most general texts on nonprofit management and governance contain only brief and relatively narrow sections on the broader ideals of serving the public interest and preserving the public trust, and I know of no books dealing exclusively with this topic. Curiously, some of the most innovative insights on accountability in nonprofit organizations (for example, understanding and responding to the expectations of multiple constituencies) are embedded in the emerging literature on nonprofit marketing (Kotler, 1982; Espy, 1993).

No Consistent Professional Ethos

Another way to understand how accountability is interpreted in the nonprofit sector is to examine the academic credentials needed to enter the world of nonprofit management. In comparison with government, these credentials are extraordinarily diverse. Therefore, they offer no common reference point or professional ethos on the notion of accountability. Private human service agencies are staffed largely by people trained in social work or clinical specialties. Cultural organizations often are managed by artists or historians. Nonprofit health care organizations sometimes are led by doctors or public health professionals. Educational and research institutions are managed by people representing a plethora of academic disciplines, sometimes with predictable results! Finally, many small nonprofits are founded and subsequently managed by people who have no formal training whatsoever. They bring the valuable attributes of passion and idealism to their work, but they may have very narrow perspectives on their accountability either in the legal sense or in the broader sense of preserving the public trust.

Trustees and others who donate their services to nonprofit organizations bring an even more diverse set of credentials. While many are professionals from the world of business or government, some are simply concerned citizens who represent the special interests of particular client or advocacy groups. Some observers have suggested that even the professionals leave their business sense and their understanding of accountability behind when they assume volunteer positions on nonprofit governing boards (Chait and Taylor, 1989; Dayton, 1987; Herzlinger, 1994).

A small number of universities now offer specialized programs of study in nonprofit management. But these programs tend to focus on building generic skills such as fundraising, financial management, and working with boards of trustees. Most of them do not contain specific courses on the broader context of accountability or social responsibility in nonprofit management. Moreover, the emergence of these specialized programs of study is a recent phenomenon, and they have not yet matured to the point of having a shared perspective on the notion of accountability or consistency in their pedagogical strategies for conveying this notion to students.

Thus, in summary, the general notion of accountability has not been as pervasive in the nonprofit sector as it has been in government. This is not to say that nonprofit professionals and volunteers are unaware of or insensitive to their obligation to preserve the public trust. Rather, the people who work and volunteer in the nonprofit sector, unlike their counterparts in government, do not have a shared value system or even a common vocabulary with which to engage in a sectorwide, intellectually coherent dialogue on the notion of accountability. In the absence of a shared value system, many nonprofit professionals and volunteers are first exposed to the principles and instruments of accountability after they begin their service. Unfortunately for some, their first exposure comes as a result of a particular controversy or accountability crisis in their organization.

Public Perceptions of Government and Nonprofit Organizations

In the United States, the nonprofit sector emerged and subsequently evolved in an environment characterized by ambiguous legal frameworks, regional idiosyncracies, and ad hoc accommodation between government and charities. This stands in sharp contrast with our government institutions, which were founded upon relatively explicit and widely endorsed principles of accountability. In effect, the nonprofit sector has been allowed to evolve and grow according to a free-market philosophy, not unlike the competitive environment in which business organizations exist (see, for example, Steinberg, 1987). Thus the notion of accountability in the nonprofit sector has, until recently, been largely defined by the market rather than by any overarching regulatory framework.

Public Perceptions of Government

Most citizens know at least the rudimentary principles of our governmental system, and many actually know quite a bit about the foundations of our democracy as well as the administrative operations of government. Indeed, on or about April 15 of every year, most taxpayers suddenly become experts on government administration and public finance.

On a daily basis, most of us are direct beneficiaries of some government service. We travel on roads built and maintained by the government. Municipal employees or contractors collect our garbage. We send our children to public schools. A government corporation delivers our mail. When we are not satisfied with these services, we generally can find someone (if we are patient and persistent) with whom to lodge our complaint.

Also, we enjoy the privilege of voting for our representatives in government, and ultimately we have the option of voting with our feet by moving to another locality that might offer lower taxes, better services, or a more attractive business climate. In some states and municipalities, we can actually propose laws to change things when we are not satisfied. Finally, we may attend public meetings to observe the deliberations of our elected and appointed representatives.

Public Perceptions of Nonprofit Organizations

For a variety of reasons, nonprofit organizations are a mystery to the general public. First, the nonprofit sector is vast in size and diversity. The Internal Revenue Code contains nearly thirty categories of tax-exempt organizations, ranging from the familiar (religious, charitable, and educational organizations) to the arcane (cemetery companies). Few people understand how deeply their lives are affected by the nonprofit organizations they encounter on a daily basis. Perhaps they think the nonprofit sector is dominated by charities to serve the poor. They forget that the nonprofit sector includes the Girl Scouts, the Boy Scouts, the YMCA, many hospitals and universities, industrial development corporations, public television and radio stations, and even the National Football League.

Second, the revenues of nonprofit organizations (typically some mixture of philanthropic donations, fees for service, and contracts and grants) are complicated and not terribly interesting to the average person. Few citizens fully understand how their tax dollars subsidize, either directly or indirectly, the activities of nonprofit organizations. Even fewer understand that nonprofits are legally permitted to generate profits, form subsidiary corporations, and engage in other commercial activities. And fewer still have even a cursory understanding of the type of fiscal pressures that are forcing more and more nonprofit organizations to diversify their revenues through entrepreneurial strategies like commercial enterprises, subsidiary corporations, and more aggressive investment strategies.

Third, the governance structures of nonprofit organizations more closely resemble those found in business than those in government. Trustees of nonprofit organizations rarely are in the public spotlight. They do not run for election, their meetings are not necessarily open to the public, and few citizens understand how they obtain their positions of public trust.

In sum, most average citizens do not feel the same kind of ownership of the nonprofit sector that they feel toward government agencies. On a day-to-day basis, the nonprofit sector is relatively invisible to the general public. This is both a blessing and a curse for the people who work and volunteer in nonprofits. On the one hand, the relative invisibility of these organizations can insulate them from the distraction and drain of dealing with public inquiries. On the other hand, widespread misunderstanding of the nonprofit sector can lead to pseudocontroversies in which nonprofits are forced to defend actions that are entirely legal and appropriate.

Some New Notions of Accountability

The discussion thus far has demonstrated that there are important differences in the accountability environments of government and the nonprofit sector. In both sectors, however, accountability can be a moving target that can frustrate even the most committed professionals and volunteers.

Customer Service

Managing for greater accountability is made more challenging by recent thinking in management theory that suggests that public serving organizations need to be "reinvented" (Osborne and Gaebler, 1992) or "reengineered" (Hammer and Champy, 1993) to better serve the needs of customers. Customer service has emerged as a dominant theme in business management, and this theme is rapidly spreading to government and nonprofit organizations as well.

The publication in 1992 of *Reinventing Government* by Osborne and Gaebler sent shock waves through bureaucratic and political circles. The book became a best-seller, provided some of the political rhetoric of the 1992 Presidential campaign, and was an intellectual blueprint for Vice President Al Gore's *From Red Tape to Results* (1993), which recommended actions to improve the effectiveness and efficiency of the federal government.

Osborne and Gaebler believe that government organizations must be liberated from the stranglehold of regulations, bureaucratic procedures, line-item budgets, and risk-averse organizational cultures if they are to be more entrepreneurial and customer focused. They argue persuasively and with many examples that bureaucracy is the ultimate obstacle to improving government responsiveness and performance. Among their many recommendations are that management systems in government should be less rule driven and more mission focused. Public officials, they argue, should be given more discretion and authority to develop entrepreneurial programs and strategies for government agencies to earn money rather than simply spend money. Essentially, they say that governments can and should adapt business management principles to the public sector context to more effectively meet the needs of citizens, taxpayers, and future generations.

Intellectually, these are very attractive and exciting themes. In practice, however, they require fundamental shifts in the accountability environment of government agencies at the federal, state, and local levels (Terry, 1993; Moe, 1994). Osborne and Gaebler claim that their management philosophy does not supplant the traditional notion of accountability, but rather redefines it by freeing public officials to manage more strategically in response to rapidly changing conditions and emerging public needs. In effect, the Osborne and Gaebler philosophy calls for broader standards of accountability based on professionalism, expertise, responsiveness to changing needs, and empowerment of citizens to play a larger and more meaningful role in public affairs.

The bureaucratic structures and red tape, which Osborne and Gaebler denounce, do indeed inhibit the flexibility and entrepreneurship of government agencies. But, for better or worse, they also are the primary instruments of public accountability designed to prevent abuse of power and to limit the autonomy of public officials (Goodsell, 1985). Government officials cannot consult with citizens on every decision they make, so we have historically relied on these bureaucratic mechanisms to constrain administrative discretion and abuse of power. For example, regulations on government procurement are loaded with red tape that often significantly inflates the cost of goods and services used by the government. But the flip side is that many of these regulations are designed to ensure that government officials exercise their purchasing authority with detached professionalism, thereby guaranteeing fairness and equity in the treatment of government contractors.

Eliminating this red tape and the larger bureaucratic framework that produces it will require the development of new instruments of accountability. Osborne and Gaebler do not offer a detailed explanation of what these new instruments of accountability might look like. But they suggest that a new framework of accountability must include mechanisms to empower citizens to play a more meaningful role in setting government goals and measuring progress toward their achievement. Obviously, this demands a much deeper commitment on the part of public officials to educate citizens, to identify their customers, and to answer for their actions under more fluid and ambiguous conditions.

I believe that the Osborne and Gaebler thesis raises important questions about the role of accountability in an entrepreneurial paradigm of public management. The case of the Orange County investment fund, which declared bankruptcy in December 1994, illustrates some of the pitfalls of an entrepreneurial management philosophy. The Orange County case is discussed in Chapter Seven.

States and localities also are being held to higher standards of accountability, reflecting the general principles of customer service and quality management (National Commission on State and Local Public Service, 1993). Consider, for example, the following exchange of viewpoints reported recently in the *Pittsburgh Post-Gazette*. In a news story on logistical problems encountered in a new public housing project, the executive director of the City's Urban Redevelopment Authority (URA) was quoted as saying that minor glitches were inevitable in any new project, "Just like when you buy a new car and take it back for servicing" (Rotstein, 1994). Not long ago, such an excuse might have passed without notice. In this case, however, the explanation of the URA director prompted a stinging letter to the editor from a private citizen, obviously well-versed in the vocabulary of Total Quality Management (TQM). The citizen wrote: "[The URA's explanation] is exactly the type of thinking that should be obsolete in the 1990s—expecting things to be wrong (even when new) and then having to fix them. . . . The URA should do things right the first time, and demand the same from its suppliers. To tolerate shoddy quality is the mentality that allowed the Japanese to kick us in the global market place. . . . Bureaucrats . . . should learn what private industry is now realizing—getting it right the first time is better for everyone in the long run" (Goldberg, 1994).

Perhaps the person who wrote the letter is not a typical citizen. Clearly, he is informed on national and international business trends and he uses the vocabulary associated with the quality revolution. Still, his informed perspective on TQM, and his ability to relate it to government services, may be a harbinger of things to come as citizens become more vigilant consumers of public services just as they have become more discriminating consumers of privately produced goods and services.

The nonprofit sector also is under growing pressure do a better job of identifying and meeting customer needs (Kearns, Krasman, and Meyer, 1994). The United Way, for example, has responded to growing demands for consumer choice by allowing donors to designate annual gifts to specific agencies or classes of agencies rather than giving the United Way unlimited discretion in its allocations. Beyond this, the local campaigns of United Way affiliates are themselves facing more intense competition from other fundraising federations that are challenging the quasi-monopoly that the United Way has enjoyed. On the granting side, foundations are

demanding greater accountability from the nonprofits they support by requiring more sophisticated methods of outcome measurement, more advanced management systems, stricter
compliance with a growing array of reporting requirements, and
greater commitment to diversity and quality in governance structures (for example, O'Connell, 1988).

Increased Public Awareness of the Nonprofit Sector

Finally, there are two other forces emerging especially in the nonprofit sector that are likely to have lasting impact on how accountability is defined and assessed. First, the debate on accountability
in the nonprofit sector has emerged from the chambers of legislatures and the courts and entered the living rooms of citizens
across the country. Issues of compliance with complicated tax laws
and regulations will, of course, continue. But increasingly these
controversies are spilling over into broader discussions of lucrative
compensation packages for nonprofit executives, the proliferation
of nonprofit organizations, excessive commercialism in the nonprofit sector, and fraudulent or misleading fundraising practices.
One does not need to be a lawyer or a tax accountant to participate in dialogue on these issues (for example, Nielsen, 1992).

The second broad trend has to do with historic distinctions
between the public and nonprofit sectors, which are becoming
increasingly blurred. Prior to the War on Poverty in the 1960s, government relied very little on the nonprofit sector as a partner in
human service delivery. Today, the situation is far different. On average, nonprofit organizations receive 31 percent of their annual revenues from government grants, contracts, and reimbursements
(Salamon, 1992, p. 27). Consequently, their spending on social welfare programs (excluding education, pensions, and veterans' benefits) is slightly higher than that of the federal government and far
exceeds the spending of state and local governments combined
(Salamon, 1992, p. 37). In the 1980s, the role of nonprofits in delivering public services increased as the Reagan and Bush administra-
tions sought to divest and privatize many domestic government
programs. Similarly, the Republican Congress elected to office in
1994 turned quickly to the nonprofit sector as a potential safety valve
for anticipated reductions in domestic spending on social programs.

This evolving partnership between government and the nonprofit sector will have implications for the accountability of both sectors. At a minimum, professionals in each sector will need to know far more about the accountability environments in which the other operates. Nonprofits, therefore, can learn a great deal from government officials about fishbowl life. Also, the public sector can provide valuable lessons to nonprofits in the development of stricter internal management controls and more rigorous governance policies.

Conversely, governments have much to learn from nonprofit organizations about the role of accountability in a competitive, market-driven environment. Nonprofits tend to have more experience than governments in developing entrepreneurial responses to public problems, in monitoring customer needs and satisfaction, and in assessing the impacts and outcomes of their services.

Summary

In this chapter, we have illustrated some contrasting perspectives on accountability in the public and nonprofit sectors. But the basic challenge is the same for both government and nonprofit organizations: to manage resources, internal processes, and services in ways that serve the public interest and preserve the public trust. The history and traditions of the two sectors (and, consequently, their respective views of accountability) are different. But these parallel streams are beginning to converge in a new accountability environment that is more dynamic and complex than at any time in history. It is an environment in which emerging themes of customer service and responsive entrepreneurship are beginning to compete with the more traditional reporting mechanisms for ensuring accountability. It is an environment in which historical distinctions between the public and nonprofit sectors are beginning to disappear. It is an environment of intense public scrutiny that has spilled over from the public sector to the nonprofit sector. It is an environment of constant change.

Preserving the Public Trust
The Challenge of Accountability

Chapter One explored the philosophy of accountability in terms of historical precedents and contemporary trends. This chapter extends that discussion by examining how this philosophy has been operationalized through formal definitions of accountability and specific mechanisms for ensuring that public and nonprofit organizations do serve the public interest and preserve the public trust.

The accountability environment is a constellation of forces—legal, political, sociocultural, and economic—that place pressure on organizations and the people who work in them to engage in certain activities and refrain from engaging in others.

Legal and regulatory forces comprise a major portion of the accountability environment. They mandate certain organizational actions and prohibit others with a vast array of rules, procedures, reporting requirements, and sanctions by outside entities. Within an organization, the bureaucracy imposes its own rules and operating procedures designed to enforce accountability by bureaus, departments, field offices, and individual workers to higher authority within the organizational chain of command.

Another important mechanism for enforcing accountability is the court of public opinion, which can be heavily influenced by the news media and a growing number of watchdog organizations that monitor and report the activities of public and nonprofit organizations. The verdicts issued by this court often are expressed in terms of economic and political support for the organization. Clients, donors, and other stakeholders have at their disposal a powerful mechanism to voice their opinion by granting or withholding valued resources. For example, downward trends in

United Way donations can be traced, at least in part, to the 1992 controversy surrounding the former president of United Way of America and, perhaps, the erosion of confidence in the stewardship of that organization.

Resources. One type of public trust is served when government and nonprofit officials exercise appropriate stewardship over funds and property, thereby demonstrating accountability for the resources or assets of the organization. Can the organization account for its revenues and expenditures? Are there appropriate controls to prevent fraud, waste, and abuse?

Outcomes. Another type of accountability focuses on the outcomes produced by public and nonprofit organizations. Did the services reach their intended beneficiaries? What benefits were achieved by these services in relation to their cost? These questions often are addressed through a type of program evaluation known as summative evaluation.

Processes. Finally, there is accountability for the processes of the organization. Did decision makers follow mandated or otherwise defensible procedures? Did they exercise appropriate professional judgment when necessary? What checks and balances are in place to ensure accountability to an internal chain of command? These questions are addressed either through performance audits or through a type of program evaluation known as formative evaluation.

Two Brief Examples of Accountability Challenges

Several brief examples will illustrate these and other concepts. The first example concerns the audit of a county health department. The second describes a controversy involving a nonprofit mental health center.

A Public Sector Case

The headline was designed to catch the reader's attention: "Unhealthy Situation: Audit Raises Questions About Food-Inspection Practices." The newspaper editorial summarized several problems uncovered by a routine audit of the Allegheny County (Pennsylvania) Health Department conducted by the county controller. The controller found: (1) that some restaurants had been deliberately and inappropriately reclassified to relieve them of the need for frequent inspection; (2) that several instances of imminent health hazards in restaurants had not been investigated within the required twenty-four-hour time frame; and (3) that health department personnel had submitted false expense reports.

The newspaper naturally deplored these abuses, but it was also critical of the corrective actions promised by the executive director of the health department. The director acknowledged that problems of accountability existed and pledged to correct them by implementing more rigorous operating procedures and internal controls to prevent further fraud, waste, and abuse. But the newspaper editors apparently believed that the director was focusing too much attention on a formal, rule-driven system of accountability and too little on the moral and professional responsibility of workers to police themselves. The newspaper also implied that some employees soon would discover ways to circumvent the new rules and reporting procedures to serve their own interests rather than those of the tax-paying public.

A Nonprofit Sector Case

The headline read, "Mental Health Facility's Priorities Draw Fire," but the first part of the news article seemed out of sync with it. (This anecdote was adapted from French and Howey, 1993.) The opening paragraphs described a tragic series of events in painful detail. A woman who suffered from severe paranoia had killed her son, ostensibly to protect him from mobsters she was convinced wanted to torture him. At the time of the murder, the woman was receiving outpatient psychiatric counseling from a nonprofit mental health center in a midwestern city. Ironically, it was her son who had convinced her to seek psychiatric treatment.

In the previous year, other tragedies had occurred in the center's outpatient program. Several patients had committed suicide, one molested a child, and another committed arson. Curiously, none of these patients had been admitted to the center's acute care residential facility. Instead, all of them were treated as outpatients.

After recounting these incidents, the news story highlighted several more general criticisms of the mental health center.

Observers alleged that the center (1) regularly "dumped" uninsured patients on neighboring hospitals even though it received government money to treat the indigent; (2) offered fewer beds for inpatient care than most mental health centers of comparable size; (3) failed to provide twenty-four-hour emergency service; (4) devoted too much effort to serving people with relatively minor problems (like low self-esteem) at the expense of seriously and acutely afflicted patients; and (5) paid its chief executive officer roughly one-third more than CEOs in other mental health centers of comparable size. The story questioned the absence of governmental oversight of the center, noting that the last audit by the state oversight agency was in the mid 1970s.

Comparisons

Let us briefly compare and contrast these two cases to illustrate a few important aspects of accountability. Obviously, both cases involve public controversies regarding the extent to which an organization fulfilled its expressed or implied promise to serve the public interest and preserve the public trust. But while both cases involve issues of accountability, there are important differences between the two.

The county health department presents a classic case of accountability. A clear chain of authority exists between the county and state health departments, and the audit conducted by the county controller represents a formal and relatively precise mechanism for reporting to the higher authority. There is also a relatively explicit set of performance criteria for which the county health department must literally account, and both internal checks and balances and an outside oversight agency to enforce the accountability standards.

Moreover, in the case of the county health department, there was no ambiguity in the controller's audit, and any reasonable person would quickly conclude that the public trust had been violated. The health department itself quickly accepted the controller's findings and immediately implemented some corrective actions. Finally, the nature of the trust relationship between the general public and county health department is very clear—citizens rely upon and trust such agencies to protect them from certain health hazards. Public notices in restaurants attest to the fact that the eating establishment has been inspected by the county health department and meets codified health standards. These notices are the department's statement of accountability to restaurant patrons. This is a relatively explicit standard of accountability, clearly defined in the state and county regulations that the health department is charged to enforce.

In contrast, the case of the mental health center involves subjective and wide-ranging criticism of the center's priorities, the quality of its services, its cooperation with peer agencies, and its executive compensation policies. The catalyst for this criticism is not a formal audit by an authorized oversight agency. In fact, a major concern in this case is the absence of rigorous oversight and formal chains of accountability. This controversy was brought to light by a murder that captured the attention of the news media and the general public. Significantly, some of the strongest critics of the mental health center are not government oversight agencies but other nonprofit health care organizations, which under certain circumstances might even be viewed as competing service providers.

Finally, unlike the county health department, the nature of the trust relationship between the mental health center and the general public is ambiguous, as are the associated performance criteria. Public expectations of such centers typically are diverse, ranging from clinical treatment and rehabilitation to education, advocacy, and even public safety. Consequently, reasonable people might have vastly different opinions on whether or not the public trust has been violated in this case. Should the center be held responsible for the actions of its patients—who, by definition, are emotionally unstable? Should it be held accountable for the processes it uses to determine whether patients are be admitted to the acute care facility or merely treated on an outpatient basis? Does the center have a moral obligation to provide more indigent care than is legally required? If not, does the center have a civic obligation for a certain level of indigent care in return for exemption from most local, state, and federal taxes? What salary should be paid to the CEO of such an organization? (See Kahn, 1992, for a discussion of the salary question.) What are the criteria? Should salary policies be considered part of the governing board's accountability to donors, patients, and the community at large?

Clearly, these questions involve implicit standards of responsibility and professional obligation within a rather loosely coupled accountability infrastructure. Consequently, the test of compliance rests as much on public opinion as on any outside audit or objective test of performance. Moreover, it is not clear to whom the mental health center is accountable (answerable) or which decision makers within the center bear the burden of answering to a higher authority. Is the center primarily accountable to its patients or to the community at large? To peer agencies or to the state mental health department? To the newspaper reporters who wrote the story? Does the CEO bear the burden of accountability or does it rest on the board of trustees?

The responses of the two organizations also show some interesting differences. The director of the county health department immediately promised to take corrective action by tightening procedures and internal controls. While this response certainly was warranted, it is interesting to note that the newspaper criticized the director for not taking more sweeping actions to address the causes as well as the symptoms of this problem. The director took a reactive or tactical approach by making immediate changes in the internal operating procedures. The newspaper suggested that he take an adaptive or strategic approach by trying to instill a new professional culture in the county health department wherein accountability would be ensured less by bureaucratic rules and more by the personal values and professional norms of a motivated workforce.

The mental health center, on the other hand, mobilized a set of public relations resources to defend its actions—also a reactive or tactical approach but vastly different from that of the county health department. The chairperson of its board of trustees, a respected community leader, supplied reporters with data to justify the center's patient screening procedures. Also, he explained the board's procedures for determining the CEO's salary. Ultimately, he defended the center by claiming it was in full compliance with the letter of the law in all of its activities.

The two cases illustrate that both public and nonprofit organizations are vulnerable to a wide variety of accountability challenges. Moreover, they are held accountable to a variety of performance standards on a continuum from explicit rules and procedures to implicit expectations of diverse stakeholders. Also, they are accountable to diverse constituencies, from oversight agencies to the general public, peer agencies, and the news media. Finally, their responses to these controversies can be categorized along a continuum from reactive tactics to adaptive strategies.

Some Definitions of Accountability

With these two illustrations in mind, let us review some formal definitions of accountability. Most formal definitions of accountability are found in the literature of public administration, political science, and law. It is not surprising, therefore, that these definitions seem to be more directly applicable in government bureaucracies than in private nonprofit corporations.

Narrow Definitions

The *HarperCollins Dictionary of American Government and Politics* (Shafritz, 1992, p. 4) contains the following entry: "*Accountability:* (1) The extent to which one must answer to higher authority—legal or organizational—for one's actions in society at large or within one's organization. (2) An obligation for keeping accurate records of property, documents, or funds." Similarly, Starling (1986, p. 123) says, "A good synonym for (accountability) is *answerability.* The organization must be answerable to someone or something outside themselves." Here are several other definitions of accountability:

- White (1926) views accountability as both a reporting mechanism and as an instrument of managerial and political control. The accountability criteria are different at each level in the organizational hierarchy. "The [professional] levels of the administrative system are accountable to the [governance] command for policy conformity of the whole organization. Officials . . . to whom public funds are advanced are accountable for their use . . . which is enforced . . . by final determination of the auditing office. Top management levels must be responsible for gaining expected results from the expenditure of funds and energy" (p. 221).

- Gruber (1987) views accountability as an instrument of control in a democratic society. "Bureaucracies threaten democracy when they abuse their power by acting corruptly, inefficiently or unfairly and . . . procedural safeguards, or limits, must be advocated to ensure that such abuses do not take place" (p. 22).

- Smith (1971, p. 26) says, "Accountability is the central objective of democratic government: how can control be exercised over those to whom power is delegated?"

- Mansfield (1982, p. 61) says, "[The] very meaning [of accountability] is a showing . . . that an agent has done what he had been told to do, whether well or badly." But he adds, "The notion of accountability reaches beyond obeying instructions faithfully to include a responsibility for behavior and actions that are judged by standards [such as] . . . competency, integrity, judgement, prudence, vision, courage, and other like qualities" (p. 62).

- Paul (1991, p. 2) defines accountability as "Holding individuals and organizations responsible for performance measured as objectively as possible."

These definitions provide a useful starting point because they illustrate three core elements that are at the heart of any accountability system: a higher authority vested with the power of oversight and supervision, a measure or criterion used by the higher authority to assess compliance or performance of mandated activities, and an explicit reporting mechanism for conveying information to the higher authority. Table 2.1 provides some examples of each of these elements.

A precise operational definition of accountability is quite helpful in analyzing a clear-cut case like the county health department summarized earlier. The higher authority in that case is the state health department and, by extension, the state legislature. The measures of performance are codified in public health regulations governing restaurant safety. And the reporting mechanism is the audit conducted by the county controller and the supporting documentation supplied by the county health department.

But the definitions of accountability discussed thus far contain a strong bureaucratic bias that makes them less applicable to ambiguous cases. Thus, these formal definitions are not very useful in cases where there is no formal chain of command in which

Table 2.1.   The Accountability Infrastructure: A Narrow View.

Higher authority	Performance criteria	Reporting mechanisms
External	External	External
Higher levels of government	Laws	Audits of financial and procedural
Regulatory agencies	Regulations	compliance
Accrediting agencies	Administrative mandates	Self-study reports
The courts	Contractual obligations	Site visits
	Accrediting guidelines	Contractual reports
Internal	Internal	Internal
Supervisors	Standard operating procedures	Internal audits
Volunteer board of trustees	Organizational policy	Chain of command
Elected officials	Job descriptions	Formal communication channels
	Assignments and tasks	Internal checks and balances
		Performance evaluations

a higher authority oversees and regulates the activities of those below it. The definitions are also difficult to apply when standards of compliance or performance are implicit, subjective, or not acknowledged by all stakeholders, or where there are no specific and institutionalized procedures for reporting (accounting) for performance or compliance.

But even under these ambiguous conditions (unfortunately typical of the day-to-day context of management), public and nonprofit officials still are asked to account for their actions. Citizens, legislators, journalists, and self-appointed watchdog groups rarely premise their investigations on formal academic definitions. In the case of the mental health center, the trustees and staff were asked to account for their actions not through a formal and well-functioning chain of command, but rather through news media that forced the issue by running a splashy front-page story on the tragedy. The performance criteria in this case involved a few objective (legal) standards, but most of the attention focused on subjective judgments about agency priorities, community needs, executive compensation, and collaboration with related organizations. Finally, the reporting mechanism in the case of the mental health center consisted primarily of public relations and damage control strategies mobilized hastily by the trustees and the staff in response to the critical newspaper article.

Broad Definitions

For cases like the mental health center, we must look for broader definitions of accountability. For example, Kingsley (1944, p. 282) suggests that accountability is achieved when an organization assumes responsibility for responding to the needs of society. Similarly, Krislov and Rosenbloom (1981, p. 22) say that accountability is achieved when the organization is responsive to and identifies with the general public. Also, Levine, Peters, and Thompson (1990, pp. 5–6) discuss accountability in terms that bridge the notions of answerability, responsibility, and responsiveness: "[Citizens] want administrators to be held accountable to their wishes—to their personal definitions of the problem and the best way to solve it. In this way citizens make administrators responsible to their particular needs."

Finally, Shafritz (1992, p. 10) proposes the following definition: "*Administrative accountability:* The concept that officials are to be held answerable for general notions of democracy and morality as well as for specific legal mandates."

Thus, the scholarly literature presents us with some fairly clear distinctions between strict accountability (answerability) and broader notions such as responsiveness to public needs and adherence to democratic and moral principles. Gortner, Mahler, and Nicholson (1987, p. 393) use the notions of legal control and hierarchical control to describe a continuum from strict *accountability* to *responsibility*. In their framework, a formal system of accountability is ensured when (1) decisions and actions are determined and checked by superiors (hierarchical control) and (2) actions are mandated or forbidden by law (legal control). When these two conditions are absent, then the system of strict accountability is replaced by one of responsibility and discretionary judgment.

The broader definitions introduced in this section draw our attention to important aspects of accountability that are not necessarily codified in laws, regulations, bureaucratic procedures, or hierarchical reporting relationships.

Were the actions of the mental health center consistent with what Shafritz calls "general notions of democracy and morality"? We may not be able to answer this question conclusively, but at least the broader definitions of accountability encourage us to consider a more diverse set of performance criteria—something beyond mere compliance and reporting. Also, these definitions help us pose additional questions to clarify those criteria. For example, what are the trade-offs between the obligation of the mental health center to treat indigent patients and the board's fiduciary responsibilities to ensure the center's financial viability? What about the CEO's annual salary? Should charitable organizations pay their employees less than other types of organizations simply because they are nonprofit? Can a compensation policy be justified in terms of "general notions of democracy and morality"? And what are we to make of the elusive priorities of the mental health center? Is it a violation of democratic or moral principles for the center to target some of its services to people with minor psychological problems in addition to seriously and acutely afflicted patients? Are both types of services consistent with the charter and the mission of the organization? Are both types of services responsive to the needs of society?

And, finally, to whom is the mental health center accountable on these and other issues? Under a strict definition of accountability, the center must answer only to the state oversight agency and, in a limited way, to the Internal Revenue Service. But in reality, the center has been forced to answer to a much wider set of constituents via its response to the newspaper article.

To some extent, these are rhetorical questions that do not lead us to conclusive findings about the accountability of the mental health center. On the other hand, they are exactly the questions that must be asked when the accountability infrastructure is loosely coupled or does not contain the three core elements described earlier—higher authority, clear performance criteria, and an explicit reporting procedure. The narrow definitions of accountability do not allow us to address these questions because they focus on compliance with explicit legal or bureaucratic mandates. The broader definitions of accountability, while perhaps distasteful to theoretical purists, bring these questions to the surface for reasoned debate.

Public Trust and Public Interest

The questions we have raised about the mental health center illuminate issues that span the boundary between two important concepts underlying the notion of accountability: public trust and public interest.

In one sense, accountability involves preserving the public trust—being able to account for the organization's implied promises to its constituencies by pursuing its stated mission in good faith and with defensible management and governance practices. The public interest, on the other hand, is not so easily defined; it involves diverse perceptions and values regarding public needs and priorities. Theoretically, therefore, it is possible for the mental health center to preserve the public trust (be accountable in a technical sense) without necessarily serving the public interest as defined by at least a subgroup of people in the community. Alternatively, it is conceivable that the public interest could be pursued in ways that violate regulatory or bureaucratic definitions of the public trust. Do the ends justify the means?

While public trust and public interest are separate theoretical concepts, they generally become indistinguishable in any practical discussion of accountability. Again, the general public does not make clear distinctions between public trust and public interest when assessing the performance of government and nonprofit organizations. People want to know not only that we are doing what we promised to do or what we are legally obligated to do, but what they expect us to do, what they want us to do, what they think we should do.

Who Is the Higher Authority?

Finally, the broader definitions of accountability expand the notion of a higher authority by implying that the general public, not some oversight agency, is the ultimate guardian of democratic values and morality. Thus, accountability involves not only formal oversight but also public scrutiny in terms of citizen confidence and trust. This is consistent with Rosen's view (1989, p. 4) that accountability involves the exercise of "lawful and sensible administrative discretion" and efforts to "enhance citizen confidence in . . . administrative institutions."

Which View Is More Salient?

The definitions presented thus far illustrate that the notion of accountability may be interpreted narrowly or broadly. The narrow view focuses attention on answerability—demonstrating compliance with explicit mandates through a chain of command to a higher authority. The broad view, on the other hand, opens the door for scrutiny by the general public according to standards that may be implicit, subjective, and constantly changing.

Many accountability controversies in government and the nonprofit sector involve violations of both explicit and implicit standards of behavior. Several years ago, for example, some of the most prestigious research universities in the country (many of which are chartered as private nonprofit corporations) came under scrutiny from Congress for alleged misappropriation of overhead expenses charged to government-funded research contracts. Overhead funds are earmarked to cover indirect expenses associated with research projects such as personnel administration, insurance, utility costs, depreciation of capital assets, and so on. Accountability for these funds is enforced by agencies of the federal government through periodic audits. As a result of these audits and subsequent hearings in Congress, some institutions were criticized for accounting practices that seemed to violate the spirit if not the letter of the law.

For example, Stanford University was criticized for depreciating a University-owned yacht that it considered a "building" (a fixed asset) for accounting purposes. As the controversy gained momentum through highly publicized congressional hearings and investigative reports in the national news media, public attention began to shift away from the technical (and sometimes arcane) details of compliance with financial accounting rules and toward more nebulous (but more titillating) issues such as the salaries and lifestyles of university presidents, the location and financing of management retreats for top-level university administrators, and so on. Obviously, these are issues that include, but extend well beyond, regulations governing expenditures and accounting systems.

Thus, both views of accountability—the narrow view and the broad view—are equally salient in the contemporary environment of public and nonprofit organizations.

A Strategic Definition

Both the narrow and broad perspectives on accountability presented thus far assume that organizations are essentially reactive in their efforts to serve the public trust. In other words, once the standard of accountability (whether explicit or implicit) has emerged, the organization is pressured to react by demonstrating its compliance to specific rules or responsiveness to public needs.

There is a another perspective that suggests that accountability involves not only reactive responses, but also efforts to anticipate emerging performance standards and expectations and to take proactive steps to ensure that the public trust is served. Romzek and Dubnick (1987, p. 228) state that "accountability involves the means by which public agencies and their workers *manage* the diverse expectations generated within and outside the organization" (emphasis added). This perspective contains an important element not found in the previous definitions— the implication that public expectations can be managed. Theoretically, then, government and nonprofit officials may take proactive steps to respond to the accountability environment in which they operate. At a minimum, they can strategically position themselves by implementing accountability systems that build on their strengths and are appropriate for the environment in which they work.

In the case of overhead expenses cited above, universities across the country attempt to influence the standards by which they are judged. They do this by negotiating their respective overhead rates with executive agencies of the federal government. Consequently, the overhead paid on government research contracts varies among the universities according to factors such as the age and condition of campus facilities, the state of the local economy, the types of research the university undertakes, and so on.

But the criteria are imprecise and there is a political calculus to these negotiations. Just prior to the national controversy on this issue, the senior executives of my own institution debated the merits of asking for the significantly higher overhead rate they believed was justified, or for a moderately higher rate that might have been more feasible in the context of the growing congressional scrutiny.

Dimensions of Accountability: An Integrating Framework

The discussion thus far has illustrated that the notion of accountability contains as many as three dimensions: the higher authority to whom organizations and individuals are accountable, the standards of performance—explicit or implicit—for which organizations are held accountable, and the responses to the accountability environment—tactical or strategic—from inside the organization.

One way to visualize the accountability environment is with a three-dimensional representation like the "accountability cube" in Figure 2.1.

Summary

Accountability is a concept with many dimensions. As a result, public dialogue about accountability often is hindered because the term itself means different things to different people. It is

Figure 2.1. The Accountability Cube.

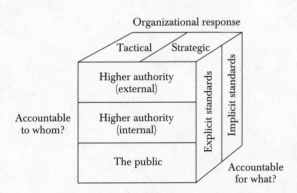

important, therefore, that we try to map these various dimensions in order to understand the complexity of the topic. But mapping the dimensions of accountability is more than an interesting intellectual exercise. In Part Two, we will see how the mapping process can uncover important tactical and strategic issues for public and nonprofit organizations that want to do a better job of managing their accountability environment.

Part Two

Tools for Managing Accountability

The next four chapters present conceptual and analytical tools for preserving and enhancing accountability. These tools are designed to guide decision makers through a strategic management process for anticipating, interpreting, and responding to their accountability environment.

Chapter Three reviews the core principles of strategic management and relates them to the notion of accountability. In any organization, strategy evolves from four activities: looking backward to the organization's legal mandate; looking forward toward its mission and espoused values; looking outward for environmental opportunities and challenges; and looking inward for distinctive strengths and limitations. While there is nothing dramatically new about these four activities, which can be found in most strategic planning texts, this is the first book on the topic of accountability to make extensive use of this template in a pragmatic but theoretically sound way.

Chapter Four introduces the notion of the accountability environment and shows how managers and leaders can analyze and dissect it in search of specific types of strategic challenges and opportunities. The framework presented in Chapter Four is really the intellectual heart of the book. It shows that compliance with legal and regulatory mandates is only one of four dimensions in the accountability environment of any organization. The other three dimensions involve what I call negotiated accountability, discretionary accountability, and administrative advocacy. Chapter

Four discusses specific types of opportunities and challenges in each of the four dimensions and suggests how managers and leaders can scan their own accountability environment for factors that may be unique to their organization.

Chapter Five describes how to conduct an accountability audit by focusing on the organization's strengths and vulnerabilities with respect to preserving the public trust. In this chapter, I describe the components of the organization's accountability infrastructure and present a set of questions for assessing how well (or how poorly) the organization is positioned to respond effectively to events and trends in the world outside.

Chapter Six presents a framework to help managers and leaders make sense of the information they have gathered via the tools presented in the previous two chapters. The objective of Chapter Six is to help organizations uncover and clarify their strategic issues and choices related to accountability. In general, these strategic issues tend to cluster into four types. Comparative advantage issues result from the intersection of external opportunities and internal strengths, and they present the organization with specific types of choices regarding the preservation or enhancement of its accountability. Mobilization issues arise when the organization faces accountability challenges but has certain strengths with which to address them. The question is how to use these strengths and allocate resources most effectively. Damage control issues must be addressed when the organization is especially vulnerable by virtue of its weaknesses to certain types of accountability challenges from the outside world. Finally, comparative disadvantage issues arise when the organization is unable to pursue certain strategic opportunities because of its inherent weaknesses. Clarification of strategic issues is essential prior to the development of viable strategies and tactics.

Chapter Three

A Strategic Management Approach
Core Principles

The prime objective of any strategic management system is to achieve a good fit between the organization and its environment. As such, strategic management is more outward looking, more inclusive, and less introspective than traditional long-range planning systems. Also, strategic management is concerned with how the parts of the organization relate to each other and to the whole—how they work in concert to support the mission, the goals, and the strategies of the organization.

Typically, we think of strategic management as a holistic approach because of its focus on external trends and events—opportunities and threats—as well as the organization's internal environment—its strengths and weaknesses. But the holistic philosophy of strategic management does not preclude using it for parts of the organization or in selected policy areas, like accountability, that typically transcend departmental boundaries and functional specialties.

This chapter presents an overview of strategic management concepts and methods. It is intended especially for readers who are not familiar with the strategic paradigm, and for those who want a refresher on basic terminology. Chapter Four then builds on these concepts by presenting a framework for analyzing an organization's accountability environment. Then, Chapter Five describes how to conduct an accountability audit based on the organization's internal strengths and weaknesses. Finally, Chapter

Six presents a method for identifying and clarifying the strategic accountability issues facing public and nonprofit organizations. These issues are illuminated and clarified when decision makers synthesize their assessments of external opportunities and threats and internal strengths and weaknesses.

Strategic Management Principles and Accountability

The core principles of strategic management are well documented and formalized (see for example, Bryson, 1988; Grant and King, 1982; Hart, 1992; King and Cleland, 1978; Porter, 1985; Wheelen and Hunger, 1990; Thompson and Strickland, 1992). While formal models and templates for strategic management vary in complexity, there are five essential steps that all of them have in common:

- *Looking backward:* The organization's mandate
- *Looking forward:* The organization's mission and values
- *Looking outward and inward:* The results of SWOT analysis
- *Thinking strategically:* The issues and choices facing the organization
- *Strategy development:* The organization's goals and objectives

Let us briefly examine each of these generic steps in relation to accountability.

Looking Backward

Managers and policy makers must first know what the organization is required or authorized to do before they can develop new strategic directions, initiatives, or programs. The organization's mandate specifies this formal purpose—the reason for its creation and the obligations to which it is legally bound.

The mandate can take several forms—charter, articles of incorporation, by-laws, legal statutes, ordinances, or administrative regulations. For example, when creating a new jurisdiction such as a municipality or a school district, a state legislature will grant a charter delegating to the jurisdiction certain powers and obligations outlined in the state constitution and in statutory law. Typically, in the governmental sector, these underlying legal frameworks are the heart of an organization's mandate because they outline (sometimes in excruciating detail) nearly all facets of the jurisdiction's functions, its organizational structure, its policy-making procedures, the sources of its revenue, and (in terms of accountability) its reporting relationships to other organizations in the hierarchy of command. For example, the Borough Code for the Commonwealth of Pennsylvania is a document of several hundred pages covering everything from the allowable sources of tax revenue to procedures for awarding public contracts.

The mandate is a critically important instrument of accountability, especially from a legal perspective, and can be used to enforce all dimensions of accountability. It can be used to account for the resources of an organization by clearly designating, and perhaps limiting, the sources of its revenues. The mandate also controls the processes of an organization by specifying certain governance and policy-making procedures as well as administrative procedures. Finally, the mandate accounts for the outputs and outcomes of the organization because it outlines the fundamental purposes and scope of activities to which the organization is committing itself.

While the mandate is technically a public document, it generally is not widely distributed. It is the type of document that is kept tucked away (out of sight and out of mind) until a challenge or controversy arises. It is advisable, therefore, to periodically review the mandate and the organization's portfolio of activities to ensure that they are still consistent with each other. Nonprofit organizations are, in fact, required to review their mandate and to declare on Form 990, filed annually with the Internal Revenue Service, whether the core purpose of the organization has changed from that specified in the original charter. There is a significant level of concern, however, that even these mandated reports are not taken seriously by nonprofit organizations (Levis, 1992).

Beyond legalistic oversight, both public and nonprofit organizations should review their mandate early in their strategic planning process (Bryson, 1988, pp 92–94). Some questions to ask when examining the mandate are:

- What does the mandate require in terms of scope of service, internal procedures, resource generation and so on?

- What limits or constraints does the mandate place upon the organization? Does the mandate explicitly or implicitly forbid certain activities or programs?
- What degrees of freedom, if any, are presented by the mandate?
- What reporting relationships and channels of accountability are specified by the mandate?
- Would a reasonable person conclude that the organization's existing programs and procedures are consistent with and supportive of the mandate?

A careful review of the mandate is an important step in an accountability audit, which we will discuss in detail in Chapter Five.

Looking Forward

An organization's mission statement is an extension and interpretation of its mandate. If the mandate is a statement of legal requirements and authorization, then the mission is a statement of intentions, goals, and strategic directions. The mission statement, therefore, should provide a concise interpretation of the mandate in terms that people can easily understand.

- What business are we in?
- What are our principal products and services?
- Who are our primary clients or beneficiaries?
- What needs do we fill?
- What operating philosophies do we follow?
- What are our priorities for the future?

The mission statement should dwell less on technical or legal obligations and more on what the organization is committing itself to do within whatever discretionary authority is granted by the mandate.

The mission statement should also provide a guide to daily decision making as well as long-term planning. In other words, an effective mission statement should provide much more than eloquent but meaningless rhetoric about the organization's purpose. Rather, it should provide an explicit statement of the organization's operating philosophy and core values. For example, the mission statement of a prestigious research university contains a section that states, among other things, that the institution will pursue only those initiatives in which it has a "comparative advantage," and that all of its activities in teaching and research will be designed to enhance its position of national leadership by "influencing the behavior of other institutions." In other words, this institution is publicly stating, to both internal and external audiences, that it will not attempt to be all things to all people. Such an explicit operating philosophy can have a powerful impact on strategic decision making and long-term resource allocation.

Some operating philosophies may have immediate effects on short-term (versus long-term) decision making. For example, the mission statement may say something about the organization's commitment to employee development, to measuring the quality of client services, or to a certain philosophy of resource management.

Finally, the mission statement should be the foundation for the organization's strategic plan by providing a concise overview of the organization's goals and aspirations for the future. Often, the strategic direction of the organization is expressed in a separate *vision statement* appended to the mission. Whether as a separate vision statement or as part of the mission statement, the organization's priorities and strategic direction should be stated publicly.

Thus, the mission statement should include at least three distinct sections as follows:

1. The purpose of the organization, expressed in terms of products, services, targeted customers, and needs filled
2. The operating philosophies and values, expressed in terms of the organization's self-image, how it perceives its niche or distinctive characteristics in the marketplace, how it makes decisions and manages resources to preserve or enhance its accountability
3. The aspirations for the future, expressed in terms of broad strategic goals and priorities

Missions are slightly more fluid and dynamic than mandates because they reflect the organization's interpretation of its role in society, its relationship to its constituents, its position in the marketplace, and its aspirations for the future. Also, old missions can be accomplished and new missions can be formulated to take their place. Or as dramatically demonstrated by the Association for Children's Television (ACT) in 1992, the organization may choose to close its doors after accomplishing its stated mission (Moore, 1992). While the mission statement should not be changed haphazardly, it should be updated as needed each time the strategic plan is reviewed.

Like the mandate, the mission statement is a powerful instrument of accountability. Peter Drucker, in fact, suggests that the mission statement is *the* instrument of accountability for public and nonprofit organizations, because they do not have a bottom line like profit and loss to measure performance. He writes, "A well-defined mission serves as a constant reminder of the need to look outside the organization not only for 'customers' but also for measures of success. The temptation to content oneself with the 'goodness of our cause'—and thus to substitute good intentions for results—always exists in nonprofit organizations. It is precisely because of this that the successful . . . nonprofits have learned to define clearly what changes outside the organizations constitute 'results' and to focus on them" (Drucker, 1989, p. 89).

Unlike the mandate, the mission statement is a highly public document. Generally, it is distributed to employees, foundations, citizens, and perhaps included in annual reports and other documents. Portions of the mission statement might be extracted in the form of slogans or mottos printed on business cards, marketing materials, and letterheads. Consequently, the mission is one of an organization's primary accountability contracts with the public. It is the document in which we say to the public, "Here is what we promise to do for you. You may hold us accountable for this."

There are several triggers or symptoms that may suggest that effort should be invested in the development of a new or revised mission statement:

- Recurring and unproductive debates within the organization (line versus staff, headquarters versus field offices, and so on) regarding interpretation of the mandate, core purpose, resource allocation, operating philosophies, and goals
- A pattern of apparently ad hoc decision making at the top of the organization or goal displacement in the middle of the

organization wherein key decisions do not seem to be guided
by an overarching purpose or vision
- An unfocused or disjointed portfolio of services without clear
  and consistent priorities
- A pattern of confusion or misunderstanding among key
  constituencies—elected officials, oversight agencies, citizens,
  and funders—regarding the core purpose and goals of the
  organization

Any of these symptoms can suggest that the organization
should refine its mission statement, develop a new one, or take
concerted steps to ensure that the existing mission statement serves
as a guide for decision making. The process of developing a mission statement should include a variety of stakeholders—executive
staff, middle management, and key external constituencies.

I have found nonprofits and other private sector organizations
to be somewhat more committed to the value of mission statements than governmental jurisdictions or agencies. I have no
empirical evidence to support this claim, but it is something I have
noticed again and again in consulting assignments and executive
seminars. Many of my nonprofit clients take great pride in their
mission statements. They display them in public places. They invite
comments on them. They talk with enthusiasm about how the mission was developed and its evolution over time. In contrast, when I
ask government officials to show me their mission statement, they
often pull out a copy of their charter or the authorizing legislation,
saying: "This is our mission. This is what guides us."

This difference in attitude (if, indeed, there really is a difference) between government and nonprofit professionals might be
attributed to their respective perceptions of accountability, which
we discussed in Chapter One. Nonprofit administrators seem to
feel a greater sense of autonomy and control over their own des-
tiny and they may view the mission statement as a way to express
this autonomy. Also, they probably have learned that entrepreneurship and responsiveness are keys to survival in the increasingly
competitive environment of the nonprofit sector. In the relatively
unregulated environment of nonprofit organizations, accountability is viewed from the perspective of performance in meeting
self-determined objectives (the mission) rather than reporting

compliance with legal dictates (the mandate) through a formal chain of command.

Government officials, on the other hand, have a professional ethos that has been shaped by the history and evolution of accountability in the public sector. To them, accountability traditionally has been defined in legal terms, and the mandate, not the mission statement, is the best expression of that legal framework. In many instances, government officials have been trained to think in terms of the limits on their administrative discretion rather than in terms of entrepreneurship. Consequently, they sometimes seem reluctant to express any organizational purpose or goals that cannot be directly traced to the formal mandate or charter of the organization.

Naturally, there is value in both of these perspectives. We concluded Chapter One by saying that nonprofit and government professionals had much to learn from each other with respect to accountability. As nonprofit professionals begin to experience a tighter regulatory environment, they can learn much from government officials who have lived in such an environment throughout their careers. Conversely, government officials have much to learn from nonprofits regarding a broader notion of accountability that is based on performance, not just compliance.

Looking Outward and Inward

In the jargon of strategic management, the term SWOT analysis refers to the identification of the organization's:

- *Strengths:* Aspects of organizational infrastructure, resources, and portfolio of services that contribute to the effective and efficient pursuit of its mission and thereby enhance its accountability to the public trust
- *Weaknesses:* Aspects of organizational infrastructure, resources, and portfolio of services that detract from the effective and efficient pursuit of its mission and thereby tend to diminish its accountability
- *Opportunities:* Events or trends in the external environment that have the potential, if acted upon, to assist the organization in pursuit of its mission, thereby enhancing its ability to serve the public interest and preserve the public trust

- *Threats:* Events or trends in the external environment that have the potential to hinder the organization in pursuit of its mission and threaten its accountability to the public

Typically, organizations begin with a scan of the external environment for opportunities and threats before looking inward for strengths and weaknesses. In fact, Koteen (1989) transposes the SWOT acronym (using "TOWS" instead) to highlight the desirability of looking outward first.

The scan of the external environment might focus on specific trends and factors related to accountability. In the nonprofit sector, for example, executives and trustees might focus on recent legislative and political trends related to the regulation of nonprofit organizations. What types of issues are capturing the attention of congressional oversight committees in Washington? What regulatory mechanisms are being debated in the state capitol? Is the organization especially vulnerable to any of these issues? Do any of these developments offer opportunities for the organization to demonstrate its accountability to legislators, constituents, or the general public? Do these legislative initiatives represent a real trend or are they merely isolated events?

This scan of the political and legislative environment should be accompanied by a similar scan for economic factors, sociocultural factors, and even technological factors that may affect the organization's ability to serve the public trust. Bryson (1988, p. 54) uses the acronym "PESTs" as a reminder of the four components of the external environment—political, economic, social, and technological factors—that should be scanned for threats and opportunities.

When the focus is on accountability, the scan of the external environment ought to be driven by several carefully constructed questions:

- What external events and trends could affect how accountability is defined and perceived by the organization's constituents and other stakeholders?
- What external events and trends could threaten the ability of the organization to continue serving the public trust?
- What external events and trends could damage the credibility of the organization in the eyes of the public?

- What types of accountability challenges have arisen for other similar organizations?
- What trends are occurring in the political, economic, social, and technological environments that will affect the organization's efforts to serve the public trust and, in turn, the public's ability to assess its accountability?

Chapter One discussed several very broad trends in the accountability environment of public and nonprofit organizations. In order to be useful, however, the questions must focus not only on broad trends in the environment, but on specific segments of the organization's accountability environment. Chapter Four describes a way to segment the accountability environment for closer scrutiny of these opportunities and threats. The framework presented in Chapter Four suggests that legal and regulatory mandates comprise only one facet of the accountability environment. Other opportunities and threats arise when decision makers negotiate accountability standards with relevant stakeholders, when they exercise their administrative discretion in developing their own accountability standards, and finally when they play the role of policy advocates by seeking to influence the accountability agenda.

The scan of the internal environment, the accountability audit, will be discussed in Chapter Five. In general, the accountability audit involves a thorough review of strengths and weaknesses in the organization's accountability resources and its supporting infrastructure. Essentially, the accountability audit determines whether the organization's resources, its management procedures, and its governance processes are appropriately targeted to serving the public interest and preserving the public trust. The methods of benchmarking, for example, can be used to demonstrate accountability for inputs, processes, and outcomes (Davis and Patrick, 1993; Sheridan, 1993). Is the salary of the city manager comparable to that in similar cities? Does the organization use a procurement system that is comparable to that of organizations in the field generally regarded as the best or most sophisticated? Is the average response time of the police force comparable to that of other municipalities?

Thinking Strategically

At the beginning of this chapter, I said that strategic management is primarily concerned with achieving a good fit between the organization and its external environment. Thus, a strategically well-positioned organization is one that has developed certain internal strengths that allow it to capitalize on existing or emerging opportunities in its external environment. This particular type of fit between internal and external factors gives the organization a *comparative advantage* that, according to the theory of strategic management, should be protected and nurtured at almost any cost. The organization's comparative advantage represents its distinctive competencies. It is essential that decision makers build upon these in the development of accountability strategies and tactics.

A second type of fit is achieved when decision makers understand the relationship between the organization's internal strengths and the threats or challenges that exist in the external environment. This type of knowledge allows them to *mobilize* their strengths to eliminate or at least minimize the negative impacts of the threats.

A third type of fit is achieved when decision makers understand exactly how the organization's weaknesses are preventing it from capitalizing on external opportunities. Armed with this information, they can consider a variety of strategies to correct the situation—including *divesting* weak programs, *investing* in them to turn them into strengths, or *collaborating* with another organization.

Finally, a fourth type of fit (in a very negative sense) arises when decision makers realize that the organization's weaknesses make it very vulnerable to external threats. The organization is like a ship lying broadside to an oncoming torpedo. But knowledge of this vulnerability can, under certain circumstances, allow decision makers to engage in *damage control* strategies and tactics before, during, and after the crisis.

Each of these four types of fit between the organization and its external environment presents decision makers with different types of strategic issues:

- How to build upon the organization's comparative advantages in serving the public interest and preserving the public trust

- How to mobilize accountability resources to avert or minimize threats looming on the horizon
- How to address the organization's weaknesses so that it is better positioned to take advantage of opportunities
- How to identify and employ damage control strategies when the organization is especially vulnerable to accountability challenges

Chapter Six, which concludes Part Two, presents a method for clarifying these four types of strategic issues and examining each of them in greater detail.

Strategy Development

A strategy statement tells how each strategic issue will be resolved. Generally, it consists of an explicit goal and accompanying set of objectives related to each strategic issue. A strategy also includes a set of steps or tactics designed to pursue each stated strategy, including assignment of responsibilities, timetables, and resources. The strategies might be phased in over a multiyear period, with an annual business plan of goals and objectives.

But a strategy is more than a static collection of goals, objectives, and tactics. It is an organizationwide commitment to a set of values, operating philosophies, and priorities. Also, it is an organizationwide commitment to a strategic way of thinking in which all major decisions are evaluated in light of their strategic implications. Thus, strategies for managing accountability, like other types of strategies, should be continuously monitored in light of evolving circumstances and trends. This requires leaders to build a "culture of accountability" in their organizations, a topic we take up in the last chapter.

Figure 3.1 portrays steps in the strategic management process.

Assessment of Strategic Planning

While I enthusiastically support the concepts and methods of strategic management, it would be unfair to the reader not to mention and respond to several criticisms of the approach. Like any management philosophy, strategic management has its zealots and its detractors.

Figure 3.1. The Strategic Management Process.

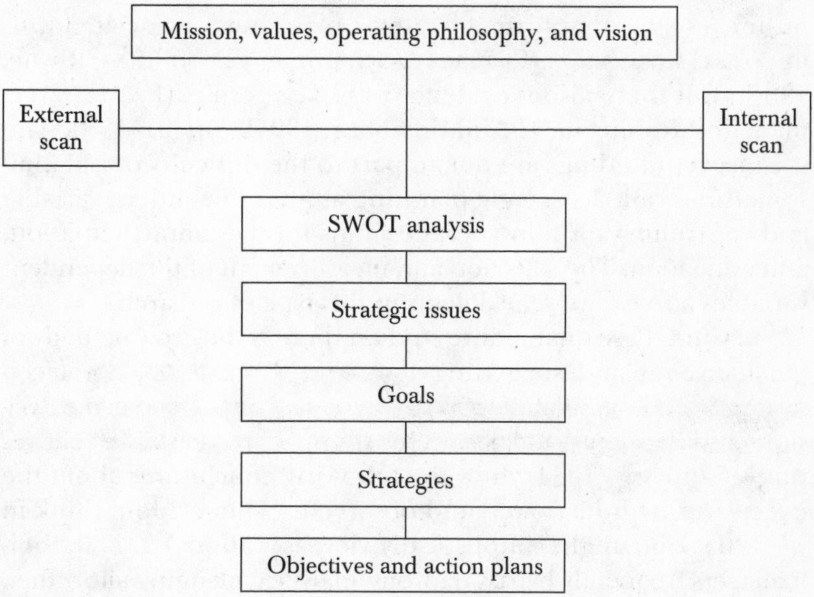

```
┌─────────────────────────────────────────────────┐
│  Mission, values, operating philosophy, and vision │
└─────────────────────────────────────────────────┘
```

| External scan | | Internal scan |

```
┌──────────────────────┐
│     SWOT analysis    │
└──────────────────────┘
┌──────────────────────┐
│    Strategic issues  │
└──────────────────────┘
┌──────────────────────┐
│         Goals        │
└──────────────────────┘
┌──────────────────────┐
│      Strategies      │
└──────────────────────┘
┌──────────────────────┐
│ Objectives and action plans │
└──────────────────────┘
```

Critiques

The general model of strategic planning described in this chapter dates back to the 1960s, when it was embraced as a panacea by many executives and management scholars. Like other management philosophies before and after, strategic planning was placed on a pedestal and hailed as the best way—perhaps the only way—to design and implement effective strategies. The approach spread quickly through businesses, governments, and nonprofit agencies. Like Total Quality Management in the 1980s and Reengineering in the 1990s, there were countless executive seminars, books, journal articles, and university courses on the strategic management approach. Actually, given the fickle tastes of management gurus and the proliferating alphabet soup of management philosophies (MBO, OD, T-groups, Q-circles, and so on), the strategic management philosophy has demonstrated remarkable durability.

But in the past ten years or so, some scholars and executives have become disenchanted with the philosophy and methods of strategic management. One line of criticism says that strategic planning is not strongly correlated with improved organizational performance. True, there is some empirical evidence from the business sector that formal strategic planning is associated with improved financial performance (Schaffir and Lobe, 1984; Rhyne, 1986). But there also is evidence of mixed results (Pearce, Freeman, and Robinson, 1987; Mintzberg, 1994b, pp. 91–158). The inconsistent findings are due in part to the difficulty of isolating something called strategic planning as an independent variable and controlling for idiosyncrasies in its format, implementation, and evaluation. The selection and measurement of the dependent variables also can pose problems in this type of research.

Beyond these quantitative studies, there is the growing body of qualitative research suggesting that decision makers do not necessarily rely on a rational, step-by-step model or process to make decisions and develop strategies. In his study of how senior executives think, Isenberg (1984) drew the following conclusions about the executives he interviewed and observed: "They seldom think in ways that one might simplistically view as 'rational.' . . . Rather, managers frequently bypass rigorous analytical planning altogether, particularly when they face difficult, novel, or extremely entangled problems. When they do use analysis for a prolonged time, it is always in conjunction with intuition" (p. 82).

Mintzberg's research (1994a, 1994b) shows similar results. He believes that disenchantment with strategic planning can be traced to one source: "*Strategic planning* is not *strategic thinking*. Indeed, strategic planning often spoils strategic thinking, causing managers to confuse real vision with the manipulation of numbers. . . . Most successful strategies are visions, not plans" (1994a, p. 107).

Mintzberg observes that strategic thinking and strategic management require creativity, synthesis, and sometimes even sudden, gestaltlike experiences that provide dramatic new insights on problems that previously seemed insurmountable or that had routinely been handled in suboptimal ways. "Search all those strategic planning diagrams, all those interconnected boxes that supposedly give you strategies, and nowhere will you find a single one that explains the creative act of synthesizing experiences into a novel strategy" (1994a, p. 109).

Finally, there have been criticisms from the executive suite as well as from academia. Harold Geneen, the chief executive of ITT from 1959 to 1977, took pride in writing the shortest memo in the history of that company: "There will be no more long-range planning" (1984, p. 49). Under Geneen's leadership, ITT made detailed plans for only the next four quarters. "No one," he said, "is wise enough to see five or ten years into the future and plan for it with any sensible certainty" (p. 92).

Response to the Critiques

I believe Isenberg's observations on executives' use of judgment and intuition are correct. Most senior executives I have encountered display a similar style of decision making. But Isenberg takes care to point out that intuition is not used randomly or carelessly by executives and that "non-rational" decision making is not "irrational" decision making. Isenberg found that intuition is applied in five specific ways (Isenberg, 1984, pp. 85–86):

1. To *sense* when a problem exists, even when the data are inconclusive;
2. To perform *well-learned* decision-making processes (including strategic management models) very rapidly;
3. To *synthesize* bits of data and information into a total picture;
4. To *check* on the results of rational analysis; and,
5. To *bypass* in-depth analysis on problems that have been encountered in some form before.

Geneen, despite his expressed cynicism toward strategic planning, actually is a perfect example of the type of informed intuition that Isenberg discovered in his studies. Soon after he took the helm, Geneen launched a strategy to transform ITT from an antiquated telephone and telegraph company into an international management conglomerate. This strategy did not come from a formal organizationwide strategic planning process. But it did reflect Geneen's careful analysis of the company's historical evolution, its traditional mission and niche in the marketplace, the external forces (especially political, economic, and technological) that had emerged to threaten the company's long-term viability, and its internal strengths and weaknesses vis-a-vis those external forces (Geneen, 1984, pp. 46–50). Thus, despite his expressed cynicism toward strategic planning, Geneen actually followed an approach almost identical to the one summarized in this chapter. His strategy was part rational and part intuitive.

Mintzberg's observations also are correct. But he seems to set up a straw man for easy attack by assuming that strategic planning is performed by professional planners who are separate from strategic thinkers and managers. It goes almost without saying that professional planners can only inform the process of strategy development by collecting relevant data and perhaps posing challenging questions to the people—executives, managers, and trustees—who are formally responsible for strategy development and implementation. Professional strategic planners, however talented they may be, cannot and should not be the framers of organizational strategy. They are merely the technical support staff for the decision-making process.

Also, it should be obvious that the concepts and methods of strategic planning—the diagrams and interconnected boxes so glibly criticized by Mintzberg—cannot and should not prescribe specific strategies. At best, they are heuristic tools to help illuminate choices and pose challenging questions to decision makers who must interpret them and formulate strategies using a mix of rational and intuitive judgment. The reader will see plenty of these interconnected boxes in the following chapters of this book. Keep in mind that they are designed to pose questions, not to offer solutions. In fact, the reader will soon discover (perhaps with some frustration) that the next three chapters focus more on posing questions than on offering solutions or strategies. I agree with Mintzberg—there is no conceptual or methodological framework, however rigorous, that is capable of actually formulating strategies.

Naturally, there are certain rudimentary strategies that all organizations should follow to enhance their accountability, especially when ensuring compliance with legal mandates and regulatory constraints. But, unfortunately, there are no universal answers to the more complicated accountability issues in serving the public interest and preserving the public trust. I do believe, however, that there are guidelines for the types of questions decision makers should ask themselves and their constituencies so that the accountability issues can be appropriately defined and resolved.

Summary

The product of the strategic management model outlined in this chapter is a strategic plan for accountability that includes results of the following activities:

- An assessment of the external accountability environment for emerging opportunities and threats
- An accountability audit that examines the mandate, the mission, and a variety of internal factors in order to uncover the organization's strengths and weaknesses vis-a-vis the notion of accountability
- A clarification of the organization's key strategic issues related to accountability
- A statement of accountability strategies, including goals, objectives, and action plans

The chapters that follow present analytical tools, frameworks, and methodologies to help decision makers perform each of these tasks.

Chapter Four

Scanning the Accountability Environment

The accountability environment in which public and nonprofit organizations exist is complex and quite volatile. It is composed of a constellation of forces and stakeholders. Decision makers can quickly be overwhelmed in their efforts to identify salient forces, trends, and events affecting the accountability strategies of the organization.

This chapter presents a conceptual framework to help decision makers divide the accountability environment into more manageable pieces for closer scrutiny of specific kinds of opportunities and threats. This framework focuses attention on selected aspects of accountability that often are ignored. Also, this chapter presents several analytical techniques for mapping the interactions among forces in the accountability environment and for using scenarios to develop reasonable forecasts of opportunities and challenges.

Conceptual Framework

When public and nonprofit organizations scan their accountability environment, they must address many complicated questions:

- What are the legal or regulatory standards to which we are held accountable? Who enforces these standards?
- What are the informal or implicit standards to which we are held accountable?
- Who are the opinion leaders who define and enforce these standards?

- How, if at all, is our accountability environment changing? What forces are contributing to these changes?
- What strategies or tactics are available to help ensure the organization's accountability in a changing environment?
- What has been the experience of comparable organizations?

It can be difficult to keep all these considerations in mind without becoming confused or distracted. We need a tool to help us divide the accountability environment into manageable segments or parts for closer scrutiny and analysis. We need a way to organize our thinking and to focus our attention on particular types of opportunities and threats. The framework presented here tries to fill this need. It divides the accountability environment into four segments, each of which contains certain kinds of opportunities and threats.

The framework assumes that the accountability environment of any organization contains at least two dimensions: A set of accountability standards—explicit or implicit—generated by the organization's environment, and a response—tactical or strategic—from inside the organization.

Superimposing these two dimensions yields a matrix with four cells, as illustrated in Figure 4.1.

Consistent with the discussion in the first three chapters, the framework presented in Figure 4.1 recognizes that public and nonprofit organizations are held accountable for at least two types of performance standards.

Explicit standards. First, they are held accountable for explicit performance standards that often are codified in law, administrative regulations, bureaucratic checks and balances, or contractual obligations to other organizations. These accountability standards represent the legal, bureaucratic, and regulatory constraints that public and nonprofit officials confront on a daily basis. Here, the reporting mechanism often is some type of audit or evaluation and the mechanism of enforcement generally is a sanction for nonperformance or noncompliance.

Implicit standards. Second, public and nonprofit organizations are held accountable for implicit standards of performance that involve ill-defined and, perhaps, shifting notions of what constitutes responsible or appropriate behavior. Implicit standards of

Figure 4.1.   Four Dimensions of the Accountability Environment.

| | | Standards of Assessment | |
		Explicit (de jure)	Implicit (de facto)
Organizational Response	Tactical (reactive)	Legal accountability (compliance) –1–	Negotiated accountability (responsiveness) –2–
	Strategic (proactive)	Anticipatory accountability (advocacy) –4–	Discretionary accountability (judgment) –3–

Source: Reprinted with permission from *Public Administration Review* (Kearns, 1994, p. 188). © by the American Society for Public Administration (ASPA), 1120 G Street, N.W., Suite 700, Washington, D.C., 20005. All rights reserved.

accountability are rooted in professional norms and social values, beliefs, and assumptions about the public interest, the public trust, and how (and to whom) organizational behavior should be explained. Even though these implicit standards are not necessarily defined by laws and regulations, they can involve powerful sanctions for nonperformance or noncompliance. The organization's public image may suffer as the result of critical media attention. It may come under attack from a special constituency that feels its interests are not adequately represented by the organization. Or it may lose critically important support from elected officials, funding organizations, clients, and partner organizations. Any government official who has confronted the wrath of a taxpayer ("Who is responsible for *this* wasteful program?") is familiar with these implicit and subjective standards of accountability. Any nonprofit organization that has been scrutinized by the media for its "excessive" compensation policies, "unbalanced" board of trustees, or "grossly inflated" endowment fund also is familiar with these implicit and subjective standards. In these circumstances, the accountability mechanism is the court of popular opinion rather than a formal audit by an authorized oversight agency.

The framework in Figure 4.1 also recognizes that decision makers have several options with which to respond to accountability standards.

Tactical approach. First, they can use a tactical approach by simply responding in a timely manner to either explicit or implicit accountability standards. The tactical approach is essentially a reflexive response, driven by intense pressure from the accountability environment to take some action. For example, the organization may be contractually required to file a financial audit with an oversight agency. Or it may come under intense pressure to respond to public criticism by, for example, convening a public meeting with clients or with the editorial board of the local newspaper.

Strategic approach. Second, decision makers may take strategic actions to anticipate and position their organization within a changing accountability environment. The strategic approach requires foresight and a willingness to take corrective action before the organization is forced or pressured to do so. For example, decision makers might use their discretionary authority to make internal adjustments in the organization to enhance its accountability before it becomes the target of public scrutiny and criticism. Or decision makers might take proactive steps to advocate certain changes in legal or regulatory requirements that they believe will enhance their service to the public trust.

Subsequent sections describe each cell of Figure 4.1 in some detail. Keep in mind that these four cells are conceptual representations of important segments of the accountability environment. In the real world, the boundaries between segments may not be as clear and precise as those represented here. But this tool provides a point of departure for additional in-depth analysis and perhaps adaptation by decision makers to the unique context of their organization.

Legal Accountability: Compliance

The upper left quadrant of Figure 4.1 (Cell 1) denotes the most familiar and most narrowly interpreted form of accountability—compliance by a government or nonprofit organization with an explicit standard of performance, operational procedure, output measure, or reporting requirement. Often, the accountability standards in this cell are formally codified and enforced and therefore carry the force of law. The enforcement mechanism may be an outside oversight agency with the power to impose sanctions on the lower organization for noncompliance or nonperformance.

Alternatively, the standards in this cell might be embedded in the bureaucratic procedures, chains of command, hierarchies of authority, and checks and balances in the organization itself. In this case, the object of compliance is the organization's own performance standards and rules, and the accountability mechanisms include formal supervision, employee performance appraisals, and so on. While these internal accountability mechanisms do not necessarily carry the force of law, they are very explicit and vigorously enforced as part of the organization's management control system.

Government organizations at all levels—local, state, and national—must comply with a host of legal and regulatory constraints that filter down through the intergovernmental chain of command. Examples include procurement procedures that govern how municipal governments purchase equipment and other commodities, accounting procedures that specify how state governments keep tabs on federal grants and contracts, and human resource policies that tell federal agencies how to recruit and manage their employees.

Compliance, of course, applies to nonprofit organizations as well. They must follow a specified procedure to be formally recognized by the Internal Revenue Service as tax-exempt organizations. They must submit annual reports to federal and state oversight agencies. They are audited with respect to their use of government funds. They must comply with the standards of certain accrediting bodies. And they must comply with explicit legal and regulatory standards, such as those regarding unrelated business income and those prohibiting certain types of political activity.

Whether the accountability standards are enforced externally or internally, compliance is essentially *reactive* in nature. The organization (or the individual worker) awaits the formulation of precise and clearly articulated standards and then essentially follows the rules, subject to oversight, periodic audits, or performance evaluations. This type of accountability environment requires a clear hierarchy of authority that is recognized as legitimate by all actors. Also, this type of accountability environment is heavily reliant on the traditional notion of bureaucracy that, especially in government, has been a principal instrument for ensuring that the public trust is not abused. With all its warts, bureaucracy still serves a very real purpose in holding people and institutions accountable to rules, precise tasks, clear chains of command, and impartial administration of programs. Also, the importance of bureaucracy as a constraint on public and nonprofit organizations may be slightly overestimated by its critics. True, public and nonprofit managers often are placed in the unenviable position of being machinelike implementers of orders or bureaucratic procedures dictated from above. Just as often, however, they have at least some latitude and discretion to interpret legislative or regulatory intent in relation to their own specific contexts and needs. Their obligation in this cell of the matrix is to follow the *spirit* of the law as well as the *letter* of the law.

While compliance is always reactive, it is rarely a passive or knee-jerk response. Indeed, compliance requires active (and sometimes proactive) participation from organizations subject to explicit standards of accountability. They must design administrative and operational procedures in accordance with the laws and regulations. They must train employees and volunteers on how to comply and how to report their compliance. They must anticipate problems and barriers that may hinder compliance. They must allocate (and perhaps reallocate) sufficient resources to ensure that compliance remains a high priority. And, of course, they must monitor their own behavior and compile appropriate information in order to demonstrate (literally account for) their compliance. Still, all of these actions are essentially in response to the stimulus provided by the law, regulation, or bureaucratic standard of accountability that is imposed upon them.

Threats and opportunities in Cell 1. When scanning this segment of the accountability environment, decision makers should ask several questions:

- What are the legal, regulatory, and bureaucratic standards to which the organization is held accountable?
- Who enforces these standards? Who is the higher authority in the accountability chain?

- Over the past five years, what significant changes have taken place in the legal and regulatory environment of the organization?
- Are there any political, economic, social, or technological forces that are likely to affect the legal and regulatory environment over the next five years?
- Have comparable organizations encountered significant problems regarding their compliance with laws and regulations?
- Does the legal and regulatory environment provide opportunities to enhance the organization's performance in serving the public trust?
- Conversely, does the legal and regulatory environment pose any threats that will hinder the organization's efforts to be accountable to the public trust?

In this segment of the accountability environment, many managers will be inclined to see more threats than opportunities. After all, compliance with rules and reporting through a formal chain of authority generally are viewed as constraining factors that reduce flexibility and administrative discretion. Also, compliance often carries substantial financial and administrative burdens if scarce resources must be diverted away from the organization's core mission and devoted instead to the nuisance tasks of documentation and reporting. For years, businesses have complained— with some justification—about the hidden costs of government regulation. More recently, state and local governments expressed concern about so-called *unfunded mandates* in the intergovernmental system. In 1995, Congress took steps to reduce these types of mandates in the federal system, but they remain a problem in many states. A state legislature, for example, may pass a popular law mandating minimum jail sentences for people convicted of drunk driving. This law might demonstrate the legislature's accountability to the public interest and responsiveness to media outrage over repeat offenders. But the lawmakers may refuse to provide funds to relieve the resulting overload on local courts and jails, thereby passing the most tangible costs of accountability on to municipalities and counties.

Another type of threat is related to unanticipated consequences of an accountability mandate. A given law, regulation, or other instrument of compliance, while intended to increase accountability, may actually have the opposite effect. For example, the notion of performance contracting has been used in government-funded job training programs to provide financial incentives for private trainers to help their clients find and hold good jobs after they complete a training program. Trainers are reimbursed, in part, on the basis of their success rates. From the standpoint of accountability, what could be more reasonable? In many cases, however, this reimbursement policy led to the phenomenon known as *creaming:* selecting only the cream of the crop among the unemployed—those who would be easiest to train and easiest to place in good jobs. Obviously, this leaves the hard-core unemployed to fend for themselves.

Also, some events or trends in this cell of the matrix are perceived as threatening because an organization's prior poor performance makes it particularly vulnerable when judged by an explicit standard of accountability or performance. Moreover, the organization may have little hope of turning the situation around. Clearly, this circumstance presents a threat of the highest order because of the likelihood that it will develop into a full-blown accountability crisis (see Chapter Six).

Finally, events or trends in this cell might be threatening if they hold organizations accountable for processes or outcomes over which they have limited control. For many years, we held law enforcement agencies accountable for performance measures like arrest rates and clearance rates even though there are many forces affecting these outcomes that are well beyond the agencies' control. Human service agencies are held to standards regarding client outcomes when there are a host of factors beyond their control that can intervene to affect measures of success (Buckholdt and Gubrium, 1983).

Thus there are several types of threats that decision makers may detect when scanning Cell 1 of the matrix:

- Threats related to the administrative or financial burdens of compliance
- Threats arising from the unanticipated negative consequences of compliance
- Threats associated with the organization's historic performance and its limited prospects for compliance

- Threats associated with operational measures of accountability and the extent to which the organization can control these factors

While threats may seem pervasive in this cell, decision makers should search for opportunities as well. For example, legal mandates and even administrative regulations often are the product of extensive political bargaining and compromise. Consequently, accountability standards and the associated reporting mechanisms may be expressed in vague but politically palatable language that leaves room for interpretation and administrative discretion. A nonprofit training organization, operating fully within the letter and spirit of the law, found that it could set up a for-profit subsidiary that not only provided employment opportunities for at-risk youth—its primary clients—but also generated a modest stream of revenue for the parent nonprofit corporation. Thus, when scanning this portion of the accountability environment, it is important to ask not only how the organization is constrained by compliance obligations but also what degrees of freedom or latitude are embedded in the accountability standard.

Another type of opportunity presents itself when decision makers perceive that their organization not only meets but exceeds the formal standards of compliance. This can be a valuable marketing and public relations tool, especially for nonprofit organizations but also for government agencies. Municipalities, for example, may boast that their accounting systems not only meet standards established by the state legislature but even the more rigorous standards advocated by professional associations like the Government Finance Officers Association.

Finally, there may be opportunities in this cell related to advances in information technology and the prospects for more efficient and effective reporting to higher authorities. The development of sophisticated computer networks and the ease of access to extensive data bases may greatly ease the workload on public and nonprofit agencies in complying with a host of reporting requirements. The Internal Revenue Service has the capability to accept tax forms via electronic transfer. With appropriate safeguards, the same type of technology may soon be available for other types of reports. For example, the director of human resources for a large mental health facility is required by state law to conduct extensive background checks on prospective employ-ees, especially those who will have professional contact with minors. Currently, the process involves a time-consuming sequence of writ-ten requests for information from law enforcement agencies, finan-cial institutions, former employers, and others. Controlled access to a growing array of information data bases could greatly facilitate background checks, making them more timely, more accurate, and less expensive.

Thus there are several types of opportunities that might emerge from careful analysis of Cell 1 of the matrix:

- Opportunities to interpret mandates in terms of the latitude they provide for administrative discretion
- Opportunities to demonstrate performance over and above that required by the mandates
- Opportunities arising from advances in information technol-ogy that can facilitate timely and efficient compliance with reporting requirements

Negotiated Accountability: Responsiveness

The cell in the upper right corner of Figure 4.1 (Cell 2) addresses several different accountability contexts. First, government and nonprofit organizations often are held accountable for perfor-mance standards that are implicit—those arising from shifting societal values and beliefs or from emerging political values and priorities that are not codified in law, administrative regulations, or bureaucratic controls. For example, nonprofit organizations often are urged by various stakeholder groups to diversify their boards of trustees to ensure representation of minority interests or client perspectives. But there is no legally binding requirement for nonprofits to do this. Similarly, a government agency might be under pressure from a group of constituents to form a citizen advi-sory board on a particularly pressing issue. But, again, there may be no legal requirement to do so. In such cases, the accountability standards are only loosely defined (or completely undefined) and thus open to debate.

A second circumstance in this cell, and one that also is quite familiar to public and nonprofit managers, is the need to be accountable for standards codified in laws and regulations (or other contractual arrangements) that are vaguely worded and therefore subject to interpretation and translation by administrators who are charged with their implementation. For example, the Internal Revenue Service prohibits many types of nonprofit organizations from engaging in substantial activities that are not related to the organization's tax-exempt purpose. What does *substantial* mean in this context? What criteria are used to assess whether the organization meets this standard? Are these criteria negotiable? The IRS has never defined this in precise operational terms. Rather, it has always relied on subjective judgment and interpretation of the organization's activities.

A third circumstance in Cell 2 arises when the organization's internal controls and flows of accountability are vague or when supervisors are given latitude to adapt their managerial style to the varying skills and capabilities of their subordinates. Anyone who has had any type of managerial experience knows that not all employees respond well to the same type of supervision. Some require relatively tight controls and a strict chain of accountability via frequent activity reports. Others, however, require relatively little oversight and thrive under conditions of delegated authority (Hersey and Blanchard, 1982). When a single model of delegation does not make sense, a kind of negotiated accountability can be tailored to the subordinate's skills, motivation, and prior performance.

In all three cases, the accountability standards are implicit and imprecise. Nonetheless, they are powerful enough to capture the organization's immediate attention, providing a catalyst for tactical actions that often involve some form of negotiation between the organization and a group of stakeholders in its external or internal environment.

In the first case, the negotiations may take place with a particularly powerful (or interested) constituency that has a high stake in the outcome of the dilemma. These constituencies may include citizen groups, advocacy organizations, and other coalitions of stakeholders inside or outside the organization. Generally, they are groups that have made some claim—substantiated or not—that the organization is not behaving accountably. In the second case, the negotiations generally will take place with the regulating body that enforces the vaguely worded law, regulation, or contract. In the third case, negotiations may take place with individual workers or their labor representatives.

An example of negotiated accountability is the recent national trend where nonprofit institutions—especially large institutions like hospitals and universities—are pressured to make payments in lieu of property taxes to municipal or regional governments. In these instances, the government unit holds the nonprofit institution accountable to loosely defined standards of what constitutes charitable activity. Pittsburgh, for example, has been at the forefront of municipal efforts to force large nonprofit institutions to pay their fair share to the city coffers and, accordingly, has negotiated ad hoc arrangements with most major hospitals and universities to make some payment in lieu of taxes. The city's claim does not rest on a precise legal standard or clear jurisdictional authority. In fact, both the Pennsylvania Constitution and the body of case law regarding tax-exempt organizations are based on an imprecise definition of charitable organizations. Nor has the city employed an explicit fee-for-service formula that might calculate the payment on the basis of factors like the size and location of the facility and its estimated use of municipal services. Instead, the city took its case to the public at large, through extensive media coverage, making claims about extravagant salaries and lifestyles of hospital and university executives, scrutinizing the public service ethos and track record among hospitals, and asking whether certain types of university facilities (a football stadium) are essential to the educational mission of the institution (for one such news story, see Hayllar, 1990).

In Pittsburgh, and in other localities as well, many nonprofit institutions have chosen the path of least resistance, bowing to vague and implicit notions of accountability, while genuinely acknowledging some obligation to help the city cope with its fiscal woes. Even while under severe pressure, however, these institutions played at least a marginal role—some more marginal than others—in framing and defining what are acceptable standards of contributions to the community. But this role has been played out in ad hoc, one-on-one negotiations with city officials, or in contested negotiations in the courts. Not surprisingly, those institutions that engaged in negotiations early on set a de facto standard of accountability that subsequently was applied to others. This "ad-hocracy" is the most significant and perhaps troubling attribute of negotiated accountability. The standards by which the organization (or the individual worker) is judged are imprecise and the outcome of the negotiated arrangement likely will vary from case to case. Moreover, the reporting mechanism through which accountability is ostensibly demonstrated is equally vague and often idiosyncratic.

Finally, in this segment of the accountability environment it is not always clear to whom public and nonprofit officials are literally accountable. To whom must they answer? With whom should they negotiate? In most cases, the squeakiest wheel will get the most grease, but what about those constituents who lack the political clout to make powerful demands on the organization? They may seek alternative service providers (which is not always feasible) or they may circumvent formal communication channels or seek stronger allies capable of representing them in the negotiations (see Paul, 1992; Hirschman, 1970).

Threats and opportunities in Cell 2. When scanning this segment of the accountability environment, decision makers should ask several questions:

- What are the implicit standards of accountability by which the organization is judged?
- Over the past five years, have there been significant changes in these implicit standards?
- Are there external stakeholders who are particularly interested in the enforcement of these standards?
- Is the pressure exerted by these stakeholders sufficiently strong to require an immediate tactical response? Are they widely viewed as legitimate representatives of broader interests or other stakeholders? Who is the higher authority in the accountability chain?
- Are any of these accountability standards negotiable? Is the reporting mechanism negotiable?
- What accountability issues currently are being negotiated by similar organizations? What are the likely outcomes of these negotiations? Who have been the most active and influential stakeholders in these negotiations?
- Would it be in the organization's best interest to negotiate now or later?

- On what philosophical or legal grounds should the organization negotiate?
- Does this portion of the accountability environment provide any opportunities for the organization?
- Does this portion of the accountability environment pose any threats to the organization?

These questions may highlight several types of threats. As described earlier, the accountability standards in this environment are vague and perhaps dynamic. As a result, reasonable people will disagree about what types of organizational behavior constitute accountable performance, often leading to conflict between the organization and its environment. Conflict, in turn, generally involves risk and uncertainty because the outcome of the dispute and its long-term effects cannot be controlled or predicted. Low-level conflicts can quickly and unpredictably escalate to major controversies, especially when those on one side or the other perceive that escalation will enhance their power and control of the situation.

Another threat is that negotiated solutions can have unforeseen adverse effects in the long run, especially when there is no precedent and thus no opportunity to learn from the mistakes of others. If we negotiate now, will it limit our flexibility later? If the negotiated settlement is based on some type of formula, such as number of clients served, will the formula compound our vulnerability to unforeseen demographic shifts? These unknown factors can increase the perceived risks in this cell.

Also there is the threat that participants in the controversy will resort to adversarial tactics to force a defensive reaction or, worse yet, a premature resolution. This is an especially effective tactic for stakeholders who feel disenfranchised or believe they have limited leverage in a formal and deliberate process of negotiation. They often have little to lose by raising the stakes or circumventing the formal process. Adversarial tactics also are common when there is little or no trust among the negotiating parties.

Finally, some controversies in this cell of Figure 4.1 might be perceived as zero-sum games, involving only win/lose options, extremely high stakes for all parties, and limited opportunities for spreading the risks. Clearly, these types of negotiations are threatening for all parties.

None of these negative scenarios is fully within the control of the organization, and the absence of control is inherently threatening to most public and nonprofit administrators. Thus, the threats in this cell of the accountability environment may arise from several sources:

- Threats arising from the possibility that low-level negotiations may escalate into major controversies
- Threats arising from the absence of precedents and the associated uncertainty of outcomes
- Threats arising from the absence of trust among participants and the associated risks of adversarial behavior
- Threats arising from the absence of win/win solutions that serve the interests of all parties without imposing unreasonable burdens on any of them

On the other hand, decision makers may perceive several types of opportunities in this cell of the accountability environment. Timing is one factor that may offer opportunities. As illustrated, the hospitals that launched early negotiations with the city of Pittsburgh gained some leverage because they set the standards that were followed later on. But it is easy to envision other contexts in which decision makers may want to delay negotiation, letting other negotiators set the precedent. Zartman and Berman (1982, pp. 47–54) say that negotiations may be especially timely when some type of significant change has taken place in the environment that alters the relative power of stakeholders or their respective perceptions of the situation. Also, negotiations may be timely when existing relationships between two or more parties collapse and when all parties agree that they would be better off with a new arrangement than with none at all.

Negotiations may provide the opportunity to clarify expectations and performance standards, thereby reducing uncertainty and risk. There may be an opportunity for the organization to actively participate in defining the criteria by which it will be judged and, perhaps, to educate oversight agencies, the public, the media, and other stakeholders about its constraints. Negotiations may, for example, be an appropriate way to resolve long-standing disputes or tensions that have been simmering beneath the surface. In the process, there may be opportunities to build trust among participants, especially when negotiations take place in good faith and with mutual disclosure of information.

Finally, there may be the opportunity for negotiations on one issue to have positive spin-offs on others, especially when the decision makers sense that their willingness to negotiate now will imply obligations from others to make quid pro quo concessions on other issues.

Thus, the opportunities in this cell can be grouped as follows:

- Opportunities arising from the timing of negotiations
- Opportunities to use negotiations to clarify performance expectations, thereby reducing organizational uncertainty and risk
- Opportunities to use negotiations as an educational forum
- Opportunities to resolve latent tensions, building trust and partnership
- Opportunities to use negotiations on relatively minor issues to obtain concessions on other, more important issues

Discretionary Accountability: Judgment

The cell in the bottom right corner of Figure 4.1 (Cell 3) portrays the context in which accountability standards and reporting mechanisms are implicit. But unlike the previous cell, the accountability forces are neither powerful enough nor sufficiently focused to demand immediate tactical negotiation with powerful constituencies in the external environment. Indeed, in this cell, there may be no identifiable parties with whom to negotiate, no specific oversight agency, and no formalized reporting mechanism. Thus this portion of the accountability environment gives public and nonprofit officials great latitude for professional judgment and is therefore labeled *discretionary accountability*.

Decision makers in this cell have the freedom to design and implement their own accountability systems, but they would be wise and prudent to prepare themselves to defend—that is, account for—these systems according to some set of criteria.

This cell recognizes knowledge and expertise as the primary instruments of accountability, rather than mandated reporting channels or checks and balances enforced by external oversight agencies or internal bureaucratic hierarchies. In fact, Cell 3 has very little meaningful oversight other than the self-defined and self-enforced norms and standards of professional practice. The enforcement body is likely to be a diverse (and diffuse) set of stakeholders with varying degrees of formal power and authority.

Even though this is a relatively unstructured segment of the accountability environment, it can still involve external pressures on the organization. For example, government and nonprofit officials may feel peer pressure via their professional networks to adopt management systems like Total Quality Management, benchmarking, or performance budgeting. In such a case, the organization is under pressure to respond to two intersecting external forces: societal expectations calling for improved quality of government and nonprofit services, and standards of performance within the profession driven by peer networks, which may lead to wide acceptance of certain management philosophies like TQM as surrogate measures of accountability. Ultimately, however, this cell of the framework recognizes that the decision to adopt or reject these methods rests on the discretionary judgment of the public or nonprofit official.

Also, this cell calls for prudent action that can simplistically be described as doing the right thing even when the right thing is technically unenforceable (Independent Sector, 1991). For example, an organization that operates relatively free of regulatory constraints on its financial management and investment activities may find it prudent to reinforce its own checks and balances or to convene an advisory body as a mechanism of self-policing. Or the organization might take the initiative to conduct a salary survey to ensure that its compensation policies are in line with those of comparable organizations. Also, prudent organizations often are the first to adopt codes of ethics, conflict of interest policies, or special training programs for employees and volunteers to sensitize them to the ethical dimensions (and possible ethical dilemmas) in their work.

Thus, when there is neither a legal obligation (Cell 1), nor even focused social pressure (Cell 2), prudent organizations take proactive steps to voluntarily develop their own accountability mechanisms to ensure that the public trust is served.

Threats and opportunities in Cell 3. When scanning this segment of the accountability environment, there are several relevant questions:

- In what types of activities related to serving the public trust is the organization free to exercise substantial discretion, flexibility, and autonomy?
- Within these domains of activity, are there any implicit performance standards that are defined by social values, assumptions, or professional norms of practice? While formal chains of accountability may not exist, are there any stakeholders who have particular interest in promulgating higher standards of voluntary accountability?
- Over the past five years, has there been any change in the legal or regulatory environment that allows for greater discretion, flexibility, and autonomy in serving the public trust?
- Over the past five years, have new management or governance tools emerged that are related to voluntarily serving the public trust and voluntarily reporting organizational activities and outcomes? Are these tools becoming widely accepted on a voluntary basis among comparable organizations?
- Are there any external stakeholders, like voluntary watchdog organizations, who are particularly interested in monitoring the organization's exercise of its discretion, flexibility, and autonomy?
- Can the organization take proactive steps to improve administrative behavior or organizational performance?
- Have other comparable organizations encountered significant accountability crises due to the inappropriate exercise of administrative discretion or as the result of an entrepreneurial venture?
- Does this portion of the accountability environment present any opportunities for the organization to maintain or enhance its accountability?
- Does this portion of the accountability environment pose any threats that may hinder the organization's efforts to be accountable?

Unlike the previous two cells, Cell 3 may seem to offer decision makers more opportunities than threats. This is the cell in which accountability standards are defined primarily by the organization itself rather than by its external environment. There is a relatively high level of freedom and many opportunities for professional judgment in this cell compared with those discussed above. But there are threats in this cell that can be attributed directly to the freedom that public and nonprofit organizations enjoy under these conditions.

One important type of threat in this cell is related to competition. In an environment relatively free of regulatory oversight, nonprofit and even government organizations will face increased competition from organizations for whom the so-called entry costs and compliance costs are low. One of the startling findings from the Gaul and Borowski study of the nonprofit sector (1993b, p. 2) is that, on average, 29,000 new nonprofit organizations are recognized each year by the Internal Revenue Service. Many grantmaking organizations apparently have noticed this trend of proliferation and now are challenging nonprofit organizations to demonstrate that they are not duplicating services or otherwise engaging in unproductive competition with other organizations. A relatively unregulated environment also opens the door for unscrupulous organizations—or even well-intentioned but incompetent organizations—to enter the market, thereby increasing the burden on legitimate and effective organizations to distance themselves from the crowd. In the public sector as well, the deregulated entrepreneurial spirit not only allows competition, but encourages it. To cite one of the best-known examples, the city of Phoenix allowed private firms to bid against its own department for the city's refuse collection contract (Osborne and Gaebler, 1992, pp. 76–80). Initially, a private firm was awarded the contract, but after several subsequent bidding processes, it was again awarded to the city's own agency. Essentially, the city won back its own contract after making administrative and operational reforms.

Another type of threat in this cell involves increased exposure to risk. What happens when a discretionary program fails, when public funds are wasted or lost, or when a mistake slips through the organization's own internal control system? In this cell, the organization must assume full and complete responsibility for its actions and may be more greatly exposed to legal and financial liability. When initiatives fail in this cell, the organization cannot hide behind the skirts of a formal regulatory framework by saying, "Well, yes, things did go dreadfully wrong, but we were only following the directives from above!" In effect, this segment of the accountability environment sometimes gives public and nonprofit professionals enough rope to hang themselves. As illustrated in Chapter Seven, this can be a very volatile sector of the accountability environment.

A third type of threat in this cell relates to the culture of the organization. In an unregulated environment, organizations are relatively free to engage in entrepreneurial activities to generate new revenues or to address emerging needs of clients. In his review of the literature on profit-making enterprises in the nonprofit sector, Young (1988) notes that this entrepreneurial spirit can distract the organization from its public service mission. Also, entrepreneurship can carry substantial costs in legal and administrative support services and can create conflict and goal displacement among members of the organization. In an unregulated environment, the organization can become inebriated with the seemingly endless possibilities to enhance or diversify revenues, to reallocate resources, to revise programs and procedures, to reach out to new clients, and so on. In the process, the organization can gradually drift from its traditional values and comparative advantages. Also, it can lose sight of its ultimate accountability to the public when other measures of performance such as market share become increasingly important. It can even drift from its legal mandate.

A related type of threat concerns the core competencies of the organization. Some government and nonprofit professionals are accustomed to working in an unregulated, market-driven environment but many are not. They are more comfortable and more competent in an environment structured by guidelines, rules, regulations, and other explicit parameters of accountability.

Finally, there are threats related to the public image of the organization. The notion of administrative discretion may be at odds with prevailing perceptions (and stereotypes) of government and nonprofit organizations. Government organizations often are perceived as rigid bureaucracies staffed by machinelike people who show no initiative, exercise no discretion, and certainly are not entrepreneurs. Nonprofits, on the other hand, often are stereotyped as charities staffed entirely by idealistic do-gooders with no management skills whatsoever. Consequently, this segment of the

accountability environment often is disrupted by pseudocontroversies that can be very damaging. For example, a nonprofit organization might be criticized by the news media for regularly
showing surplus revenues (profit) at the end of the fiscal year. This
approach to financial management is not only legal, it is prudent.
Still, it is at odds with the literal interpretation of the word nonprofit. During the Aramony scandal at the national office of the
United Way, the news media repeatedly referred to the spin-off corporations of the United Way as if to suggest something inherently
evil about such corporate structures. There were plenty of things
to criticize in the Aramony case, but the simple existence of spin-
off corporations was not one of them.

Thus, the threats in this segment of the accountability environment can be summarized as follows:

- Threats related to the prospect of increased competition from
  comparable organizations
- Threats related to the prospect of increased exposure to risk
  by the organization or its employees
- Threats arising from the impact of unregulated activities on
  the culture of the organization
- Threats related to the core competencies in the organization
  and its inability to manage accountability in an unregulated
  environment
- Threats to the public image of the organization

The opportunities in this environment are more intuitively
clear than the threats. In this cell, the organization is uncon-
strained by tight external controls. Moreover, it is not experiencing substantial pressure to negotiate standards with outside
stakeholders. This relatively unregulated environment naturally
provides the organization with opportunities for greater flexibility
and responsiveness to changing needs. It is free to develop measures of performance and accountability mechanisms tailored to
various components of its mission and to different segments of its
client population. One of the key shortcomings of almost all
bureaucratic or legal standards of accountability is that they tend
to follow a one-size-fits-all philosophy by lumping disparate organizations (and perhaps disparate consumers) into large categories

to ensure identical treatment of all. But in Cell 3 of the framework, organizations have substantial freedom to define standards of accountability appropriate for their context, their mission, and subsets of clients. It is also free to report (literally account) for its performance via whatever communication channel it desires because there is no formal reporting mechanism to which it must adhere.

Another type of opportunity in this cell is for officials to use information technology to periodically (and proactively) inform constituents regarding accomplishment of organizational goals and objectives (Egol, 1988). Businesses routinely produce annual reports for stockholders and potential investors, but this practice is relatively rare in public and nonprofit organizations. Advances in management information systems and decision support systems make compilation of regular public reports relatively easy. And new distribution technologies such as electronic mail and fax machines offer opportunities for cost-effective communication to targeted stakeholders.

A related opportunity involves the prospect of seeking input and meaningful participation from clients, donors, and other stakeholders in designing accountability measures relevant to their needs and their perceptions of the public interest. This approach holds the prospect of building support and trust for the organization as well as generating creative ideas that would otherwise not be explored.

Another type of opportunity involves exercising leadership by serving as a benchmark of excellence for comparable organizations. This may be a prerequisite for being an effective advocate for new policies or management procedures designed to enhance accountability.

Finally, this environment provides organizations with the opportunity to invest in the professional development of staff and volunteers. As described above, this segment of the accountability environment requires new skills and perhaps new perspectives to fulfill professional obligations and responsibilities. It requires people who are self-starters and proactive in their efforts to serve the public trust. It requires creativity and innovation. It requires vision and leadership.

Thus the opportunities in this segment of the accountability environment can be summarized as follows:

- Opportunities for enhanced flexibility and responsiveness to changing needs
- Opportunities to regularly and proactively inform key constituencies on progress toward goals and objectives
- Opportunities to broaden participation in organizational decision making
- Opportunities to serve as a benchmark of excellence, influencing the behavior of other organizations
- Opportunities to enhance the skills of professional staff members and volunteers

Anticipatory Accountability: Advocacy

Finally, the bottom left cell of Figure 4.1 (Cell 4) portrays situations in which government and nonprofit agencies must try to anticipate changes in the explicit standards to which they may soon be held accountable and the reporting channels for formal oversight. They may try to prepare themselves for compliance with these emerging standards or, perhaps, actively participate in the legislative or regulatory processes leading to their design and implementation. Thus, this cell is labeled *anticipatory accountability.*

Suppose a state legislature is considering steps to tighten regulatory controls on certain types of nonprofit commercial activities and fundraising strategies. The lawmakers will need to address many questions: What is the desired outcome of the stricter regulations? What types of controls will achieve these outcomes? What enforcement mechanisms should be established? How should compliance be reported and through what chain of accountability? In this cell, the affected organizations should try to anticipate the formulation of these new standards in order to prepare for eventual compliance (Cell 1). These organizations may even play an advocacy role in shaping and defining the standards they believe eventually will be (or should be) imposed.

What if the anticipated changes in the accountability environment are expected to loosen rather than tighten regulatory constraints? Here too, decision makers would be wise to strategically prepare their organization for these new and more flexible standards. For example, using the discretionary model of accountability (Cell 3), they might anticipate the need to develop stronger internal controls and self-imposed checks and balances within their agencies to compensate for the deregulated external environment. Also, using the concept of negotiated accountability (Cell 2), they might anticipate that the emerging legislative or regulatory standards will be vaguely stated, thereby creating a need for negotiation and clarification of standards with relevant stakeholders. Here they may begin to formulate their negotiable interests and strategies in advance.

The notion of anticipatory accountability requires that public and nonprofit officials try to stay ahead of the curve by preparing for likely changes in their accountability environment. It also places added responsibility on administrators to educate elected officials, board members, and other policy actors on emerging public needs and the risks and benefits associated with contemplated legal or regulatory actions. Thus, the notion of anticipatory accountability is consistent with the concept of "administrative advocacy" (Shafritz, 1992, p. 10) wherein public managers not only are responsible for implementing policy initiatives dictated from above, but also for advocating legislative or administrative initiatives to serve the public interest.

Clearly, this responsibility implies additional burdens of accountability. Baily (1988, p. 480) says that "politics and hierarchy induce the public servant to search imaginatively for a *public-will-to-be*. In this search, the public servant is often a leader in the creation of a new public will, so he is in part accountable to what he in part creates" (emphasis added).

Threats and opportunities in Cell 4. There are several relevant questions to be answered when scanning this segment of the accountability environment:

- What legislative or regulatory actions—pending or emerging—are likely to have the greatest strategic importance for the organization?
- Can the organization influence the outcome or participate in deliberations on these issues?
- Should the organization propose formal standards or reporting channels of accountability to fill a void in the current system?
- Does this portion of the accountability environment present any opportunities for the organization?

- Does this portion of the accountability environment pose any threats?

The threats and opportunities in this segment of the accountability environment are, in some respects, similar to those related to compliance (Cell 1). Certainly there is the possibility that the anticipated formal standards will somehow be disadvantageous to the organization. They may carry compliance costs or impose inappropriate or unattainable standards of accountability. But there are several other threats as well that are unique to this segment of the accountability environment.

First, there are political risks associated with any form of advocacy. The organization's direct involvement in the formal policy-making process can galvanize widespread debate and controversy, potentially focusing unwanted attention and scrutiny on the organization itself. Also, there is the risk of alienating powerful constituencies and jeopardizing the organization's traditional base of support. It is especially threatening if the organization's name becomes affiliated with a particular legislative or regulatory proposal. For example, a statewide association of nonprofit hospitals (call it the XYZ Association) advocated a legislative initiative regarding tax exemptions that was particularly beneficial to its members. But the name of this organization became informally attached to the initiative—it became widely known as the XYZ Bill rather than by its legislative reference number. This focused some unwanted attention on the association, especially from other nonprofit organizations who opposed the proposal.

Also, there are potential legal threats, especially for private nonprofit organizations that operate under strict restrictions on political activity. For these organizations, it is wise to seek professional legal counsel before engaging in any political activity.

Thus, the threats in this segment of the accountability environment are essentially related to the political risks of advocacy:

- Threats arising from polarized debate on an issue
- Threats associated with the loss of traditional bases of support
- Threats associated with the public visibility of the organization
- Threats related to the legality of political activities, especially for private nonprofit organizations

The political context of this cell presents opportunities as well as threats. There is the opportunity to build advocacy networks and coalitions of other stakeholders who share similar interests and objectives. These coalitions can have beneficial effects long after the political issue has been resolved.

Also, there is the opportunity to exercise leadership and to focus favorable attention on the organization if its motives are widely perceived to advance the public interest. As in Cell 2 (negotiation) there are opportunities use advocacy to educate relevant stakeholders and to preempt events that might lead to the imposition of inappropriate standards.

Finally, as in several other cells, there is the opportunity to use information technology to support and enhance the organization's advocacy efforts. Common Cause uses a computer network to alert members to important congressional votes and to respond to queries about legislative issues. Even very small organizations with limited staff and budgets have discovered that access to the information highway can significantly enhance their efforts to anticipate and participate in dialogue on political and legislative initiatives (Moore, 1994).

Thus, the opportunities in this segment of the accountability environment include:

- Opportunities to build networks and coalitions of support that could have long-lasting beneficial impacts
- Opportunities to exercise leadership
- Opportunities to focus favorable attention on the organization
- Opportunities to use the political process to educate important stakeholders
- Opportunities to use information technology to enhance anticipatory accountability and advocacy

Environmental Scanning Using the Framework

The conceptual framework outlined here can help decision makers ask some important and probing questions about their accountability environment. In the broadest sense, decision makers should ask which of the four types of accountability environments applies to their organization and whether any of the four types is more pervasive and important than the others. For many organizations, of course, the notion of legal accountability (Cell 1) will initially be perceived as most pervasive. They may, for example, perceive that the environment is dominated by strict regulatory standards and formal lines of accountability through the interorganizational chain of authority. But even these organizations may discover after some reflection that they must also deal—if only occasionally—with the other three segments of the accountability environment.

Also, it is important to remember that the framework is not a static diagnostic device. That is, organizations will move from one cell to another as their accountability environment changes. For example, as we discussed in Chapter One, many nonprofit organizations have historically been relatively unregulated, allowing them to operate primarily in the domain of negotiated accountability (Cell 2) or discretionary accountability (Cell 3). But, the trend in the nonprofit sector is toward greater oversight and control by government agencies and private watchdog organizations, especially concerning the activities of large commercial nonprofit organizations (see Mehegan, 1995). This may suggest that a nonprofit organization will view its environment as shifting increasingly toward legal accountability (Cell 1) or anticipatory accountability (Cell 4). If such a shift is perceived by decision makers, they may want to adjust their behavior and their management systems accordingly.

Conversely, the trend within agencies of the federal government, and in many state and municipal governments as well, is toward less hierarchical and less regulated structures that, ostensibly, are more effective in meeting the needs of internal and external customers.

Thus, decision makers should be concerned not only with plotting the organization at a particular time, but also assessing trends that may suggest movement from one cell to another within the framework.

Also, some components or programs of the organization may be plotted in one cell of the framework, while other parts are mapped elsewhere. In universities, for example, teaching is a relatively decentralized and unregulated activity—while personnel administration generally is managed centrally and within a more regulated environment.

Clearly, there is no precise metric or instrument with which to determine the organization's placement within the framework. What separates a highly regulated organization from a moderately regulated one may be a matter of opinion or perception. Teachers in public school districts, for example, may feel they are tightly regulated, especially in states moving toward the concept of outcome-based education. But compared with police departments, where the actions of law enforcement officers are closely scrutinized by a hierarchical chain of command leading ultimately to the courts, school districts still offer their personnel a very substantial amount of autonomy and discretionary authority.

Sources of Information on the Accountability Environment

Decision makers who are well-informed about events and trends in each segment of the accountability environment might be successful in using qualitative techniques like brainstorming to generate lists of opportunities and threats. Brainstorming sessions can be either extremely productive or a complete waste of time. In my experience, brainstorming too often is approached in a casual way with little advance preparation and no attention to the process. Under these circumstances, brainstorming is little more than a group bull session contaminated by unfounded speculations and little real clarity of thought. Advance preparation for a brainstorming session should focus on careful selection of participants and drafting clear and focused questions for the participants to consider (see Nutt and Backoff, 1992, pp. 225–272).

The insights gained from a brainstorming session will be enhanced when the group includes diverse expertise and perspectives. The executive staff of the organization, including the legal staff, will have familiarity with the legal and regulatory environment and, therefore, will be able to identify threats and opportunities related to legal accountability (Cell 1) and anticipatory accountability (Cell 4). Boards of trustees and elected officials, on the other hand, may have relatively more expertise in interpreting subtle shifts in societal values and expectations that are related to the notions of negotiated accountability (Cell 2) and discretionary accountability (Cell 3).

Clients, service recipients, local watchdog organizations, and representatives from the news media also will have their own perspectives on each segment of the accountability environment and should be invited to participate in the brainstorming sessions. As a general rule, it is helpful to tap the perspectives of at least some people who have no vested interest in the organization. By virtue of their detached perspective, these outsiders can challenge the assumptions of staff members, who naturally are inclined to see opportunities and threats from their own perspective.

Regardless of who participates in the brainstorming session, its value can be diminished by vague or open-ended questions like *"What are the major threats and opportunities in our accountability environment?"* Such a question will not focus attention on specific types of issues. It is likely to lead to unproductive speculation when what is needed is targeted analysis that truly taps the participants' expertise and insights. Questions should be targeted on each cell of the accountability environment to achieve maximum benefit of the group's collective knowledge.

Even with well-informed participants and well-focused questions, brainstorming alone may not be sufficient to thoroughly scan the accountability environment for opportunities and threats. There is no substitute for a rigorous and systematic effort to tap every available source of hard data on events and trends in the accountability environment. Legal and regulatory trends, for example, can be evaluated by regularly scanning government documents like the *Federal Register,* the *Congressional Record,* and the *Congressional Quarterly.* Many state legislatures also have on-line data bases or periodic reports that provide updates on legislative debates and actions in the state capitol. Professional associations like municipal leagues or statewide associations of nonprofit organizations also are a valuable source of timely information on legal and political trends. National organizations, like Independent Sector, the National Center for Nonprofit Boards, or the International City Management Association are yet another source of information on accountability trends and often provide legislative updates for their members. Also, professional newsletters and journals can provide objective information and insights into trends and events in the accountability environment. These are really too numerous to list, but they include publications like *Public Administration Review, Public Administration Times, The Chronicle of Philanthropy, Nonprofit Management and Leadership,* and *Nonprofit Times.*

Finally, it is prudent to keep abreast of trends and issues among watchdog organizations like the Better Business Bureau, the National Committee for Responsive Philanthropy, and locally organized groups. What accountability issues are most important to these watchdog groups? Are they shifting their attention away from some issues and toward others?

How to Assess Events and Trends

Environmental scanning is an art as well as a science. In fact, it may be more art than science because of the inherent subjectivity of distinguishing threats from opportunities. Nonetheless, there are a few valuable tools to use in the scanning process.

Focusing on Priority Events

Lederman (1984) presents a priority matrix for segmenting high-, medium-, and low-priority events and trends in the external environment (Figure 4.2).

This matrix suggests that not all threats and opportunities in the accountability environment are equally important from a strategic point of view. To develop priorities, decision makers should first try to assess the likelihood that a threat or opportunity will occur, and then assess its potential impact on the orga-

Figure 4.2. Event Priority Matrix.

		High	Medium	Low
	High	High priority	High priority	Medium priority
Probability of Occurrence	Medium	High priority	Medium priority	Low priority
	Low	Medium priority	Low priority	Low priority

Impact on the Agency

Source: Reprinted from *Long Range Planning, 17*(3), Lederman, L. L., "Foresight Activities in the U.S.A.: Time for a Reassessment?" p. 46, copyright 1984 with kind permission from Elsevier Science Ltd., The Boulevard, Langford Lane, Kidlington 0X5 1GB, UK.

nization. For example, in the cell of Figure 4.1 we have labeled anticipatory accountability (Cell 4). Decision makers naturally will assess the probability that a legislative or regulatory proposal will be implemented as well as the strategic impact on the organization if it is implemented. These will be important considerations when formulating a strategy to address the issue. The same approach can be followed with the other three segments of the accountability environment to rank-order events from high to low priority.

Mapping Linkages Among Events

Opportunities and threats in the accountability environment do not necessarily occur independently of each other. Rather, they sometimes interact in systemic ways creating a situation in which the whole is more than the sum of its parts. Cross-impact analysis is a useful method for mapping these interactions (Gordon and Hayward, 1968; Dunn, 1994, pp. 249–258). Suppose, for example, that a nonprofit organization detects the following trends in its accountability environment:

SAL: National and local newspaper articles on "excessive" salaries paid to nonprofit executives

LEG: Proposed legislation in the state capitol requiring nonprofit organizations to file more extensive annual reports on revenues and expenditures

COMP: Pressure from small business associations for regulatory agencies to investigate "unfair competition" by nonprofit organizations that run commercial enterprises

PHIL: Philanthropic contributions from corporate foundations in the region

FEES: Use of service fees by nonprofit organizations as a method of stabilizing and diversifying revenues

There may be a synergy among some of these trends that can be graphically portrayed for closer scrutiny.

In Table 4.1, a plus sign (+) indicates that the occurrence of one event is presumed to enhance the probability of a related event. A zero (0) indicates that two events appear to be unrelated. A minus sign (–) indicates that the occurrence of one event will inhibit the probability of a related event. Thus, working across the

**Table 4.1.   Cross-Impact Analysis of Trends
in the Accountability Environment.**

Trends	SAL	LEG	COMP	PHIL	FEES
SAL	none	+	+	–	0
LEG	+ +	none	+	–	0
COMP	+ +	+ +	none	–	0
PHIL	0	0	0	none	–
FEES	+	+	+	– –	none

first row, decision makers may conclude that newspaper articles on "excessive" salaries are likely to: fuel political support for more extensive reporting requirements, provide more motivation for businesses to challenge the tax advantages enjoyed by commercial nonprofits, and contribute to a decline in contributions from corporate foundations. Below the diagonal vector, a double-plus sign (++) or a double-minus sign (– –) indicates a reciprocal reaction where *A* not only affects *B* in a positive (or negative) way, but *B* affects *A* in the same direction. Thus, working across the third row, decision makers may believe that pressure from small businesses to eliminate "unfair competition" is likely to: be a catalyst for newspaper articles on executive salaries, fuel political support for stricter reporting requirements, and contribute to the decline in donations from corporate foundations.

The cross-impact matrix can be used to develop scenarios of how one event in the accountability environment may lead to others. For example, the following scenario might be constructed based on the judgments in Table 4.1: A change in any one of three events—newspaper articles on executive salaries, legislated reporting requirements, or challenges from small businesses—is likely to have reciprocal effects on the other two. These three events, in turn, will contribute to declining support from corporate foundations, thereby placing pressure on nonprofit organizations to increase service fees in a effort to stabilize revenues.

The example provided here is a simple one designed to illustrate possible applications. More sophisticated applications of cross-impact analysis might make use of available quantitative data or judgments that would allow conditional probabilities to be attached to each event or trend. Also, there are more complex methods for constructing scenarios that utilize expert judgments translated into quantitative measures (see Saaty and Kearns, 1985, pp. 140–151).

Scenarios also can be developed with simple brainstorming methods, but cross-impact analysis is a good way to visualize the interactions among events and can help focus attention on the underlying assumptions within each of the cells.

Some Suggestions on Process and Procedure

When should decision makers apply methods like the ones presented in this chapter? Who should be involved in the process?

If the organization regularly engages in a strategic planning process, the methods presented in this chapter should be incorporated into the environmental scanning phase of that process. In other words, as the organization looks outward for threats and opportunities related to its overall corporate strategy, it should also use methods like those described here to focus specifically on the accountability environment. Decision makers will find that there is an economy of effort when they combine their scan of the accountability environment with their scan of the broader strategic environment. This is because much of the information they would typically gather for general strategic planning will overlap information germane to the specialized topic of accountability.

Whether or not an organization follows a cyclical (three- to five-year) strategic planning process, I strongly recommend that decision makers conduct a scan of the accountability environment frequently—at least once a year, and more often when the accountability environment is in flux. As noted earlier, the accountability environment can change rapidly and dramatically, especially after the occurrence of a highly publicized controversy or scandal. Today, for example, the accountability environment of nonprofit organizations is in a turbulent state as lawmakers and watchdog groups are reacting to the rash of recent controversies. Thus, under current circumstances, it would be prudent for nonprofit organizations to update their scans of the accountability environment very frequently if they want to be well positioned for the rapidly changing opportunities and threats.

Regarding participation in the process, I recommend that the scan of the accountability environment be driven by the professional staff of the organization, but with leadership from the governing board and broad participation from many other stakeholders. In nonprofit organizations, for example, the board of trustees must play a central role in the process because they are ultimately the last stop in the accountability chain of command. Similarly, in government jurisdictions, elected officials should be personally involved in the scanning process.

Clearly, trustees and elected officials will rely, in part, on the technical expertise of professional staff in gathering and interpreting information in the scanning process. But they themselves will bring a unique and valuable perspective to the process and therefore they should avoid becoming excessively reliant on input from the staff.

The process described here provides a good opportunity for organizations to seek input from a variety of sources—citizens, clients, special interest groups, media representatives, peer organizations, regulatory agencies. These and other stakeholders might be convened as an accountability advisory committee to provide regular input and feedback on the organization's environmental scanning process and its accountability plan.

Summary

The accountability environment of public and nonprofit organizations is inherently complex and ever-changing. The search for opportunities and threats in this environment can be overwhelming unless decision makers segment the environment for closer scrutiny. This chapter has presented and illustrated a method for segmenting the accountability environment and isolating specific types of opportunities and threats.

While the framework presented here is a useful starting point, readers are encouraged to experiment with this approach and adapt it to their own needs and contexts. As I said in Chapter Three, no strategic management tool or framework can actually design and implement strategies. The key is to find a method that helps decision makers ask the right questions about their accountability environment.

The focus in this chapter has been on the external environment. In the next chapter, we turn our attention inward to look for organizational strengths and weaknesses and assess how well (or poorly) the organization is positioned to respond to external opportunities and threats. Chapter Six then describes how to isolate strategic issues related to accountability by synthesizing information from the external scan and internal audit.

Chapter Five

Conducting an Accountability Audit

The previous chapter explained how the external accountability environment can be segmented for close scrutiny of opportunities and threats. In this chapter, we will turn our attention inward to assess the organization's strengths and weaknesses in terms of the resources at its disposal to serve the public interest and preserve the public trust. Just as the external environment can be segmented, so too can the internal environment. The internal environment consists of the organization's accountability infrastructure—the resources, policies, and processes that either support or detract from the organization's accountability to the public.

In accountability auditing, it is especially important to assess strengths and weaknesses with respect to the events and trends in the accountability environment. *Strengths* are defined here as assets the organization can mobilize in response to its accountability environment. Strengths allow the organization to position itself to respond in a timely and effective manner when opportunities or threats arise. *Weaknesses,* on the other hand, are potential liabilities that can inhibit or even prevent the organization from responding appropriately to its accountability environment. They are the factors that can cause the organization to be out of step with the world around it and vulnerable to criticism or even to a full-blown accountability crisis.

Note that this approach to accountability auditing differs from traditional approaches that focus primarily on documenting accountability policies and procedures such as ethics policies, conflict of interest policies, checks and balances, and so on. To be sure,

these traditional components of an accountability audit are important and, as such, are discussed in this chapter. But it also is important, especially from a strategic perspective, to examine other types
of accountability resources that can be mobilized in response to
changing circumstances in the external environment.

Accountability Resources

An accountability audit revolves around several targeted questions:

- How well has the organization performed in meeting explicit
  and implicit accountability standards? Has the organization
  demonstrated that it is especially effective in meeting certain
  kinds of accountability standards and, perhaps, less effective in
  meeting other standards?
- Does the organization have appropriate accountability controls and are they working properly? What components of the
  organization's accountability infrastructure are especially
  strong? Are any components vulnerable to criticism?
- Is the organization devoting sufficient resources to maintaining
  and enhancing its accountability? If there is need for additional
  investment of resources, where would these best be spent?
- Is the organization positioned to respond effectively to new or
  emerging performance standards or reporting requirements
  arising from shifts in the accountability environment?
- What is the organization's current image among key
  stakeholders? How is the organization currently perceived
  by key audiences?
- Are there gaps between what the organization wants its constituencies to believe and what they actually believe? If so, what
  are the probable causes of those gaps?

The leaders of the organization may have a strong intuitive
sense of where the organization is weak and where it is strong
with respect to interpreting and serving the public trust. If so,
they may decide that the questions above are sufficient to guide
their discussion. It is more likely, however, that decision makers
will need to examine specific aspects of the organization's
accountability infrastructure in order to zero in on selected
strengths and weaknesses.

What does this infrastructure look like? Can it be segmented for closer scrutiny? The organization's accountability infrastructure can be organized as follows:

- *Financial Resources:* The extent to which the organization has slack resources, or the potential to secure additional resources, for a timely response to changes in the accountability environment. Examples include reserve funds, a dedicated crisis fund, access to special-purpose grants and awards, or the ability to generate new revenues on short notice.

- *Human Resources:* The extent to which paid professionals and volunteers have both the skill and the commitment to respond effectively to emerging trends and events in the accountability environment. Examples include leadership among the staff and on the board, motivation of staff and volunteers, and ability of staff and volunteers to acquire and use skills needed to respond effectively to the accountability environment.

- *Information Resources:* The extent to which the organization has ready access to data with which to scan the accountability environment and formulate appropriate responses to challenges and opportunities. Examples include information on emerging legislative and regulatory standards, information on the activities of comparable organizations, information on client demographics and needs, and—most importantly—information about the outcomes and impacts of the organization's work.

- *Legal Mandate:* The extent to which the organization is legally authorized to respond to changes in its accountability environment. Examples include the degree of freedom provided by the organization's mandate to interpret and adapt legal and regulatory standards, the legal authority of the organization to engage in advocacy and other political activities, and the legal authority of the organization to establish its own accountability standards and reporting mechanisms.

- *Networks:* The extent to which the organization, either alone or with others, can influence the accountability environment via collaboration, persuasion, or other means. Examples include formal membership in professional associations, informal channels with peers, and contacts with political actors.

- *Public Image and Credibility:* The extent to which the organization can rely on its reputation and its record of prior performance to respond to accountability threats and opportunities. Examples include prestigious awards for prior performance, rankings among peer organizations, perceived moral value of the mission, and ability to mobilize clients and other constituencies.

• *Management Controls and Governance Procedures:* The extent to which the organization can rely on its infrastructure and support systems to mobilize and direct all other accountability resources outlined above. Examples include budgeting procedures, strategic planning systems, quality assurance systems, recruitment and training procedures, performance appraisal systems, internal checks and balances, codes of ethics, formal dissent procedures, and other relevant policies and procedures.

Clearly, these internal resources are not necessarily independent of each other or mutually exclusive. The public image and credibility of the organization could affect its political power, which in turn could affect its networks with other organizations. But there are broad distinctions among these accountability resources. More importantly, they will come into play in different ways in response to forces in the accountability environment. Table 5.1 illustrates how each resource group might relate to the segments of the accountability environment discussed in Chapter Four.

Each cell of Table 5.1 contains an example of how the organization's resources might be assessed when confronted with threats or opportunities from each segment of the accountability environment. Naturally, each cell could contain many more examples.

Some Illustrations

Sometimes accountability audits should be conducted in a tactical manner in response to specific threats or opportunities. Other times the audit should be conducted in a strategic manner in an effort to anticipate changes in the environment. Let us examine both types of applications.

Tactical Audit

Juvenile Center, a nonprofit half-way house for juvenile offenders, has come under attack from residents and businesses in its

Table 5.1. Accountability Resources and the Accountability Environment.

Accountability Resources	The Accountability Environment			
	Compliance accountability	*Negotiated accountability*	*Discretionary authority*	*Anticipatory accountability*
Financial resources	Cost of compliance and impact on budget	Use of financial resources to strengthen negotiating position	Slack resources to invest in discretionary programs	Slack resources to invest in advocacy
Human resources	Skills in complying with laws and regulations	Skills in negotiating	Ability to use discretion and judgment	Skills in advocacy
Information resources	Use of information to demonstrate compliance	Use of information to strengthen negotiating position	Access to information on standards of professional practice	Use of information to strengthen advocacy
Legal mandate	Legal authority of the organization to interpret laws and regulations or to challenge account- ability standards that are harmful to the organization or its constituents	Legal authority of the organization to negotiate standards of accountability	Legal authority of the organization to establish its own standards of accountability	Legal authority of the organization to advocate the interests of its constituents

(continues)

Table 5.1. *(continued)*

Accountability Resources	Compliance accountability	Negotiated accountability	Discretionary authority	Anticipatory accountability
			The Accountability Environment	
Networks	Use of networks to enhance compliance	Use of networks to strengthen negotiating position	Use of networks to establish benchmarks of professional practice	Use of networks to strengthen advocacy
Image	Use of image to build credibility with oversight organizations	Use of image to strengthen negotiating position	Use of image to defend discretionary judgments	Use of image to strengthen advocacy
Management controls and governance processes	Use of internal quality assurance systems to demonstrate performance exceeding mere compliance	Use of professional development systems to build skills in negotiating	Use of internal checks and balances even when not required by law	Use of professional development systems to build skills in advocacy

neighborhood. The citizens and business owners claim the center has violated the city's zoning ordinance by not taking required steps to secure the facility, thereby jeopardizing the health and safety of the neighborhood. While this clearly is a threat, let us assume that the leaders of the center believe this standard of accountability is negotiable—the zoning ordinance is vaguely worded and the operational definition of a secure facility is open to debate. Still, the neighbors are threatening to take legal action if their concerns are not addressed.

The Juvenile Center might assess its accountability resources (strengths and weaknesses) as follows:

- *Financial Resources:* The center's own resources are fully committed for this fiscal year and it cannot afford to make all the structural changes needed to enhance the security of its facility (weakness).
- *Human Resources:* The executive director of the center is a skilled negotiator (strength), but she has little staff support and her time and energy are fully consumed by several critical grant proposals due next month (weakness).
- *Information Resources:* The center has not kept very good records regarding incidents involving its clients, visitors, and neighborhood residents. Therefore, it is not in a very strong position to counter the residents' arguments that the center presents a security problem to the neighborhood (weakness). On the other hand, the center has reliable information suggesting that neighborhood residents will settle for far less than what they have publicly demanded as concessions (strength).
- *Legal Mandate:* Legal counsel believes the Juvenile Center is in technical compliance with the zoning ordinance (strength), but acknowledges that the ordinance contains some vague language and that neighborhood residents have several valid concerns (weakness). Trustees of the center have authorized the executive director to negotiate any agreement she believes is in the best interest of the center and its clients (strength).
- *Networks:* The center has the support of another nonprofit organization—a neighborhood development corporation—that enjoys high credibility and has significant political clout with the city council and the zoning board (strength). Moreover, one of the

trustees of the center is an active member of the neighborhood chamber of commerce and may be able to persuade the chamber to soften its negotiating position (strength).

• *Image:* The image of the center has been damaged by several controversies over the past five years, including a financial crisis and accusations of mismanagement under the previous director. These events tarnished the image of the organization (weakness). On the other hand, the local newspaper recently published an editorial saying that the center is gradually "turning the tide" under new leadership and expressing hope that this controversy can be resolved without threatening the center's viability or distracting it from its "worthy mission" (strength).

• *Procedures:* The center's new strategic plan, adopted last year, outlined a series of steps to improve community relations, including the establishment of a community advisory board that will hold its first meeting next month (strength).

The accountability audit described in this example relates to a specific and immediate threat from the external environment. Thus the primary purpose of the audit would be to develop a tactical approach to negotiations with the neighborhood residents and business owners. For example, the Juvenile Center might join forces with the neighborhood development corporation to expand the dialogue on neighborhood security to include property crimes, vandalism, gang violence, and so on. It might use its contacts with the chamber of commerce to explore the interests and objectives of the business owners. It might suggest that this issue be explored at next month's inaugural meeting of the community advisory board, thereby buying time for the executive director to finish the grant proposals before turning her full attention to this issue.

Strategic Audit

Suppose a municipal government was scanning its accountability environment as part of its strategic planning process. Let us assume that the decision makers have detected specific opportunities and threats in each segment of the accountability environment, but that their overarching scenario for the next three to five years is as follows:

The federal government (Congress, the President, and regulatory agencies) will continue their efforts to give states and localities more discretionary authority in determining spending priorities and service delivery mechanisms. The state legislature and the governor will follow the lead of the federal government by relaxing state regulatory standards in areas like procurement, contracting, and managing public investments. Overall, the intergovernmental environment will be significantly deregulated compared with current conditions. Locally, citizens will demand higher quality services with less bureaucracy and more user friendliness. While most citizens will not play a significantly larger role in government affairs, several citizen advocacy groups will emerge to exert greater influence. There will also be much more interaction between the municipal government and private nonprofit organizations. Most of these interactions will be collaborative (in planning and delivering social services), but some will be competitive.

With this type of scenario in mind, the decision makers proceeded to examine their strengths and weaknesses, but they did so in a slightly more general way than the Juvenile Center in the prior example. Here is what they came up with:

- *Financial Resources:* Overall, the municipality's financial position is strong. It maintains a modest reserve fund for special initiatives and is nowhere near the legal limit on its taxing capacity (strength).
- *Human Resources:* The city manager has prior experience in other organizations—public and private—that have successfully implemented various quality assurance initiatives like Total Quality Management. He is known to be an innovator and a public sector entrepreneur (strength). But, on the whole, the middle managers and rank and file employees in City Hall are not skilled in these methods and have expressed skepticism regarding their value (weakness).
- *Information Resources:* Several years ago, the municipality quietly launched an effort to develop a data base on the efficiency and effectiveness of its various departments and bureaus. It now has the capability to track these measures over time and to benchmark with other comparably sized municipalities around the country (strength).

- *Legal Mandate:* The municipality is governed by a home rule charter that gives it substantial latitude regarding its sources of revenue and its operational procedures (strength). But the municipal workforce is heavily unionized and current union contracts place some severe restrictions on its freedom to redesign jobs or make other procedural changes (weakness).
- *Networks:* On the whole, the municipality does not enjoy good relations with surrounding communities or with nonprofit social service organizations (weakness). But one of the city council members is a former state legislator who maintains close contacts with his former colleagues in the state capitol. He could be a powerful advocate for the community with the state legislature (strength). Also, the city manager is active in several professional associations and maintains contact with his peers around the country (strength).
- *Image:* Overall, the public image of the organization is not very good. The local news media regularly criticize the "impenetrable bureaucracy of City Hall" and there are several minor lawsuits pending that allege various types of discrimination, violation of procedures, and general mismanagement (weakness).
- *Procedures:* Nearly all of the municipality's procedures are stifled by its growing bureaucracy. A recent internal analysis by a group of volunteer business professionals found evidence of duplication, unnecessary paperwork, delays, and outdated procedures in nearly all facets of the organization (weakness).

Clearly, from a macro perspective, this municipality is not very well positioned to respond effectively to the anticipated deregulation and other changes in its accountability environment. The culture of the workforce appears to mirror the organization's bureaucratic inertia, and substantial investments will be required to infuse more flexibility and entrepreneurship into the organization. Even in the current bureaucratic environment (with its emphasis on uniform procedures), the accountability of the organization is suspect. Citizens might be even more distrustful if municipal employees are given more discretionary authority in a deregulated environment.

Nonetheless, this municipality has some important strengths that might be mobilized to prepare for anticipated changes in its accountability environment. It has slack resources to launch new initiatives and perhaps to invest in training and professional development programs. It has a very competent city manager and also a broad legal mandate (its home rule charter) to restructure its operations. Also, it has a powerful information base with which to identify priorities and to focus its energies on a few projects at a time. Such an approach might gradually build credibility both inside and outside the organization.

Before the municipality can develop strategies or tactics, the decision makers should try to isolate the important strategic issues:

- Can the strengths of the organization—its financial resources, its city manager, and its information resources—be leveraged to capitalize on emerging opportunities?
- How could the leaders of the employee union be persuaded to work with the administration in reexamining work rules, job descriptions, and procedures?
- How could the newspapers be persuaded to support the city's efforts to restructure its operations?
- How could the citizen advocacy groups be involved in the process?

The articulation of strategic issues is critical to the success of any strategic management system and therefore deserves special attention. A detailed discussion of strategic issue analysis is provided in Chapter Six.

Prior Performance: Evidence and Supporting Documentation

Thus far, we have discussed accountability from the perspective of resource mobilization. We have focused on particular accountability resources (finances, people, information, and so on) and how each can be mobilized to address emerging trends in the external environment. In accordance with the strategic management perspective, the guiding paradigm for this book, the discussion in this chapter has had a prospective flavor—searching for strategies and tactics.

But we cannot escape the fact that accountability auditing must also have a retrospective component, which demands evidence and supporting documentation on prior performance in serving the public trust. We are dealing with accountability, and there is no substitute for a formal accounting of strengths and weaknesses supported by evidence and documentation.

In retrospective auditing, the same categories of accountability resources described above can be used to guide the investigation. But the questions should be designed to assess how well the organization has historically performed in meeting accountability standards rather than how the organization might mobilize these resources to address emerging trends. In some cases, the organization's performance can be measured directly, while in others, the reviewer will need to look for indirect evidence. In general, the following standards should apply:

- Financial Resources

    There is evidence that the organization is regularly audited by an independent professional in accordance with generally accepted accounting principles, and that problems or shortcomings raised in management letters from the auditor are promptly addressed by the administrators and trustees.

    There is evidence that individual services and program categories also are audited as required by statutory or contractual agreement.

    There is evidence that the organization uses its budgeting and accounting procedures to assess the relative cost-effectiveness of its programs, not just a line-item listing of expenditures and revenues.

    There is evidence that the organization manages its finances in accordance with generally accepted accounting principles and legal requirements.

    There is evidence that the organization follows internal procedures, with appropriate checks and balances, to minimize the risk of fraud, waste, and abuse in managing its financial resources.

    The organization plans its resource development activities with a view to ensuring its long-term solvency.

There is evidence that the majority of the organization's income is spent on programs and activities directly related to the mandate and mission.

- Human Resources

  There is evidence that the organization employs personnel who are competent, ethical, and qualified to contribute to the mission.

  There is evidence that the organization follows personnel policies and procedures that promote effective and accountable performance.

  There is evidence that employees are trained to follow internal and external chains of accountability.

  There is evidence that the organization applies appropriate standards of accountability to its volunteers and has volunteer recruitment and management policies to promote effective and accountable performance.

- Information Resources

  There is evidence that the organization's information system is designed to provide readily accessible proof of compliance with accountability standards.

  There is evidence that the organization's information system is designed to provide documented program outputs, outcomes, and impacts.

  There is evidence that information on program outputs, outcomes, and impacts is used by decision makers to improve efficiency, effectiveness, and accountability.

  There is evidence that information is regularly shared with relevant stakeholders inside and outside the organization where appropriate.

  There is evidence that the organization regularly reports its performance to inside and outside stakeholders in annual reports, audited financial statements, and program evaluation reports.

  Where appropriate, the organization has taken steps to ensure confidentiality and security of its information system.

- Legal Mandate

  There is evidence that appropriate documentation establishing the organization's legal authority is in place and up to date.

There is evidence that appropriate documentation regarding policies and procedures is in place and followed by the organization.

There is evidence that the organization is in compliance with relevant legal and regulatory requirements.

There is evidence that the organization is in compliance with all contractual arrangements with internal and external stakeholders.

- Networks

There is evidence that the organization maintains contact with relevant professional associations to keep abreast of standards of professional practice.

There is evidence that the organization regularly utilizes formal methods and procedures to monitor the needs of current and prospective clients.

Where appropriate, the organization seeks ways to work in collaboration with other organizations to achieve its mission.

- Image

The organization regularly communicates its mission, its goals, its strategies, and its actual performance to relevant constituencies.

There is evidence of ongoing two-way communication between the organization and relevant constituencies.

- Procedures

The organization's mission and operating philosophies demonstrate a commitment to quality and accountability.

There is evidence that the pursuit of accountability permeates all levels of the organization.

The organization and its governing body are structured to achieve the mission, and these structures are consistent with the expressed operating philosophies.

Program goals are clearly defined, with observable outputs, outcomes, and impacts.

There is evidence that resources are allocated and managed so as to achieve goals and desired outputs, outcomes, and impacts.

There is evidence that responsiveness to explicit and implicit standards of accountability is a focus of the organization and is reflected in all of its management and governance procedures.

A Special Word of Caution to Private Nonprofit Organizations

Many of the most highly publicized accountability challenges for nonprofit organizations have concerned subjective standards of appropriate behavior applied by the general public and the news media to executives and board members (Pratt, 1992). Consequently, in addition to the criteria already discussed, private nonprofit organizations should pay close attention to the following issues:

- *Compensation policies:* What is the total compensation (salary and benefits) of the chief executive officer and other top executives of the organization? How was this compensation determined? Can it be defended in terms of national averages or in comparison with salaries at comparable organizations? Would the trustees be forced to defend the compensation package in terms of special skills and attributes of the executive? Would the organization be embarrassed to have this compensation package made public? Why? Does the organization have a position classification and compensation system for all employees?

- *Commercial enterprises and excess revenues:* What portion of the organization's annual revenue is derived from fees for service and profit-making enterprises? Are any profit-making enterprises unrelated to the core mission? Is the portion of revenue from commercial enterprises growing at an unusually high rate? Is the organization in danger of letting these commercial enterprises distract it from the charitable mission of the organization? Even if the commercial enterprises are entirely legal and appropriate, would the organization find it difficult to explain them to the media or to the public at large? Does the organization have a defensible procedure for determining prices and fees for its services?

- *Fundraising policies:* Do the fundraising materials provide prospective donors with accurate and truthful information regarding the purpose of the solicitation and how their donation will be used? Is the organization engaged in any fundraising strategy that might be criticized as misleading, coercive, or otherwise inappropriate? Does the organization produce a regular report of its fundraising activities and results? If the organization employs fundraising consultants, are they members of the National Society of Fundraising Executives and do they abide by the professional code of ethics of that organization or a similar professional society? Are there explicit written contracts with fundraising consultants that specify the controls retained by the organization?

• *Endowment funds:* Does the organization have an endowment that might appear to the general public to be excessively large? Can the organization easily defend the size of its endowment and the uses of endowment funds?

• *Governance policies:* Are policies in place and followed that help ensure that the volunteer board of directors (trustees) exercises its legal responsibilities in stewardship of the organization? Does the organization have a board recruitment strategy that is tied to its strategic plan? Are newly recruited board members fully oriented to the mission, goals, and operations of the agency? Does the board display a mix of skills and attributes that will help the organization fulfill its core mission? Does the board have at least some members who represent the interests of clients? Does the board display diversity of gender, ethnicity, and so on?

• *Grant administration:* If the organization has restricted revenues from grants and contracts, does it follow internal procedures to ensure that grant money is spent on the purposes for which it was intended? If salaries and other expenses in the organization are allocated among grant sources, can the organization ensure that these percentage distributions represent actual levels of effort on the programs and projects supported by the several grants?

• *Volunteer management:* Does the organization have a comprehensive policy for volunteer management that addresses recruitment, screening, training, assignment of duties, supervision, and performance evaluation? Do the volunteers have direct contact with clients? If so, are they properly trained for these interactions?

• *Use of funds:* Does the organization spend most of its total income on programs directly related to the mandate and mission? What portion of its total budget is spent on fundraising? What portion of its total budget is spent on administration? Would these proportions be perceived as reasonable and appropriate by outside observers?

• *Public information:* Does the organization provide on request a report on its purposes, current activities, governance, finances, and tax-exempt status? Does it provide on request complete financial statements for both the parent organization and any controlled or affiliated entities?

- *Outcome measurement:* Does the organization regularly assess its impacts on clients in addition to traditional output measures such as number of clients served?
- *Collaboration and duplication:* Does the organization follow policies and procedures to ensure that it is not unnecessarily duplicating the services of another agency? Can the organization demonstrate that it regularly collaborates with other agencies for maximum efficiency and effectiveness?

Some of these standards are similar to those used by the Better Business Bureau (see Mehegan, 1995) and the National Charities Information Bureau to monitor the accountability of nonprofit organizations. Also, many of these questions are relevant to government organizations as well as private tax-exempt agencies, but they are directly related to several of the most prominent accountability challenges that nonprofits have confronted in recent years.

Ethics Audits

Earlier in this book, I said that ethics and accountability were not synonymous even though the terms sometimes are used interchangeably. But ethical considerations are an important subset of a more general effort to serve the public trust. Lewis (1991, pp. 199–202) has developed an "ethics audit" that specifies certain criteria for determining the ethical health of public organizations. Her audit is divided into three sections that can be summarized briefly as follows:

- *Explicit policy:* This portion of the ethics audit requires decision makers to document and assess the organization's ethics policies and procedures. Are these policies proscriptive (punitive) or prescriptive (encouraging personal responsibility)? Are they widely distributed and understood by employees? Do these policies provide a guide to decision making?
- *Operations and procedures:* This portion of the audit examines the role of ethical considerations in decision making, organizational

structure, and support systems. Are employees encouraged to raise ethical issues during deliberations on operations and programming? Are ethical considerations reflected in recruitment, development, and appraisal of employees? Do public documents (including budgets and annual reports) faithfully and accurately represent the true picture of the organization?

- *Internal control:* This portion of the audit addresses internal monitoring and control mechanisms related to ethical conduct. Is there a serious commitment to reducing the risk of fraud, waste, and abuse of public resources? Is appropriate ethical training provided to employees and volunteers? Are there mechanisms in place and followed for investigation of alleged abuses?

Lewis's book contains an extensive bibliography on ethics in the public service, including reference to various professional codes of behavior and other sources on taking ethical inventories in organizations.

Conducting an Accountability Audit: The Process

The accountability audit will be most time consuming the first time it is conducted because the necessary documents and information may not be readily available. As experience is gained, however, the time needed to complete the accountability audit should decrease.

When Should An Accountability Audit Be Conducted?

From the standpoint of logistics and logic, it is desirable to conduct the accountability audit as part of the organization's regular strategic planning process. During this process, the organization will already have committed staff resources to the compilation of historical documents and information such as missions and mandates that will also be highly relevant to the accountability audit. Logistically, therefore, it makes sense to integrate and coordinate the two activities. Also, the activities of strategic planning and accountability auditing are logically linked and therefore should be conducted simultaneously if possible. Both activities, for example, require environmental scanning and investigation of internal strengths and weaknesses. Much of the information gathered via

organizationwide strategic planning is directly relevant to accountability auditing and vice versa. Therefore, there should be procedures for cross-referencing both sets of activities.

However, an accountability audit can be conducted independently of a strategic planning process—and should be conducted
separately under certain circumstances. For example, if the organization recently has completed its strategic planning process, and
if the accountability environment seems to be changing in especially significant ways, decision makers may appropriately decide
not to wait for the next strategic planning cycle to conduct an
accountability audit.

Like environmental scanning, accountability auditing should
be a continuous, not a cyclical, activity. This is what distinguishes
strategic management from strategic planning (see Chapter Three).
Moreover, as in annual business planning derived from long-range
strategic planning, the organization should establish annual performance goals and objectives derived from its accountability audits.
These annual goals and objectives will relate to specific initiatives
designed to correct weaknesses and to build on strengths in serving
the public trust. They should be reviewed and updated as part of
the organization's strategic management process.

Who Should Conduct the Audit?

The question of who should conduct the accountability audit is
critical because it may have significant effects on the success or failure of the endeavor.

The least formal option is for the organization's staff to conduct the accountability audit. This option has the advantage of giving the staff significant ownership of the process and the results.
This is important when developing strategies for enhancing
accountability because the employees themselves have helped
frame the problems and opportunities that demand attention.
There is more subjectivity involved in an accountability audit than
in a financial audit, and the staff may be more committed to implementing corrective actions if they themselves have had a role in
defining the problems.

The other advantage of this option is that it is less threatening
to the staff and the leadership of the organization. Remember, the

idea of conducting an accountability audit is a relatively new notion in the public and nonprofit sectors and change generally is threatening to some people. Moreover, like other types of auditing, the organization's credibility is on the line. In addition, the term *accountability* may for some people raise the specter of unethical behavior, abuse of trust, or constraints on professional discretion. All of these can be threatening, especially the first time an accountability audit is conducted. For these reasons, the organization may opt for an internal audit, especially the first time, to ease fears and tensions about the process and to build a culture of self-reflection and self-criticism.

But, of course, there are certain disadvantages to the internal approach to accountability auditing. First, the staff may have difficulty being objective about their accountability strengths and liabilities. Second, the accountability audit may take longer if conducted by staff, who will inevitably be distracted by their daily routines and obligations.

If the organization decides to conduct the accountability audit internally, it should be a widely shared responsibility involving a team representing all levels of the organization—top executives, midlevel staff, supervisors, line personnel, and support staff. While this team might be guided by a team leader, it is not advisable to assign overall responsibility for the audit to one or several people. That strategy runs the danger of setting those people up as the bad guys in the organization. A team with shared responsibility will spread ownership of the process and the results beyond one or several people.

The second, and most formal, option for conducting an accountability audit is to hire an outside consultant to compile and interpret the data. This option is analogous to hiring an accounting firm to conduct an independent financial audit. Naturally, this option has the advantage of adding objectivity and credibility to the process. An outside auditor will add a fresh perspective to the organization and might be able to challenge some of the implicit assumptions that staff members make about their accountability environment.

Also, the consultant will bring certain types of expertise to the process and will probably be able to conduct the audit more efficiently and perhaps more quickly than a team of staff members.

Relatedly, the consultant will have familiarity with other comparable organizations and industry standards and will be able to bring that knowledge to the auditing process.

Finally, there is a third option—a middle ground between an internal staff-driven audit and an external independent audit. The middle option, perhaps the ideal option, is to have the staff conduct the accountability audit, but with advice and guidance from an outside facilitator. This option represents the best of both worlds by giving the staff significant ownership of the process but with all the benefits of a consultant who can provide objectivity and expertise.

Summary

A strategic approach to accountability requires a special type of internal auditing that is both prospective and retrospective. The approach presented in this chapter differs from traditional methods of compliance auditing or performance auditing because it views the organization's accountability infrastructure not as a static collection of rules, procedures, and so on, but as a dynamic set of strategic resources that can be mobilized in response to perceived threats or opportunities.

This chapter and Chapter Four should provide decision makers with the framework they need to identify the organization's strengths, weaknesses, opportunities, and threats—the SWOT analysis, in the jargon of strategic planning. The following chapter describes how to identify strategic issues related to accountability and how to formulate strategies to address those issues.

Chapter Six

Clarifying Strategic Accountability Issues

In Chapter Three, I said that the objective of any strategic management system is to help the organization achieve a better fit with its external environment by understanding how its strengths and weaknesses interact with the opportunities and threats presented by the world outside.

Naturally, the most desirable type of fit is one that maximizes the organization's comparative advantages by using its strengths or assets to capitalize on an opportunity in the accountability environment. But the organization also should know something about how its weaknesses and vulnerabilities interact with specific trends and events in its environment. Knowledge of these shortcomings is helpful when developing damage control strategies to prevent or minimize an accountability crisis that may be looming on the horizon. Also, the organization should be able to target certain of its weaknesses for long-term and perhaps incremental investments to take advantage of opportunities. Finally, from the perspective of strategic resource allocation, the organization should be able to identify external factors that might require rapid mobilization of its accountability mechanisms to avert potential challenges or threats.

Understanding these various types of fit between the organization and its environment is a prerequisite for developing effective accountability strategies and tactics. It is not advisable to leap ahead to the development of accountability strategies based solely on a simple listing of strengths, weaknesses, opportunities, and threats as developed in Chapters Four and Five. It is far better to take some time to evaluate how internal strengths and weaknesses interact with external opportunities and threats, thereby illuminating specific types of goals and objectives to be achieved by the strategies that are eventually developed. In other words, it is important to ask the right questions (What objectives are we trying to achieve?) before searching for the right answers (What strategies will help us achieve those objectives?).

Taking the time to identify and articulate a set of accountability issues facing the organization will help ensure that decision makers ask the right questions and thereby avoid the phenomenon of solving the wrong problem. *Accountability issues* are defined here as the strategic choices an organization must make, either to sustain its exemplary performance in serving the public trust or to bolster areas in which it has been less successful in meeting accountability standards and expectations.

These accountability issues are not always intuitively obvious and they do not simply emerge from lists of opportunities, threats, strengths, and weaknesses. In order to identify and clarify these strategic choices, we need another framework for synthesizing the findings from the environmental scan (Chapter Four) and the accountability audit (Chapter Five). This chapter presents such a framework. It is a simple yet powerful tool for synthesizing information and for clarifying the key accountability issues facing public and nonprofit organizations.

Assessing the Fit Between Organization and Accountability Environment

After doing a scan of the accountability environment and assessing organizational strengths and weaknesses, decision makers will want to know if their current accountability systems are tailored appropriately to the organization's strengths and whether they are in tune with opportunities and challenges in the accountability environment.

The fit between an organization and its accountability environment has been examined in a very interesting and revealing way by Romzek and Dubnick (1987). The case they have analyzed is the National Aeronautics and Space Administration (NASA), especially the events leading up to the tragic explosion of the space shuttle *Challenger* in 1986. Many readers will vividly recall the horrifying television images of the spacecraft exploding moments after takeoff resulting in the deaths of everyone on board. Subsequent investigations revealed that synthetic seals (O-rings) on the *Challenger's* huge rocket booster had become brittle in the unusually cold weather, allowing the highly volatile and combustible rocket fuel to leak and explode. While NASA officials knew there was a risk of O-ring failure in the chilly conditions forecast for the launch, they took a calculated risk and gave authorization for the flight to proceed as scheduled.

Romzek and Dubnick suggest that the *Challenger* explosion can be explained, at least in part, as a tragic consequence of shifting standards of accountability imposed by NASA's external environment. These changing standards led to NASA's gradual drift away from the type of accountability systems and controls that had served it well throughout its history.

In the early years of NASA, the locus of control over its activities was primarily internal. The agency enjoyed relatively strong political support with little meaningful oversight by anyone. NASA's relationship to its accountability environment, which included Congress, the President, the media, and the general public, was that of "expert to lay-person" (Romzek and Dubnick, 1987, p. 231). In the 1960s, there was a prevailing belief that landing a man on the moon within the decade required almost total deference to the technical experts in NASA.

Early on, NASA's accountability systems resembled those often seen in high-technology research and development organizations. The most crucial decisions in NASA were driven by technological considerations such as safety and advancement of scientific knowledge, and not by bureaucratic or political objectives. True, NASA used a very complex system of internal checks and balances, with explicit chains of command and other bureaucratic mechanisms of accountability. And of course, from its inception, the agency was acutely aware of its political constituencies and its vulnerability to shifting national priorities. But ultimately, NASA's accountability system was designed to serve technological objectives rather than bureaucratic, political, or administrative ends. In effect, NASA had historically operated in the domain of discretionary authority (Figure 4.1, Cell 3), although Romzek and Dubnick use their own conceptual framework with different terms and variables.

Gradually, however, NASA's accountability environment began to shift. In the 1970s, public disenchantment (or perhaps bore-dom) with space exploration grew as the nation turned its atten-tion to pressing priorities at home and abroad. By the early 1980s, NASA was experiencing intense political pressure from key con-stituents, especially Congress and the President, to make its new space shuttle program fully operational and to fulfill its promise as a routine, commercialized, and cost-effective method for space exploration (or perhaps space exploitation). Numerous delays of shuttle flights had placed additional political pressure on NASA. In the budget-cutting environment of the early 1980s, the agency found itself, perhaps for the first time, fighting hard for political and financial survival.

Romzek and Dubnick suggest that NASA responded by gradu-ally drifting away from its historical accountability systems and toward other strategies that played to its weaknesses, not its strengths. Organizationally, for example, NASA began to look and behave more like a large government bureaucracy than a high-tech research and development institute. Familiar "bureaupathologi-cal" (Romzek and Dubnick, 1987, p. 233) behaviors, like goal dis-placement and communication breakdowns, began to occur with disturbing frequency. Also, NASA seemed to become more and more concerned with responding to pressures from external con-stituencies including Congress, the President, the news media, and a growing cadre of subcontractors.

It was in this context, according to Romzek and Dubnick, that the decision was made to launch the ill-fated *Challenger,* despite con-trary advice from flight engineers. Pressure from NASA's powerful constituents, combined with internal breakdowns in communica-tion, led NASA officials to take a calculated risk that the infamous O-rings on *Challenger's* rocket boosters would hold, even in the unusually cold weather forecast for the launch date. When the deci-sion was being made the evening before the launch, the technical experts were asked to put on their "management hat"—to consider the ramifications of their decision from the perspective of NASA's political vulnerability. Using the framework presented in Chapter Four, an internal system of negotiated accountability apparently had supplanted the system of discretionary accountability that had previously existed in NASA. In effect, NASA had gradually and unintentionally abandoned its comparative advantage, drifting instead toward a system of accountability in which it had little experience and which, in many ways, was in contradiction with its mission, goals, and organizational culture.

The case of the *Challenger* space shuttle is a powerful illustration of how organizations can have comparative advantages (and disadvantages) in their accountability systems, just as they have advantages and shortcomings in their product and service portfolios, information technology, facilities, and so on. The system of accountability upon which an organization depends is, in a very real way, a major component of its resource portfolio. As such, the accountability system should be subjected to the same type of scrutiny and periodic updating as, say, a management information system, a human resource system, or any other facet of the organization. Unfortunately, too many organizations discover too late that their accountability controls are mismatched with their mission, goals, objectives, and tasks. The following questions are especially important:

- What key opportunities and threats were uncovered in the scan of the accountability environment?
- Is the organization's accountability strategy in line with these opportunities and threats? Is the strategy appropriate for the type of accountability environment in which the organization operates?
- If the environment provides the organization with substantial discretion to set its own accountability standards, have appropriate steps been taken to ensure that discretionary decision making is not abused?
- Conversely, if the accountability environment is primarily rule driven and dominated by regulatory controls, have proper internal procedures and reporting routines been implemented to comply with these requirements?
- What key strengths and weaknesses were uncovered in the accountability audit?
- Is the organization's accountability strategy well matched to its mission, goals, objectives, and tasks?
- Is the organization's accountability strategy consistent with its professional culture, its values, and its historical evolution?
- Does the accountability strategy play to the organization's strengths or to its weaknesses?

These questions can be useful when decision makers suspect that their accountability environment is demanding (or allowing) them to behave in ways that are not consistent with the organization's comparative advantage—that is, in ways that are out of sync with the organization's mission, its goals, its management systems, and its historical culture. The *Challenger* tragedy illustrates how an organization can respond strategically (or drift incrementally) to what the environment offers. At NASA, decision makers responded to economic and political pressures in the accountability environment by suspending their normal criteria and protocols regarding decisions to launch or scrub a mission.

Some of the questions provide a kind of check and balance on unfettered opportunism. In other words, the accountability environment does not always present the correct or appropriate standards of performance on the organization. There are times when decision makers must ask the difficult question: *"If the accountability environment does not impose appropriate constraints, should we take steps to protect our agency (and the public) from ourselves?"*

A Tool for Assessing Fit

In Chapter Three, I suggested that SWOT analysis is the conceptual and methodological core of strategic planning and, in effect, sets strategic planning apart from other decision-making processes that are less concerned with finding the appropriate fit between the organization and its environment.

But what information emerges at the end of a SWOT analysis and how is it useful to the organization? When performed correctly, SWOT analysis can help government and nonprofit executives clarify the most important accountability issues and choices facing their organization. When performed poorly, however, SWOT analysis can degenerate into a superficial list-generating exercise resulting in the production of four unconnected lists of strengths, weaknesses, opportunities, and threats. Without a systematic effort to relate the lists to each other—to synthesize them—they are of limited utility, especially with regard to the clarification of accountability issues and choices facing the organization.

Decision makers often have difficulty moving from their four lists to the formulation of strategies. Part of the problem is the common failure to use SWOT as a tool for clarifying key issues and choices prior to the development of new strategies and initiatives. When the issues are unclear, decision makers may unwittingly solve problems that have not been adequately defined, thereby increasing the likelihood of solving the wrong problem (Raiffa, 1968, p. 264; Ackoff, 1974, pp. 237–239; Dunn, 1994, p. 151).

Some Common Pitfalls

For maximum benefit, SWOT analysis demands rigorous discipline and sometimes tedious iteration. Here are some common pitfalls of SWOT analysis (Kearns, 1992).

Missing Link

The most frequent, and potentially most costly, error in SWOT analysis is the failure to link the assessments of the external and internal environments. There is a temptation to deal with the internal and external environments separately, using only one or the other as a foundation for strategies to enhance accountability. For example, the federal government is taking steps to give states and localities more discretionary authority in critically important domains like welfare reform, environmental policy, and health care financing. Some local and state officials will enthusiastically embrace the many opportunities presented by this deregulated environment. But they should also think carefully about whether they have the internal resources to fill the accountability vacuum created by the federal government's delegation (or divestment) of authority.

Blue Sky

Blue sky thinking results from unfounded optimism. It can manifest itself in various ways in SWOT analysis, contaminating assessments of both the internal and external environments. Initially, opportunities might look very promising until decision makers realistically assess what internal conditions would have to prevail before the organization could take advantage of the opportunity. Conversely, internal strengths can be exaggerated and weaknesses overlooked or underestimated, especially when they are considered in isolation from trends in the world outside.

Silver Lining

It is said that every cloud has a silver lining, but it can be dangerous to interpret this folk wisdom literally. Decision makers run into trouble when they underestimate threats or challenges in the accountability environment. For example, the chief executive officer of a large nonprofit research institution stated publicly that he welcomed a congressional investigation of whether federal research funds were being appropriately spent. He viewed the investigation as an opportunity to demonstrate his institution's superior financial controls and accountability for federal grants. But he was not familiar with the operational details of his organization's complex record-keeping and accounting procedures—and was surprised and publicly embarrassed when the investigation uncovered several relatively minor (but newsworthy) discrepancies where funds intended for research overhead had actually been spent on various administrative activities.

Cart Before the Horse

Decision makers are often tempted to develop strategies and action plans before they have sufficiently clarified the accountability issues and choices facing the organization. This can lead to serious problems when decision makers respond prematurely to strategic issues that have not been adequately formulated and defined.

It is essential to formulate strategic issues prior to the development of strategies. After all, "an answer without an issue is not an answer" (Bryson, 1988, p. 160). Bryson defines a strategic issue as: "A fundamental policy choice affecting an organization's mandate, mission, values, product . . . , clients or users, costs, financing, organization or management . . . The way these choices are framed can have a profound effect on decisions that define what the organization is, what it does, and why it does it" (p. 139).

With the integrating framework presented in this chapter, SWOT analysis can help nonprofit agencies ask the right questions before implementing strategies.

Avoiding the Pitfalls

The pitfalls outlined in the previous section can be avoided with the use of a simple yet powerful framework for integrating the analysis of external and internal factors (Kearns, 1992).

SWOT Analysis Round One: Organizing Findings

First, decision makers should organize the findings from the scan of the accountability environment and the internal accountability audit. As suggested earlier, they should begin by identifying external opportunities and threats in the accountability environment using categories like those suggested in Chapter Four. But the process of identifying external opportunities and threats should be iterative and closely coordinated with the analysis of internal strengths and weaknesses like those discussed in Chapter Five. Thus, as each opportunity or threat is identified, decision makers should immediately begin the process of integration and synthesis by asking: "What accountability resources or strengths does the organization have to help it capitalize on this opportunity or avert this threat?" and "What accountability weaknesses will prevent the organization from capitalizing on this opportunity or averting this threat?" Table 6.1 offers a useful way to organize these findings.

This iterative process is a departure from the manner in which SWOT analysis sometimes is described in the literature (see, for example, Koteen, 1989; Espy, 1986; Barry, 1986). Decision makers can address the pitfalls discussed in the previous section by following this procedure, because it forces them to try to relate each external opportunity or threat to a corresponding internal strength or weakness.

Naturally, there will be some miscellaneous factors, both external and internal, that cannot be related to each other. The organization may believe it has certain strengths (or weaknesses) in its accountability system that are not directly related to particular opportunities or challenges in the external environment. While it is useful to isolate these unconnected factors for more careful scrutiny, it is unlikely that they will present the most important strategic issues to the organization.

SWOT Analysis Round Two: Mapping Interactions

Round One of this SWOT framework constitutes a matching exercise wherein the objective is to identify salient links between internal strengths and weaknesses and external opportunities and threats. In Round Two, the decision makers try to map these links

Table 6.1. Organizing Findings: Strengths, Weaknesses, Opportunities, and Threats.

Opportunities and Threats	Strengths and Weaknesses
Compliance accountability	*Compliance accountability*
Opportunities (Example: "Some organizations like ours have received public praise for demonstrating performance over and above that required by the law.")	What strengths does the organization have to help it follow a similar strategy?
	What weaknesses would inhibit the organization's efforts?
Threats (Example: "A recently enacted mandate will impose significant financial and administrative burdens on the organization.")	What strengths will help the organization respond to this mandate?
	What weaknesses will inhibit the organization's response?
Negotiated accountability	*Negotiated accountability*
Opportunities (Example: "A regulatory agency has demonstrated its willingness to negotiate certain standards of assessment and oversight.")	What strengths does the organization have to negotiate a set of standards that best serve the public's interest?
	What weaknesses will inhibit the organization's ability to negotiate?
Threats (Example: "There is a trend toward costly litigation regarding legal definitions of charitable, tax-exempt organizations.")	What strengths does the organization have in adversarial negotiations?
	What weaknesses does the organization have in adversarial negotiations?

Table 6.1. *(continued)*

Discretionary accountability	*Discretionary accountability*
Opportunities (Example: "Deregulation in a certain domain of accountability provides an opportunity to manage in a more entrepreneurial way with greater autonomy and administrative discretion.")	What strengths does the organization have that will protect or even enhance its accountability in a deregulated environment?
	What weaknesses may diminish the organization's accountability in a deregulated environment?
Threats (Example: "Public outcry over perceived abuses of administrative discretion may lead to restrictions.")	What strengths does the organization have to combat perceptions?
	What weaknesses may fuel the public's negative perception?
Anticipatory accountability	*Anticipatory accountability*
Opportunities (Example: "Passage of new law would be advantageous to the organization.")	What strengths does the organization have to help influence passage of the legislation?
	What weaknesses inhibit the organization's ability to influence political action?
Threats (Example: "Passage of new law would be disadvantageous to the organization.")	What strengths does the organization have to help influence defeat or modification of the legislation?
	What weaknesses inhibit the organization's ability to influence defeat or modification of the legislation?

using a simple two-by-two matrix like the one presented in Figure 6.1, which portrays four classes of accountability issues likely to affect strategy development and goal setting in public and non-profit organizations.

Comparative Advantage

The upper left quadrant (Cell 1) highlights the mix of circumstances in which the organization enjoys an exceptionally strong position, by virtue of its strengths and demonstrated performance, to capitalize on certain perceived opportunities in the accountability environment. Thus, in the vocabulary of strategic planning, the organization has a *comparative advantage* in demonstrating certain types of accountability to external or internal constituencies.

For example, to adapt an anecdote from Ford (1991), a library consortium in a large metropolitan area once observed an important trend in its accountability environment. Its decision makers noticed that foundations, government agencies, and other organizations that made grants to libraries—and to the consortium itself—were beginning to stress the importance of interlibrary cooperation and regional approaches to resource sharing. Some grant-making organizations even insisted on cooperative approaches as a condition for receiving funds. Thus, this trend could be categorized within the domain of compliance accountability (see Chapter Four). The trend was perceived by the library consortium as a potential opportunity that coincided nicely with its own demonstrated record of promoting and facilitating cooperative ventures

Figure 6.1. Classifying Accountability Issues.

	Opportunities	*Threats*
Strengths	Comparative advantage –1–	Mobilization –2–
Weaknesses	Comparative disadvantage –4–	Damage control –3–

Source: Adapted from Kearns (1992, p. 13).

among several of the region's largest academic libraries, traditionally known for their independence. The detected trend in funding criteria (opportunity), in combination with the consortium's reputation as an effective liaison (strength), produced a comparative advantage that the consortium could use in developing its accountability plan.

The comparative advantage cell represents the set of desirable circumstances toward which all organizations aspire. But it is not sufficient to merely identify these happy circumstances—no organization can afford to rest on its laurels. There are countless examples of how seemingly invincible organizations neglected (or worse yet, squandered) their comparative advantages and fell prey to equally neglected vulnerabilities. Critical choices remain as to how the organization can nurture, protect, or solidify its comparative advantages in a constantly changing accountability environment. Thus, in generic terms, the comparative advantage issue facing decision makers is: *"How can the organization leverage its strengths to achieve or enhance its comparative advantage, thereby capitalizing on a perceived opportunity in its accountability environment?"*

This very general formulation of a strategic issue must be given more precision and clarity according to the specific circumstances of the organization in relation to its environment. Inevitably, conflicting goals and assumptions need to be clarified and often trade-offs must be resolved. This process of issue clarification is discussed later in this chapter, after further explanation of the matrix.

Mobilization

The upper right quadrant of Figure 6.1 (Cell 2) directs attention to issues of mobilization. Here the organization faces perceived threats from its accountability environment. But decision makers have reason to believe that their organization is in a relatively strong position to avert these threats if they can effectively mobilize their accountability resources or assets in a timely and effective manner. An exceptionally strong organization may even try to manage its environment by transforming certain threats into opportunities for its long-term advantage.

For example, as discussed in Chapter Four, a large nonprofit hospital once came under public scrutiny as part of a regional effort to force nonprofit institutions to make payments in lieu of taxes to municipal jurisdictions in which they were located. One criticism was that many of the region's nonprofit hospitals did not provide sufficient levels of charitable care to justify their exemption from local property taxes. This particular hospital, however, had done a better job than others in keeping meticulous records of its uncompensated medical care. It could show that it had provided millions of dollars worth of health care to the indigent, and had also voluntarily cared for inmates in the county jail. In addition, it had an impressive portfolio of charitable outreach activities to the high-risk neighborhood in which it was located. These included a variety of special programs related to gang violence as well as public health programs targeted to the special needs and circumstances of low-income residents in the neighborhood. Finally, the hospital had an outstanding staff of government affairs and public relations professionals, some of whom enjoyed especially high levels of credibility in the community.

Through a variety of strategies, the hospital mobilized these accountability assets to gently but firmly combat accusations regarding inadequate commitment to its charitable mission. In fact, the hospital used the public forum provided by this accountability threat to enhance (not just defend) its public image and to build advantageous partnerships with other institutions.

Thus, the generic issue in the mobilization cell is: *"How can the organization mobilize its accountability assets to avert a perceived threat or even transform that threat into an opportunity?"*

Damage Control

The bottom right quadrant of Figure 6.1 (Cell 3) portrays a situation that may be very troublesome, even catastrophic, for the organization. Here, decision makers are forced to confront the unpleasant fact that the organization is poorly prepared to address one or more ominous accountability threats. The organization's weaknesses make it especially vulnerable, and its best hope may be to engage in tactics or strategies of damage control.

Many United Way affiliates around the country were forced into damage control mode when the *Washington Post* revealed that William Aramony, former president of the United Way of America, was being paid over $460,000 in salary and benefits and had accumulated a pension worth approximately $4 million. Some local affiliates immediately condemned Aramony's behavior and tried to distance themselves from the United Way of America, threatening to withhold their dues payments and making other demands for substantive and procedural changes in the national organization (for example, see Millar, 1992). Some local affiliates launched emergency public information campaigns and intensive efforts to educate the general public and the news media regarding the complicated corporate structure of the United Way of America and their own "dotted line" affiliation with the national office.

But when pleading their case to their constituencies, many of these local affiliates found it difficult to distinguish themselves in the minds of the general public from the national organization—and even more difficult to separate the national organization from its forceful and charismatic leader. Most affiliates, after all, had derived at least some benefits from Aramony's aggressively entrepreneurial management style, including a sophisticated national marketing campaign and the United Way's lucrative affiliation with the National Football League. Moreover, they were utterly unprepared for an accountability crisis of this magnitude and lacked the management resources to deal with it effectively. Thus, they found themselves confronting all the typical obstacles of a damage control strategy.

Organizations operating in the damage control quadrant often are forced to engage in crisis management because they have discovered the accountability threat only after its disruptive effects have occurred. Like battleships struck by torpedoes, their best hope may be simply to try to remain afloat while limping to the nearest safe port. However, there may be a slim chance for more optimistic scenarios for an organization with either the time and resources to transform its accountability weaknesses into strengths or the collective will to take extraordinary action to restore public trust and confidence. In rare instances, an organization's credibility may even be restored and enhanced by its crisis management behavior.

Consider the performance of Johnson & Johnson, the health products manufacturer. The public image of that company was severely threatened in 1982 when seven people in the Chicago area died after consuming Tylenol capsules laced with lethal doses of cyanide. The company immediately pulled that product from retail outlets, provided technical and logistical assistance to federal investigators, offered a reward for information leading to the arrest and conviction of the culprit, and subsequently led national efforts toward tamper-resistant products and packaging. Johnson & Johnson was widely praised for its actions and, remarkably, Tylenol recaptured its market share as public confidence was restored.

Technically, it could be said that the response of Johnson & Johnson was actually one of mobilization (Cell 2) rather than damage control, because the company had many accountability assets, including technical and financial resources, that could quickly be applied to the crisis. Nonetheless, the sheer magnitude of the crisis and the rapid unfolding of events represented a typical damage control scenario. Moreover, Johnson & Johnson had a long history of avoiding media scrutiny of any kind and therefore was ill-prepared to be thrust into the international media spotlight. In spite of this, the company responded rapidly and effectively to protect the public interest at any cost, and in the process quickly enhanced its own reputation as a responsible corporate citizen.

The Tylenol incident inspired many people to think about strategies to help organizations plan for and energize damage control operations before threats become crises. A strategic approach to damage control involves recognizing the early signs of an impending crisis.

Meyers (1986) suggests most "unmanaged" crises display three stages: pre-crisis, crisis, and post-crisis. In the *pre-crisis stage*, the organization displays an incremental and often subtle pattern of nonperformance such as repeated cost overruns, missed deadlines, declining market share, employee turnover, and failure to meet performance goals or explicit accountability standards imposed by laws or regulations. Rather than accept and act constructively on these problems, the crisis-prone organization reacts with denial, recrimination, anger, and fear. Also, in the pre-crisis stage, there may be an inclination to view small incremental failures as isolated events instead of as part of a pattern.

For example, the local chapter of a national nonprofit organization once experienced rather modest operating deficits for several consecutive years. Fortunately, it was able to cover these losses with its reserve fund. While some trustees expressed growing concern, others dismissed the problems as a temporary phenomenon due largely to national trends beyond the control of the chapter. These national trends included a syndicated series of negative media reports focused on the national organization of which the chapter was an affiliate member. The executive director and the staff reinforced this notion, all the time keeping their fingers crossed in hopes that things would get better on their own. During this pre-crisis stage, no meaningful steps were taken to address the operating deficits or the underlying causes of the failure.

Gradually, the local chapter came under the same type of scrutiny as the national office regarding the viability of its mission and duplication of services provided by other organizations. Several board members who had earlier expressed concern resigned in frustration. Then the organization began to experience difficulty recruiting volunteers. Finally, the local United Way cut its annual allocation to the organization, gradually at first and then dramatically when the local United Way itself faced a funding shortfall. Within several years, the relatively small operating deficits increased to over $600,000. More trustees resigned in anger and frustration, the executive director was replaced, and the organization confronted a full-blown accountability crisis.

The crisis was eventually addressed, but not until the organization reduced its workforce by nearly half, cut nonessential programs, and completely restructured its service portfolio. What had begun as several minor problems in the organization's operating budget led eventually to an accountability crisis of enormous proportions. Many people who stayed with this organization throughout its torturous ordeal lamented the way early warning signs—financial, political, and interorganizational—were not given more serious or probing attention when they occurred. Here the methods of cross-impact analysis, described in Chapter Four, might have been helpful in envisioning a chain reaction of events leading ultimately to breakdown of the system.

Next, Meyers (1986) says that the *crisis stage* occurs with an actual failure of the system such as bankruptcy, breach of contract, or some other notable disaster. Incremental incidents of nonperformance reach a critical mass, resulting in a kind of "organizational melt-down." Often, of course, the failure is systemwide but manifests itself as many individual crises. At this stage, Meyers says that the unmanaged crisis is characterized by widespread panic and collapse in the organization. Confusion reigns as people frantically try to put out one fire after another with little coordination or apparent leadership of their efforts. Information leaks, conflicting actions, and duplication of efforts all help develop a general sense of chaos. Meyers suggests that the medical concept of triage can be a useful concept during the crisis stage. *Triage* is the method used by emergency medical professionals to classify trauma victims in one of three groups: the superficially wounded, the seriously wounded (with prospect for survival), and the hopelessly wounded. When resources are scarce, the superficially wounded have lowest priority. The hopelessly wounded are made as comfortable as possible with pain relievers and perhaps spiritual support. The seriously wounded are given top priority for scarce resources.

A local ballet company once followed a triage strategy when it confronted a host of management, governance, and financial problems that threatened its credibility in the community. With projections of steady reductions in revenues and rapidly escalating costs, the organization first took dramatic steps to stop the financial bleeding. It then undertook the necessary management reforms to restore the confidence of key constituencies like financial institutions. This, in turn, resulted in a line of credit that allowed the organization to invest in long-term initiatives like the search for a new performance venue. With its financial position on a more solid foundation, the organization then took more gradual steps, like streamlining and diversifying its board of trustees, to respond to demands from its accountability environment.

Finally, Meyers (1986) says that the *post-crisis stage* generally is characterized by collective shock, uncertainty, and often radical change. Departures of key personnel and post-crisis investigations contribute to self-protective behavior and efforts by survivors to distance themselves from the controversy as much as possible. Attention shifts to various salvage activities as the organization assesses its losses and begins the long process of rebuilding, dismantling, or divestiture.

Meyers suggests that organizational crises can have positive as well as negative outcomes. Often heroes and new leaders are born out of crisis where exceptionally talented people may have the opportunity to demonstrate their judgment under fire and their ability to manage ambiguity and risk. Also, needed change often is accelerated after a crisis if latent problems finally are faced and resolved. Sometimes too, organizations learn from crises by, for example, developing early warning systems to help them be better prepared the next time. Finally, a crisis can lead to fundamental changes in strategic directions and in core values and operating philosophies.

Meyers proposes a "crisis audit" methodology composed of a set of questions related to each phase of the crisis (1986, pp. 236–239):

1. Pre-crisis Phase:
   Does the organization have an early warning system?
   Are crisis management responsibilities clear?
   Is management open to surprise and criticism?
   Does bad news easily travel upward?
   Are there enough mature and talented people to withstand the sting of exposed failure?

2. Crisis Phase:
   Has a crisis team been selected and trained?
   Is the organization design flexible and open?
   Are slack resources marshalled to cope with adversity?
   Is outside help available on short notice?
   Are instructions and assignments clear, current, and rehearsed?

3. Post-crisis Phase:
   Does change happen easily in the organization?
   Is the organization capable of accepting new ways?

Here are a few other crisis management strategies that have been suggested by experts in the field (Jones, 1992):

1. Assemble a crisis management team composed of the chief executive officer, the chair of the governing body, legal counsel, a public relations professional, and other key personnel as appropriate.
2. Brainstorm a list of the worst possible scenarios and develop an action plan for dealing with each one.
3. Develop a crisis communication plan that specifies an internal chain of command as well as procedures governing external communications with the media, government officials, clients, and other key constituencies.

4. Compile and distribute an emergency telephone directory.
5. Practice emergency management procedures and involve staff and board members.

Thus, the generic strategic issue in the damage control quadrant is: *"In light of its vulnerable position, how can the organization control or at least minimize the damage that may be inflicted by impending threats in the accountability environment?"*

Comparative Disadvantage

Finally, in the bottom left quadrant of Figure 6.1, decision makers face a difficult strategic choice. In this cell, a trend or a discrete event in the accountability environment captures the attention of decision makers because it seems to offer a promising opportunity to demonstrate or enhance their accountability to the public trust. Unfortunately, the organization cannot exploit the opportunity due to acknowledged weaknesses in its accountability infrastructure. Thus, the organization displays a *comparative disadvantage* and must address a particularly vexing strategic issue: How much (if anything) should we invest in our weaknesses in order to transform them into strengths and thereby take advantage of this opportunity?

For example, a major grantmaking organization once developed a voluntary management review and enhancement process to help nonprofit agencies identify their administrative strengths and shortcomings and to develop action plans for improvement. Several nonprofit organizations announced their intention to participate in the management review and enhancement process at the earliest possible date. They saw the process as an opportunity to solidify their good standing with the grantmaking organization by demonstrating their management sophistication and accountability. Others, however, delayed the management review for as long as possible. While they recognized the potential opportunities of early participation, some said privately that their agencies might not look good under the spotlight. They wanted to see how others fared in the process, and then make their preparations accordingly. Others said that they simply did not have the spare resources to devote to the rigorous self-study and subsequent independent review. In effect, these organizations acknowledged that their accountability weaknesses prevented them, at least temporarily, from pursuing the opportunity presented by the grant-making organization.

Organizations that find themselves in the comparative disadvantage cell have several strategic choices. First, they might choose to invest in or bolster the weaknesses that are preventing them from seizing certain opportunities. This strategy is based on the assumption that these weaknesses can indeed be transformed into strengths, thereby allowing the organization to pursue the opportunity in the accountability environment. This is a particularly appropriate strategy when the perceived weaknesses are related to the organization's mandate or publicly stated mission. Under this circumstance, the organization may even be legally required to make the necessary investments.

Second, the organization might choose a wait-and-see approach; not really a strategy, this is a tactic for buying time. While this delaying tactic appears extremely conservative, it may actually be a strategically clever choice if the decision makers believe they can maintain a position just strong enough to avoid an accountability crisis. It can also be risky, however, if the opportunity becomes a threat and forces the organization into damage control mode. Consequently, the wait-and-see approach should include continuous monitoring of the situation so that the organization is prepared to move quickly and effectively when circumstances change.

Third, the organization may decide that its accountability shortcomings simply cannot be fixed without a very large infusion of new resources. If the organization cannot afford this investment or concludes that the cost-benefit ratios do not justify it, it may divest these weaknesses and allow the opportunity to pass, perhaps to another agency that already enjoys a comparative advantage.

Thus, the generic issue presented in the bottom left quadrant is: *"Should the organization invest its scarce resources to transform accountability weaknesses into strengths, or are other strategies, including divestment, more prudent?"*

SWOT Analysis Round Three: Issue Clarification

The four strategic issues in Figure 6.1 are generic representations of the types of accountability choices that emerge from a carefully conducted SWOT analysis. After mapping the issues and describing them in general terms, decision makers should try to add greater clarity and specificity to each of them so as to reflect the critical choices facing the organization as it develops its accountability strategy.

Naturally, the way these choices are framed and articulated will depend on the organization's context and its unique mixture of strengths, weaknesses, opportunities, and threats. Nevertheless, there are several principles that should guide the process of issue clarification. Before examining these principles, let us look at a brief illustration (adapted from Clark, 1991) of how one organization attempted to clarify one of its accountability issues.

As part of a strategic planning process, the board and executive staff of a nonprofit recreation and social services organization once scanned their accountability environment, using focus groups and other methods to determine what their key constituencies expected of the organization. They were gratified to discover that demand for family-oriented fitness programs and other social and educational programs remained very strong. In fact, they sensed a resurgence of demand for family-oriented programming compared with health and fitness programs offered by glitzy high-tech health clubs that catered to the needs of singles. They perceived this market demand as a potential opportunity that corresponded nicely with one of the organization's key strengths—its public image as a family-oriented facility. Thus, this organization enjoyed an apparent comparative advantage in its accountability and responsiveness to a certain set of expectations and performance standards.

The comparative advantage issue for the organization was initially framed as follows: *"How can the organization leverage its public image as a family-oriented facility to capitalize on the perceived need for more family-oriented health and fitness programs?"* However, subsequent discussion of this issue revealed that some of the decision makers did not fully agree with the way it was framed and that several important accountability issues needed to be resolved. For example, some decision makers worried that the interests of other important constituencies, such as senior citizens and singles, would suffer as a result. Others noted that so-called traditional family structures are changing with consequent effects on people's needs, activities, and schedules. Indeed, the initial framing of the issue prompted a useful discussion of what, in fact, constitutes a family.

After further discussion of critical assumptions, the organization's mission, and its accountability to the public, the decision makers reframed the issue as follows: *"How can the organization develop more family-oriented programs while continuing to meet the needs of special constituencies?*

The decision makers in this case had to address several important questions before reframing an issue on which all of them could agree:

- How is the issue related to the organization's mandate, mission, operating philosophies, and aspirations?
- How will the organization's clients be affected by the issue? Will all clients be affected in the same way?
- What assumptions are implicit in the issue and are these assumptions reasonable?
- Is the issue related in some systemic way to another issue of equal importance? Can these issues be combined or must they be addressed separately?

By addressing these and other questions (see Bryson, 1988, pp. 157–161), decision makers can clarify the key strategic choices facing the agency. It is especially important to surface and challenge the underlying assumptions implicit in each issue. In the case just described, an important assumption concerned the implied definition of a family and therefore the modified issue statement accommodated multiple interpretations. In other cases, assumptions may involve the reliability or validity of data used to forecast opportunities or threats. Mitroff and Emshoff (1979) suggest that decision makers focus most intently on those assumptions that are most important to the legitimacy of the issue and are least certain in terms of available data and other evidence.

SWOT Analysis Round Four: Issue Ranking

In the preceding steps of this framework, decision makers may develop and refine many strategic issues, perhaps three or four in each quadrant of Figure 6.1. Regardless of the number of issues generated, the organization will probably not be able to address all of them simultaneously and with equal vigor. Most often, decision makers will need to establish a priority ranking of the issues using criteria that make sense in a specific context.

The following criteria may be useful when trying to rank-order the issues, but decision makers should also explore their own criteria:

- The centrality of the issue to the organization's mandate and mission
- The urgency of the issue in terms of both time and impact
- The controllability of the issue given current organizational resources
- The cost of addressing the issue
- The public visibility of the issue to clients, donors, and other important stakeholders
- The pervasiveness of the issue in terms of its impact on organizational goals and functions
- The extent to which the issue affects fundamental values of the agency
- The extent to which the issue requires additional research in order to clarify the choices
- The extent to which comparable organizations are addressing the same issue

Whether decision makers use a sophisticated ranking process (see, for example, Saaty, 1980; Saaty and Kearns, 1985) or simple brainstorming, it is important that they consciously decide how much effort they wish to devote to pursuing the organization's comparative advantages versus mobilizing resources versus controlling damage, and so on.

SWOT Analysis Round Five: Strategy Development

The strategic issues presented in this chapter are intentionally posed as questions. The answers to these questions are, in effect, the strategies developed to address them. Strategies are explicit statements of visions, goals, objectives, programs, and activities that the organization sets in motion to address the accountability issues generated by the SWOT analysis. This chapter has suggested that if the questions (issues) are posed with intelligence and careful reflection, the answers (strategies) will flow more easily.

Strategies may involve an organizationwide commitment of resources, or action only at the departmental level. They may be designed for long-term benefits or to address immediate and pressing problems or timely opportunities. They may involve substantial reallocation of resources, perhaps even a revision of the mission, or a more modest, incremental approach. Simply stated, strategies will vary dramatically depending on the type of issue they are designed to address. Damage control strategies will naturally tend toward a shorter time horizon than strategies designed to nurture and sustain the organization's comparative advantage over the long term.

Once the strategic issue has been framed, the process of strategy development involves developing answers to the following sequence of questions:

1. With respect to each of the highest priority issues identified in Round Four, what is the organization's vision for the future? That is, what would be an optimal scenario if decision makers could look ahead, say, five years?
2. Can this vision or optimal scenario be realized if the organization does nothing at all to address the issue?
3. If not, what policies, programs, and actions can the organization take to advance the vision?
4. Which of these policies, programs, or actions are essential to advancing the vision? Which ones are merely supportive?
5. What barriers (financial, political, operational, technological) stand in the way of implementing these policies, programs, or actions? Can the barriers be overcome?
6. What benchmark measures or interim objectives will tell the organization whether or not it is making progress toward the vision?
7. What investments or reallocation of resources must the organization make to achieve the objectives and, ultimately, the vision?
8. What specific activities or tasks will be required to reach the objectives and who will perform them?

After addressing these questions with respect to each strategic issue, decision makers then need to assess how the total strategy fits together. Will investments in damage control strategies distract attention from the organization's comparative advantage? Can the organization realistically pursue all the strategies simultaneously? Bryson (1988, p. 173) poses a very useful set of questions, paraphrased below, to guide decision makers at this final phase of strategy development:

- What strategies are really reasonable and feasible within existing constraints?
- Where can the organization combine strategies in order to leverage scarce resources?
- Do any of the visions, or means to achieve them, contradict each other?
- What is the organization realistically willing to commit to over the next year?
- What specific actions and steps will the organization pursue over the next six months?

Summary

Using a matrix format like that presented in Figure 6.1, decision makers can develop a map of their SWOT analysis and, most importantly, of the accountability issues that emerge. Matrices similar to Figure 6.1 have been used for many years by multiproduct businesses to analyze the competitiveness of their product portfolios (Hedley, 1977, p. 12; Day, 1977; Wensley, 1981; Certo and Peter, 1988, pp. 96–100; Freedman and Van Ham, 1982) and have also been applied to competitive strategies for nonprofit organizations (MacMillan, 1983). But, as this chapter has tried to demonstrate, they are equally applicable to the analysis of accountability issues.

The framing of strategic issues is an important component of strategic planning. Therefore, decision makers should agree in advance to devote at least a portion of the planning process to this effort. Even in a one-day workshop, the organization can at least make some progress toward framing a set of important accountability issues and perhaps outlining strategies to address those issues.

Finally, the matrix format of issue classification can be used in the day-to-day process of management and governance, not just in the periodic (and often sporadic) cycles of formal strategic planning. For example, having a large portable matrix like Figure 6.1 available for reference at board meetings can help the executive staff and the governing board enhance the quality of their dialogue on agenda items that deal directly or indirectly with the organization's efforts to manage its accountability environment. Used in this way, the matrix can have a cognitive impact by gradually but steadily reorienting decision makers toward a continuous process of strategic thinking and strategic management versus episodic strategic planning. Also, repeated reference to the matrix format might have an important cultural impact on key decision makers by serving as a subtle yet constant reminder of their role in serving the public trust.

Part Three

Case Studies of Accountability Challenges

Examining Tactical and Strategic Approaches

The last three chapters deal with tactical and strategic approaches to managing accountability systems. Chapter Seven presents a cautionary tale—the bankruptcy of the Orange County investment pool—illustrating the benefits and risks of entrepreneurial public management. The conceptual framework presented in Chapter Four is used to analyze the accountability environment facing former County Treasurer Robert Citron. I show how the post-Proposition-13 environment in California provided Citron with extraordinary opportunities (and fiscal pressure) to develop a high-yield but high-risk investment strategy for the public funds entrusted to his stewardship. In this deregulated environment, Citron was operating solidly within the domain of discretionary judgment. The chapter concludes (in twenty-twenty hindsight) with a set of cautionary steps for managers and leaders engaged in entrepreneurial ventures relatively free of extensive oversight or formal mechanisms of accountability.

Chapter Eight presents the story of Pressley Ridge Schools and their leadership of a multi-organization effort to monitor outcomes and impacts of children's services agencies. The project, known as

SumOne for Kids, is ambitious—perhaps too ambitious, for it has suffered a variety of setbacks. It is noteworthy primarily because the participating organizations took it upon themselves to develop an accountability mechanism before the state legislature or a government oversight agency developed it for them. The case illustrates a few powerful lessons regarding strategic planning, advocacy, and discretionary accountability.

The final chapter concludes the book by discussing ways to build a culture of accountability via leadership and empowerment of employees. The argument is made that leadership for accountability must originate in the organization's governing board and work its way downward through top management and supervisors to the individual worker. The chapter includes a discussion of practical leadership skills. It concludes by illustrating the importance of leadership for all facets of accountability—from compliance to advocacy.

Chapter Seven

A Cautionary Tale
The Orange County Investment Fund

Orange County, California, is a sparkling community of prosperous high-tech firms and largely affluent residents. The streets are clean, the police are friendly, and the schools are above average. In many respects, Orange County is a model community. Until December 6, 1994, it was the envy of other municipal governments.

On that day, Orange County officials shocked the financial world by declaring bankruptcy. The county's $20 billion investment fund, representing over 180 county and municipal agencies, had experienced $1.7 billion in unrealized losses, largely due to the fund's heavy investment in derivative securities that fell steadily in value as interest rates rose in the second half of 1994. Creditors had made substantial loans to the fund to finance its aggressive investment strategies. When the book value of the fund began to fall, the creditors became nervous and liquidated $11 billion in collateral on the loans. With its leverage hopelessly constricted, the county filed for protection under Chapter 9 of the U.S. Bankruptcy Code, much as private firms seek protection under Chapter 11 of the Code. It was the largest municipal bankruptcy in the history of the law.

The news was especially shocking because the manager of the Orange County investment fund, County Treasurer Robert Citron, had built a reputation as one of the nation's most creative and successful public financial managers. Under Citron's direction, the Orange County fund had been hailed as an example of how an aggressive, entrepreneurial investment strategy could help diversify the revenues of government jurisdictions, thereby reducing their reliance on property taxes and other traditional revenue sources. Citron's philosophy included investment in long-term bonds and some high-risk securities, short-term leverage (borrowing to augment those securities), reverse repurchase arrangements that used securities in the portfolio as collateral on loans, and investment in a class of securities called *derivatives* that fluctuated inversely with interest rates. This entrepreneurial approach has been embraced by a few other California communities as well by as government agencies in several other states (Wayne, 1994).

The potential gains from such a strategy can be enormous, but the risks are proportional to the gains. For several years, Citron played the financial markets masterfully. His aggressive investment strategy may have helped Orange County jurisdictions hold their own when real estate values and tax revenues plummeted in the early 1990s (Mydans, 1994). But Citron's strategy was based on one key assumption: that interest rates would fall. Tragically, this bet backfired when rates began to climb in 1994.

Orange County investors lost millions, Citron lost his job, and the citizens lost confidence in the ability of their government to manage its financial resources.

Scanning the Accountability Environment

In some respects, the Orange County case is a story of how prevailing standards of accountability, and the management systems that support those standards, can shift in response to the economic, political, and intellectual environment.

In the field of public financial management, the prevailing standard of accountability historically has been rooted in the concept of stewardship of public money. Consequently, the priorities of public financial managers traditionally have been: first, to protect the investment principal, generally through relatively safe instruments such as government securities and certificates of deposit; second, to maintain liquidity with short-term investments so that cash is readily available to meet expenditure obligations; and, third, to derive a reasonable return on investment within the limits imposed by the first two principles. Naturally, this conservative approach does not produce dramatic returns on investment. In most cases, however, it does ensure the safety and liquidity of public funds. Some states, in fact, have laws restricting public investments to conservative instruments like government securities. These laws, of course, are an example of legal accountability discussed in Chapter Four.

In Orange County and other California communities, the shift in the accountability environment began in 1978, when voters approved Proposition 13—a ballot initiative that put a ceiling on future property tax rates. Public officials in California, as in several other tax revolt states, responded to this challenge with determination and, in some cases, with remarkable success. They found creative ways to augment and diversify government revenues and improved the efficiency and effectiveness of those services.

It was in this political and economic climate that California removed many of the regulatory constraints on financial managers like Citron, freeing them to be more entrepreneurial with public investments. In fact, Citron helped draft the state law that allowed county treasurers, with permission of their boards of supervisors, to use reverse repurchase arrangements (Hofmeister, 1994). Proposition 13 succeeded in limiting the discretionary authority of public officials to raise tax rates. Ironically, in the domain of public investment management, it helped to shift the standard of accountability away from compliance with strict legal and regulatory constraints and toward greater reliance on professional discretion and expert judgment. In this environment, an emerging generation of public sector entrepreneurs are attempting to manage government organizations like businesses—with aggressive strategies to diversify revenues, privatize operations, tailor services to customer needs, and generally enhance responsiveness and flexibility.

This free-market, entrepreneurial paradigm of public management was given intellectual credibility with the publication of *Reinventing Government* (Osborne and Gaebler, 1992). Indeed, the post-Proposition-13 environment in California provided much of the inspiration for Osborne and Gaebler. Many of the case histories and illustrations used in their book are drawn from the experiences of local governments in California.

Segmenting the Orange County Accountability Environment

Chapter Four presented a conceptual framework (see Figure 4.1) for dissecting the accountability environment for closer scrutiny.

The following discussion illustrates how each cell in that framework can be used to highlight selected issues in the Orange County case.

Legal Accountability

Recall that this is the cell of the matrix in which accountability is defined in terms of compliance with explicit legal standards.

This is the cell that many states and localities currently use to regulate the investment practices of government jurisdictions, and it is the cell in which Orange County operated prior to the liberalization of California's regulations. Also, it is the cell in which the Securities and Exchange Commission (SEC) regulates the activities of financial advisors and brokers. Did Citron, the brokers, and the Orange County Board of Supervisors follow both the letter and the spirit of California law and SEC regulations? This is a question that likely will be addressed as the investigation continues. If, however, the actors in this case believed that the relevant laws and regulations allowed room for interpretation, then the notion of compliance accountability described in Chapter Four would dictate that they make every effort to clarify the intent of these rules, which might involve various forms of negotiation with state and federal regulators.

Negotiated Accountability

This is the cell of the matrix in which accountability requires a tactical response to the demands of external stakeholders, often requiring some form of negotiation.

The concept of negotiated accountability applies to several aspects and phases of the Orange County case. First, at the front end (before the bankruptcy), there is the prospect that everyone associated with the Orange County investment pool—investors, creditors, elected officials, the SEC, and even citizens—would, in retrospect, have wanted to negotiate and reach agreement on the specified objectives of the investment pool, expressed in terms of acceptable levels of risk in relation to potential returns on investment. They might well have wanted a voice in deciding what portfolio of investment instruments would best meet the fund's objectives, how best to manage the portfolio to achieve the objectives, and what reporting mechanism would ensure accountability to the various stakeholders. We might assume that the objectives (and the associated risks) of the investment pool were specified in advance and that investors had access to relevant information about the fund's objectives. Still, immediately following the crisis, there was speculation that some investors might not have been fully informed regarding the management of the portfolio and, in particular, the use of a single broker for the fund (Knecht, 1994). Also, there is the curious aspect that school districts in Orange County were mandated to participate in the fund, thereby removing any opportunity for them to negotiate. It will never be known if a more formalized negotiation process would have helped Orange County avoid its financial catastrophe.

Second, at the back end (in the wake of the bankruptcy), there is the very real prospect that some form of negotiated accountability will be required to clarify the obligations of Orange County and the rights of investors under Chapter 9 of the U.S. Bankruptcy Code—a rarely used tool that is subject to interpretation and oversight by the courts (Herman and Lambert, 1994; Goldin, 1994).

Some people believe that Chapter 9 inappropriately relieves the jurisdiction of its legitimate accountability to its creditors. They point out that in theory the governments involved still have at their disposal certain options to generate more revenue (Petersen, 1995). According to some legal experts, it is possible that the broker for the Orange County investment pool may be liable for some of the fund's losses, just as a bartender is liable for the consequences of serving an obviously intoxicated patron (Knecht, 1994). The legal concept of fiduciary responsibility can be murky—and the broker of course denied any liability. Still, there is a precedent for financial brokers paying judgments and penalties arising from incidents similar to that which occurred in Orange County. Not surprisingly, the broker's stock (which itself is a noteworthy instrument of negotiated accountability) fell 3.4 percent following news of the Orange County problems (Knecht, 1994).

Discretionary Accountability

Recall that this cell allows public and nonprofit managers to exercise their professional judgment and discretion. Accountability is assessed in terms of their expertise, not strict legal standards.

This is the cell in which Citron operated when he was managing the Orange County investment fund. In California's deregulated environment, Citron was handed substantial discretionary authority and, in his defense, it must be said that he achieved steady gains in the portfolio's value for several years. Clearly, however, there are enormous risks as well as potential benefits associated with the notion of discretionary accountability, especially when public and nonprofit officials engage in entrepreneurial behavior.

Significantly, this is the cell of the matrix that Osborne and Gaebler (1992) suggest be enhanced by, in effect, giving government officials more discretionary authority to respond in an entrepreneurial way to public needs as they arise. The dilemma, only partially addressed by Osborne and Gaebler, is how to reconcile an entrepreneurial spirit, which requires swift unilateral responses to emerging opportunities, with the fundamental principles of representative bureaucracy, which require time-consuming efforts to build broad-based consensus on long-term as well as short-term goals. Indeed, this is the dilemma that has drawn some of the sharpest critiques of the entrepreneurial paradigm in the literature (Terry, 1993; Moe, 1994). Bellone and Goerl might well be describing the Orange County debacle when they write: "When engaged in *non-mandated risk taking,* the responsibilities of the public administrator become even more a stewardship issue. High-risk investment schemes that have gone wrong and resulted in economic losses, failed arbitrage efforts in investing federal grant funds, and short-term borrowing to pay operating costs . . . are all examples of entrepreneurial risk-taking that ignored the prudent concern for the long-term public good" (1992, p. 132, emphasis added).

But Bellone and Goerl go on to state that a "strong theory of entrepreneurship requires a strong theory of citizenship," and they suggest that the notions of entrepreneurship and democracy can be reconciled by providing more opportunities for meaningful citizen participation in the affairs of government (1992, p. 133). This argument also is made by Osborne and Gaebler. But this optimistic view of citizen participation is not shared by everyone. For example, Terry (1993) suggests that entrepreneurship requires dangerous concentrations of power and a commitment to fundamental change in the traditional notion of political authority and representative bureaucracy on which the profession of public administration is based. He concludes, "We should abandon the misconceived quest to reconcile public entrepreneurship with democracy" and points out that the Bellone and Goerl notion of civic-regarding entrepreneurship "seems to be a wolf in sheep's clothing" (Terry, 1993, pp. 394–395).

Coincidentally, there is evidence in the Orange County case that seems to confirm Terry's suspicion about the limited ability of citizens to provide a meaningful check on entrepreneurship, especially in a specialized domain like public investment strategies. Citron was reelected to the Treasurer's office in June 1994, only six months before the crisis. His opponent in the race was John Moorlach, a certified public accountant who based much of his campaign on Citron's risky investments and the vulnerability of the Orange County investment fund to fluctuating interest rates. Moorlach captured barely one-third of the vote and failed to generate any meaningful or lasting public dialogue on Citron's investment strategy. Evidently, the voters were either unconcerned about Citron's management of the investment pool or incapable of making informed judgments because of the complexity of the issues. They may also have been distracted by another political issue, Proposition 187 (limiting the rights of illegal immigrants), which had more emotional appeal than the intellectually challenging notions of reverse repurchase agreements, derivatives, and interest rates. Even after the bankruptcy, citizen reactions seemed mixed. A local radio station sponsored "an hour of rage" after the financial crisis to allow callers to vent their anger. The station received very few angry calls.

While most people readily embrace the democratic notions of citizen participation and consultation, it is highly unlikely that most citizens would be able to engage in informed and reasoned discourse on this complicated issue. Still, this cell raises important strategic issues for public managers. What opportunities (if any) exist for citizen input on a given entrepreneurial venture? Can such opportunities be created or enhanced? In the absence of citizen input, is the organization prepared to defend its actions in terms of the public interest and in both long-term and short-term perspectives? To whom would it account for its action in the absence of a formal reporting system?

In the absence of meaningful threats or sanctions from the external environment, public and nonprofit officials must take professional responsibility for anticipating and interpreting emerging standards of acceptable professional behavior and organizational performance, weighing long-term risks as well as short-term benefits. Consequently, there can be enormous pressures on public managers in this cell of the matrix. North Carolina's state treasurer, Harlan Boyles, said that prior to the Orange County incident, he was under intense political pressure from local governments in his state to liberalize investment regulations and restrictions so that they too could begin reaping the high investment dividends enjoyed by communities in California, Texas, Ohio, and elsewhere. Boyles also was receiving more than a dozen calls a month from brokers around the country hoping to sway his views. "It's a constant pressure. They'll call and say, 'Let us show you what we did in California.' Thankfully, our General Assembly has never been inclined to liberalize the investment laws" ("Public Finance Chiefs," 1994).

There also is intense peer pressure in this cell of the accountability matrix. David Bronner, director of Alabama's pension fund, said, "I remember a group outing two years ago with the Orange County people. They were very boastful about how well they were doing and how antiquated I was." Bronner also noted that, until recently, he had unilateral discretionary authority to make investments in whatever instruments he deemed appropriate, regardless of their risk ("Public Finance Chiefs," 1994).

Anticipatory Accountability

This cell requires decision makers to be advocates for the public interest and the public trust.

Significantly, the Orange County case also illustrates the pitfalls of accountability from the standpoint of administrative advocacy. In 1979, Citron, acting as head of the state association of county treasurers, was the prime architect of legal and regulatory changes that allowed the use of reverse repurchase arrangements (Hofmeister, 1994). Thus Citron and others who advocated the change bore responsibility (at the time they advocated the change) to relate it to a pressing need in the public interest, build in meaningful oversight mechanisms to monitor impacts and prevent abuse, and educate legislators (and by extension the general public) regarding risks as well as benefits. Having successfully advocated the new legislation, they bore responsibility to follow the spirit as well as the letter of the law, as suggested by the notion of compliance accountability.

In the wake of the Orange County problem, there were renewed calls for a stricter regulatory environment governing investment of public funds. Actions at the state level may once again reinvent the previous bureaucratic mechanisms designed to constrain the activities of public officials within precise and formally codified standards and prescribed behaviors. At the national level, there were calls for greater oversight of private brokers by the SEC and other regulatory bodies. Naturally, state and local agencies will be well advised to closely monitor these developments as they unfold and, if appropriate, attempt to influence the outcome of these legislative debates.

Management and Policy Implications

Embedded in each cell of the matrix presented in Chapter Four are management issues and plausible strategies that organizations might use to their advantage—and ultimately to the public advantage as they apply strategic management approaches while fulfilling their obligations as stewards of the public trust.

Legal Accountability

Public and nonprofit organizations—even those operating under an entrepreneurial paradigm—must occasionally conduct a *compliance audit*. At the most elementary level, this audit should attempt to document the organization's legal obligations as follows:

- A complete listing of oversight agencies to which the organization is generally accountable or with jurisdiction over selected portions of the organization's mandate and mission
- A compilation and analysis of the legal or regulatory standards of accountability to which the organization is bound by its mandate, charter, authorizing legislation, and contractual arrangements with other organizations
- An assessment of how well the organization has performed in meeting these standards

- An assessment of compliance with the spirit and the letter of the law
- A list of demonstrated efforts to provide full disclosure of the organization's performance in both the spirit and the letter of the law

These approaches, of course, address the most narrowly interpreted aspects of accountability—answering to a higher authority regarding performance and compliance with explicit mandates. They also are among the most important questions decision makers will ask when conducting an accountability audit.

Negotiated Accountability

Most of the literature on negotiation approaches the topic from an adversarial perspective—that any form of negotiation is, in effect, a zero-sum game wherein the interests of one or more players are advanced at the expense of others. But when attempting to enhance accountability in public management, the adversarial approach to negotiation is unacceptable. Instead, the objective of negotiated accountability is to clarify and define the public interest and to reach agreement on what mechanisms and strategies best serve those interests. A cursory list of objectives is as follows:

- To clarify the multiple and perhaps conflicting interpretations of the public interest and accountability to that interest within the context of specific programmatic activities or proposals
- To clarify what (if any) accountability issues in a specific programmatic domain are negotiable and distinguish them from those that are nonnegotiable
- To clarify the respective objectives and interests of various policy stakeholders and separate these objectives and interests from specific proposals or programs to achieve them
- To clarify and agree on reasonable standards of compliance or performance to which an organization or an individual should be held accountable
- To reach agreement on reasonable measures, behaviors, processes, or outcomes with which to assess organizational or personal accountability

- To reach agreement about any uncontrollable factors and contingencies that may affect the accountability relationship, so as to ensure, in advance, that actors are not held responsible for events beyond their control
- To reach agreement on what resources and investments are needed to maintain given levels of accountability and the marginal costs and benefits of incrementally greater (or lesser) degrees of control
- To build trust among the participants in the negotiation process

Toward these objectives, the philosophy of "principled bargaining" advanced by Fisher and Ury (1981, p. 13) seems appropriate. Among other things, this philosophy views negotiators as problem solvers, not as adversaries. The desired outcome of negotiation is to advance overriding interests and values (such as the public interest) rather than inflexible adherence to specific positions, rules, or programmatic designs. Moreover, the agreement, when ultimately reached, must contain objective criteria with which to monitor performance and to which all parties can be held accountable.

Of course, there are many conceivable contexts in which public and nonprofit administrators will work feverishly to avoid negotiation of standards for fear that it will open a Pandora's box of issues and competing interests they would rather not address or would prefer not to have out in the open for public discourse. The political or administrative philosophy may be "let sleeping dogs lie" or some variant of "what they don't know won't hurt them." It is true, under certain circumstances, that the costs of negotiation (tangible and intangible) may outweigh the benefits. From the standpoint of accountability, however, public administrators must be able to demonstrate beyond reasonable doubt that the decision not to negotiate was in the long-term as well as short-term public interest.

The general approach to negotiated accountability also is worthy of consideration for public and nonprofit administrators who, in an endless variety of contexts, may actually feel victimized by being held accountable for implicit standards they do not fully understand.

Discretionary Authority

While the entrepreneurial paradigm of public and nonprofit management has come under intense scrutiny and criticism, it is not likely to fold its tent and quietly retreat into the sunset. Managers at all levels of government and throughout the nonprofit sector are feeling the same types of pressures, to a greater or lesser degree, as those experienced by Citron in Orange County. Taxpayers are quick to demand higher levels of professional competence and improved quality of government services, but they are not inclined to provide additional resources to achieve these goals. Nonprofit organizations are being asked to assume a greater share of social services previously provided by government but again without additional public resources. These fiscal and political pressures, combined with the seemingly endless stream of antibureaucracy proposals—in the media, in the scholarly literature, in the popular literature, and in government—will ensure that public and nonprofit managers will continue to use discretionary judgment and entrepreneurial approaches.

If we assume that professional discretion and entrepreneurship will be facts of life, what principles should guide public managers to maintain accountability? Can we reconcile the notion of entrepreneurship with the imperatives of public stewardship? The following is an initial list of strategies or principles that should guide discretionary decision making and, especially, any entrepreneurial venture:

- Above all, discretionary actions or entrepreneurial ventures must be consistent with the legal mandate and authority of the organization and the public managers.
- Such actions or ventures should be mission focused and value driven, guided by an explicit and publicly stated set of goals, operating philosophies, and measures of success.
- All participants must take professional responsibility for obtaining full information on the risks as well as the potential benefits and for fully understanding the detailed mechanics of the proposed initiative—how it works as well as what it is designed to achieve.
- Discretionary programs, especially entrepreneurial ventures, should have an internal (preferably formal) system of checks

and balances with which to monitor and assess progress toward objectives as well as the procedural means of achieving those objectives.

- Less formally, participants should foster an organizational culture or climate wherein dissenting opinions among participants and stakeholders are not only tolerated but encouraged and facilitated.
- Discretionary initiatives, especially entrepreneurial ventures, should be informed by a formal process of scenario construction wherein the participants examine probabilities of various chains of events (however improbable), and consequences of those events, leading to best-case, worst-case, and most-likely scenarios.
- In the absence of meaningful citizen or client input, participants in discretionary ventures should engage in a "rehearsal of defenses" (Cooper, 1990, p. 23) by asking, "How and to whom would we defend our actions if called upon to do so?"
- In the absence of citizen or client input, there should be a mechanism for periodic disclosure of how well the initiative has performed in meeting objectives.
- The disclosure document should be prepared by an independent body.
- Discretionary initiatives, especially entrepreneurial ventures, must have a contingency plan that allows the organization to withdraw or otherwise adjust its commitment if the public interest becomes threatened by unforeseen or uncontrollable events.
- Discretionary investments should be overseen by a review body, with prohibitions against single-bet, winner-take-all investment strategies.

Mitroff and Emshoff (1979) developed a decision-making process that meets some of the objectives outlined above. Their approach involves a systematic, if tedious, set of steps designed to surface the implicit or underlying assumptions associated with policies, initiatives, or programs. Too often, these assumptions remain hidden from view until it is too late. In general, Mitroff and Emshoff recommend a flow of questions as follows:

- What is the strategy initially under consideration?
- What data provide apparent support for the strategy?
- What assumptions, when coupled with the data, allow decision makers to deduce the strategy?

Then Mitroff and Emshoff recommend a second, "dialectic" phase in which the assumptions themselves come under scrutiny and where maximum diversity of opinions is achieved:

- What counterassumptions might negate those already identified?
- What data support the counterassumptions?
- What alternative strategies can be deduced from the counterassumptions and the data that support them?

Finally, after consolidating and debating all plausible assumptions and strategies, the process again works backward from the most plausible or most acceptable assumptions, through the data that support those acceptable assumptions, to the most appropriate (best) strategy consistent with both the most plausible assumptions and the most rigorous data.

It should be readily apparent how such a model of decision making might have informed the investment strategy of the Orange County fund. Certainly, Citron and his advisers made an assumption that interest rates would remain low. This assumption should have been relatively explicit to anyone who carefully analyzed the portfolio of investments. What we do not know is whether there were mechanisms or processes built into the management system (or even the organizational culture) that allowed and facilitated the expression of counterassumptions and alternative strategies for consideration.

The professional obligation to be fully informed and knowledgeable in any entrepreneurial venture was expressed by Charles Cox, finance director of Farmers Branch, Texas, when he said, "If I don't understand it, and I don't know how it works, I'm not going to invest in it" ("Public Finance Chiefs," 1994). A recent survey of members of the Government Finance Officers Association (GFOA) found that only 4 percent were knowledgeable about derivative securities; 20 percent said that they had limited knowledge; 76 percent said they had some or no knowledge ("Public Finance Chiefs," 1994).

The Orange County case should serve as a message of caution to public and nonprofit executives who are now trying to instill an entrepreneurial and enterprising spirit in their organizations. When legal and bureaucratic mechanisms of accountability are cast aside, something must emerge to take their place. As illustrated by the Orange County case, market structures, entrepreneurship, and professional discretion may not be sufficient to ensure that the public trust is served.

Anticipatory Accountability

"Accountability tends to serve democracy best when administrators anticipate the legitimate preferences of elected officials and adjust their behavior accordingly" (Levine, Peters, and Thompson, 1990, p. 190). Certainly, there is no crystal ball issued to public managers when they take office. Still, several principles should guide their efforts to remain accountable to the public trust when operating in this type of accountability environment:

- Develop and nurture organizational routines for continuously scanning changes in the accountability environment, taking into consideration political, socioeconomic, technological, and intellectual trends.
- Utilize strategic planning methods to identify organizational strengths, weaknesses, opportunities, and threats.
- Use multiple methods to stay in touch with citizens and with elected officials to continuously monitor emerging needs.
- Develop and use networks with professional peers, striving to learn as much as possible from their experiences.
- Work with legislators in a bipartisan or nonpartisan way to craft legislative proposals that are responsive to the public interest.
- Work through alternative assumptions and options when assisting legislators in their efforts.

These steps will help ensure that public managers stay on top of emerging issues to position themselves and their organizations accordingly.

Summary

Of course hindsight is always twenty-twenty. It is relatively easy to provide retrospective explanations of what went wrong, whether in the Orange County investment pool, the New York City fiscal crisis, the United Way of America scandal, or any one of hundreds of public and nonprofit organizations that have been caught in the accountability trap. The trick is to understand shifts in the accountability environment while they are happening or, better yet, even before they emerge, and to employ accountability strategies that are well matched to the changing features of the economic and political landscape.

The irony in the Orange County case is that Citron was actually following a strategic approach to accountability management by utilizing his discretionary authority to the fullest extent allowed by California's liberalized investment laws and regulations. He correctly interpreted the political and economic climate in Southern California and responded by diversifying government revenues. He fulfilled the political mandate to hold down taxes and, for many years, he correctly anticipated and interpreted shifts in the macroeconomic landscape to the short-term benefit of his constituents—elected officials, taxpayers, investors, and creditors.

But the Orange County case also illustrates some of the pitfalls of managing in a dynamic accountability environment. The conceptual framework presented in this chapter is only marginally useful unless it helps organizations focus on strategies and policies to enhance their accountability within an ever-changing environment.

Chapter Eight

Proactive Accountability
The *SumOne for Kids* Project

A strategic approach to accountability requires anticipation and interpretation of legal and regulatory trends. Also, a strategic approach requires the ability to work effectively with stakeholders inside and outside government to advocate appropriate performance standards and reporting mechanisms. Finally, a strategic approach requires a sustained commitment of resources to develop accountability systems that are objective, valid, and reliable.

These prerequisites are especially important when public and nonprofit organizations take it upon themselves to develop measures of service outcomes or impacts that are voluntarily reported to external stakeholders. In any circumstance involving self-generated and self-reported performance data, a key consideration is credibility and integrity of the approach.

This chapter presents a brief case history of *SumOne for Kids,* a children's services outcome measurement and data base project. The case is noteworthy because it represents a strategic and proactive approach to voluntary accountability, illustrating several of the key concepts and approaches discussed in earlier chapters. This chapter is based on interviews with key personnel and a review of supporting documentation for the *SumOne for Kids* project. For descriptive information and background on the project, I drew heavily on a paper by Beck, Meadowcroft, and Kiely (forthcoming).

Background and Context

As noted earlier in this book, nonprofit human service agencies are under intense pressure to monitor, document, and report the actual outcomes and impacts of their services. Individual donors, foundations, watchdog groups, and grantmaking federations like the United Way are demanding information that goes well beyond traditional output measures such as what services are provided to how many clients at what cost. They now want to know what differences those services make in the lives of the clients who are served and, by extension, in the quality of life of the community (see Kanter and Summers, 1987; Drucker, 1990). Are clients somehow better off as a result of receiving the services? Is the community a better place as a result of the organization?

These are more than just rhetorical questions. The United Way of Allegheny County (1995), for example, requires its member agencies to analyze each program or service category according to questions such as the extent to which a program's goals and objectives are predominantly concerned with outcomes created for the clientele, and the extent to which an agency uses effective methods to evaluate both these outcomes and the quality of the program's service delivery.

The pressure to report outcomes is particularly intense in those sectors of the human service system that are perceived as crucial to the future of the nation and also those that are relatively costly from a social engineering perspective. Children's health and welfare services are a case in point. Social, economic, and demographic patterns have increased the number of children entering the health and welfare system. Today children are entering that system with increasingly serious social, psychological, and health problems, which severely restrict their potential to lead happy and productive lives. Moreover, "our most costly forms of mental health treatment (psychiatric hospitalization) and child welfare services (residential care) fail to provide payers or consumers with outcome accountability" (Beck, Meadowcroft, and Kiely, forthcoming, p. 1).

SumOne for Kids is an outcome-monitoring data base system designed by and for agencies that provide direct care, supervision, mental health, education, and social services to children and their families. It is currently being used by seventeen agencies in Pennsylvania with prospects for statewide and multistate applications.

Anticipatory Accountability: Challenges and Opportunities

The accountability environment contains many potential threats for children's services agencies—and some opportunities as well. In Pennsylvania, a particularly salient threat emerged in the late 1980s, when momentum grew in the General Assembly to pass legislation mandating outcome monitoring for children's services and making state funding for these agencies contingent upon compliance with explicit reporting procedures. In 1989, John Pierce, executive director of the Pennsylvania Council of Children's Services (PCCS), convinced his board that it would be in the best interest of the eighty-five PCCS member agencies and their clients to preempt the state-imposed monitoring system by offering to work with state authorities to develop a system that would be a management tool for the children's services agencies as well as a monitoring and reporting tool for oversight organizations and the public at large.

One of the key strategic opportunities in this environment involved developments in information technology, especially data base management, which promised to greatly facilitate the gathering, synthesis, and analysis of outcome indicators from multiple agencies. The vision was for a system that would be continuously updated as a tool for comparative analysis and benchmarking among participating organizations. In each of the participating agencies, the system would be used not only by executives and clinical specialists, but also by boards of trustees as an accountability tool for the general public. Oversight agencies in the state government would also be end users of the system.

Strengths and Limitations

In this strategic environment, PCCS had certain strengths analogous to the categories discussed in Chapter Five. With respect to leadership, for example, Pierce himself had been working for several years to advocate outcome monitoring among children's services agencies and was widely viewed as an effective champion of the concept. Also, PCCS had political credibility in the state capitol via its network of contacts with key legislators who were willing to hold off on mandated monitoring temporarily, pending an assessment of the PCCS plan. Finally, one of the members of PCCS, Pressley Ridge Schools, had experimented with its own outcome monitoring system (Pressley Ridge Schools, 1994) and agreed to be the lead agency in coordinating the design of a prototype system. Clark Luster, the executive director of Pressley Ridge Schools, had substantial experience in outcome measurement and was viewed by PCCS members as a credible broker of the outcome monitoring concept.

But along with these strengths, PCCS had certain constraints and limitations also analogous to categories discussed in Chapter Five. For example, one limiting factor was the cost of the monitoring system. The PCCS member agencies would not support a system likely to impose substantial direct or indirect costs. They were, however, moderately supportive of a system that could be relatively easily administered by existing personnel without the need for costly external consultants or support systems. Another constraint was the need for a system that could be adapted to multiple agencies with varying missions and needs. Finally, like any such organization, PCCS had a finite reservoir of political capital on which to draw, both among government oversight agencies and its own member organizations. While nearly all PCCS member agencies expressed support for moving ahead with the project, only thirty-one volunteered for direct participation in the developmental phase. The project would need to show steady (if not rapid) progress toward a practical but rigorous system that would meet the needs and expectations of multiple users.

Strategy

The development strategy for *SumOne for Kids* was based on a bottom-up/top-down philosophy. Mindful of the need for political support, the top-down component was developed early on. Even before formally launching the project, the design team met with state regulatory agencies, elected officials, educators, and researchers to secure their advice and support for the project. The involvement of these stakeholders from the very start of the project gave them some ownership of the initiative, thereby enhancing the prospects for successful implementation. Still, as we shall see later, early involvement of government officials is not necessarily a guarantee of success in a dynamic political arena.

Second, the team focused on the people who would eventually implement and use the system—the children's services agencies—to design the technical specifications. In this phase, the design team learned more about the thirty-one participating agencies, including their needs and constraints and how the system could be most useful to them.

Third, the design team had to decide what type of outcomes would be monitored and reported by the system. The tradition in health and welfare agencies is to monitor so-called clinical outcomes, such as cognitive skills or emotional stability, which typically are measured with standardized tests or direct expert observation. While the design team recognized the value of clinical outcomes, they determined that these were not necessarily the most salient final outcomes in the minds of government policy makers or citizens at large; they are, instead, intermediary outcomes that address the symptoms displayed by clients rather than their ultimate functioning in society. The team decided to develop a system based on functional outcomes that address end results or practical outcomes such as employment, school attendance, and social behavior and stability. It was believed that functional outcomes reflected the core missions of the children's services agencies. Also, from the standpoint of accountability, functional outcomes were perceived to be more politically defensible than intermediary clinical outcomes. Functional outcomes may be more subjective and, from a methodological standpoint, more problematic to measure than clinical outcomes. Still, the design team believed that the benefits of this novel approach outweighed the costs.

Fourth, to build credibility for the project and to show rapid results for government bureaucrats and policy makers, the design team quickly developed a demonstration model, incorporating data already used by some PCCS agencies and Pressley Ridge Schools into a computerized data base system. Naturally, this demonstration model was crude in comparison with the final product, but it was an effective marketing device and helped to build enthusiasm for the project.

Fifth, the design team sought input from multiple stakeholders—children, parents, teachers, judges, social workers, legislators, and community leaders—regarding the functional outcome measures that should be monitored and included in the data base (Van-DenBerg, Beck, and Howarth, 1992). It was decided that the performance standards should be those perceived as most important to the users and beneficiaries of the children's services system. After extensive surveys and interviews, followed by several rounds of synthesis and ranking, the design team selected the following five sets of functional outcomes with multiple dimensions in each:

- *Productivity:* School attendance, graduation, and/or employment
- *Antisocial Activity:* Reduction of drug and/or alcohol use rates
- *Stability of Living Environment:* Changes in the child's residence and the restrictiveness of the living environment
- *Protection from Harm:* Frequency of injury or abuse by peers or adults and frequency of threats of harm from peers or adults
- *Client Satisfaction:* Satisfaction with living arrangements, school, or work, and with life in general

The system also includes a child descriptors element that contains standardized information about the child—demographics, family history, clinical treatment plan, and so on—at the point of entry to the agency, at ninety-day intervals during treatment, and at discharge. The outcomes themselves are measured via a structured interview protocol with children and their caregivers at ninety-day intervals up to one year following treatment. The process is extensively documented with multimedia training materials and software for use on personal computers (Pressley Ridge Schools, 1995a, 1995b).

Sixth, and finally, the design team built into the system an internal accountability mechanism in the form of periodic audits to test adherence to the prescribed interview protocol and to ensure the integrity of the data. The audits of the outcome measurement system are conducted by independent firms in conjunction with annual financial and compliance audits.

Current Status: Threats and Opportunities

SumOne for Kids is being pilot-tested on a voluntary basis. Despite extensive efforts to involve agencies in the design of the system, there remain controversies and latent conflicts among the agency users—who by definition have diverse missions and needs. Some agencies, for example, believe the system is of limited utility in analyzing the success or failure of their clinical treatment programs for individual patients. This limitation derives from an agreement among the participants early on in the design process that the data on individual clients would be kept confidential to encourage honest responses from them. While aggregate data is useful in assessing effectiveness of programs or clusters of clinical modalities, some agencies believe it is less useful when evaluating the success or failure of a specific intervention with a specific child.

In the political and regulatory arena, efforts to incorporate the system into government-mandated accountability reports are proceeding through negotiations with state and federal officials. But, as is often the case, the accountability environment is a moving target. Newly emerging forces offer an ever-changing landscape of opportunities and threats for the *SumOne for Kids* project. Since the inception of the project, momentum has continued to build for various types of government-mandated outcome reports from children's services agencies. For example, the Statewide Automated Child Welfare Information System (SACWIS) is a federal matching grant program that provides incentives for states to standardize and integrate all state-operated data bases on children's services. Advocates of the *SumOne for Kids* project are finding it a major challenge to convince government regulators to nest the five functional outcome measures from *SumOne for Kids* in the SACWIS reporting mechanism. They are trying to demonstrate that the *SumOne for Kids* system is more rigorous in monitoring outcomes than the SACWIS and other mandated reports currently in use. These negotiations are proceeding, but it is not an easy sell when state officials themselves are under pressure from multiple stakeholders, including federal agencies, to address diverse and sometimes conflicting accountability standards and reporting schemes.

Also, at the national level, the Government Performance and Results Act of 1993 now requires all federal agencies to report performance outcomes in their budget requests. These requirements will gradually cascade downward to state and local agencies that receive federal funds, introducing yet another wrinkle into the accountability equation for agencies participating in the *SumOne for Kids* project.

In the strategic management terminology used throughout this book, these developments are, on balance, threats to the *SumOne for Kids* project. Ultimate success in securing statewide adoption of the system will depend, of course, on whether the advocates can effectively mobilize their collective assets or strengths (see Chapter Six) to effect political action in the state capitol and in Washington. Their reservoir of political resources will be significantly tapped in this effort.

On another front, however, the designers of *SumOne for Kids* are tentatively exploring opportunities to market the system to children's services agencies in other states on a fee-for-service basis. The success of such a venture will depend on their ability to convince these potential users that the notion of voluntary accountability (and the *SumOne for Kids* system in particular) is simply the prudent path to follow—from the standpoint of enhancing management and governance accountability—irrespective of its acceptance by government regulatory agencies.

Lessons Learned

Regardless of the future prospects, the designers of *SumOne for Kids* believe that several factors account for whatever success the project has attained so far. They feel the following measures will be important considerations in the promotion of any voluntary accountability system among multiple stakeholders:

- Involve stakeholders in the design of all aspects of the accountability system, especially the selection of outcome measures, and sustain stakeholder involvement with regular communication.
- Build on past practices, trying not to reinvent the wheel with totally new measures.
- Measure a few things very well and keep the accountability system as simple as possible.
- Develop systems that encourage self-evaluation and that help build a bottom-up culture of accountability.
- Stay abreast of external trends in the accountability environment before and during the development of the system.

This case study was not selected because *SumOne for Kids* represents an unqualified success story. Indeed, the accountability environment appears to be every bit as turbulent now as it was at the outset of the project and the advocates of this system seem to be adjusting their expectations and strategies accordingly.

This case was selected for inclusion here because embedded within it are many of the dimensions of accountability discussed throughout this book. For example, this is a case that has overtones of compliance with government-mandated reports, but the interests and motives of the various stakeholders go well beyond this narrow and technical definition of accountability. Also, the reader will quickly see how negotiation plays a role in the development of accountability standards and the associated reporting mechanisms. And, above all, the *SumOne for Kids* project represents a proactive and strategic approach to accountability that is based on professional discretion and also continuous advocacy to higher authorities as well as peer organizations. All of these dimensions of accountability were discussed in Chapter Four.

The case also illustrates several key concepts discussed in Chapters Five and Six. It is clear, for example, that PCCS and Pressley Ridge Schools had an impressive inventory of accountability assets that could be mobilized to respond to the political and regulatory challenges looming on the horizon. But while they have obvious comparative advantages as leaders and advocates of this initiative, they have limited leverage and control over their environment. At several phases of the development process (and perhaps also in the dissemination phase ahead) the need for damage control and continuous SWOT analysis is ever present.

Summary

Regarding the prerequisites for a strategic approach to accountability mentioned at the beginning of this chapter, the advocates and designers of the *SumOne for Kids* system clearly have displayed the ability to anticipate and interpret changes in their accountability environment. Their reading of the political trends among state legislators and child welfare regulatory agencies was, indeed, the impetus for designing a voluntary monitoring and reporting system.

But the advocacy skills and the long-term commitment of PCCS and Pressley Ridge Schools to this strategic initiative will be severely tested by ongoing changes in the accountability environment. As often is the case when organizations attempt to strategically manage accountability, there is no definitive end to the story.

Conclusion
Leadership for Accountability

Throughout this book, I have argued that the notion of accountability is multifaceted and therefore affects and is affected by every component of the organization—the management of its resources, the design of its processes, and the evaluation of its products and services. Also, I have said that accountability can and should be managed strategically, with a view toward prospective analysis of external opportunities and challenges as well as internal strengths and limitations.

These two attributes of accountability—its systemwide character and its strategic importance—both justify and demand the attention of organizational leaders. It is the leaders who, with their own systemwide and strategic perspective, are best able to mobilize the resources needed to sustain and enhance accountability at all levels of the organization.

Exploring the notion of leadership has been a popular pastime among executives and scholars, especially in recent years. Early research efforts (for example, Henson, 1934; Tead, 1935) laid the theoretical and conceptual foundation for the notion of leadership and paved the way for more practical (often motivational) books designed for popular consumption (Bennis, 1989; Horton, 1992; Herman and Heimovics, 1991).

In this final chapter, I will not attempt to summarize the vast and growing literature on leadership. Instead, I want to conclude with some thoughts on several key issues that link the concepts of leadership and accountability: Why is leadership essential to ensure accountability in public and nonprofit organizations? Who must assume leadership for institutional accountability? and What can leaders do to instill a culture of accountability in their organizations?

179

Why Leadership Is Essential

Richard Cyert, management scholar and former president of Carnegie Mellon University, has said that "Leadership is an attempt to capture the discretionary thinking time of organizational members, and convey to them that the ideas the leader has communicated are important" (Cyert, 1995). The operative phrase in Cyert's statement is *discretionary thinking time*—something that all workers have (in varying quantities) regardless of the context of their work or the nature of their jobs. Similarly, Bennis and Nanus (1985), two of the most prolific writers on leadership, say that effective leaders must among other things *capture and focus the attention* of their followers with a compelling vision, and *stimulate the imagination* of workers with effective communication of their vision. These two tasks are consistent with Cyert's more succinct but equally powerful definition of leadership—capturing the discretionary thinking time of followers.

Employees use discretionary thinking time whenever they choose where to focus their attention and energy among the many demands of the job. Thus, their time is not truly discretionary in the usual usage of the term because the degrees of freedom are limited in any job. And naturally, as we move down the hierarchy of authority, employees have less discretionary thinking time because their job descriptions generally require accomplishment of specific tasks rather than overarching organizational goals and strategic directions. Nonetheless, employees at all levels of the organization make choices—sometimes minute-by-minute choices—about where to direct their attention and their energy.

In this environment, the ideals of accountability and serving the public trust can easily be supplanted by more pressing concerns and tasks. Even among the governing board and the senior staff, who ostensibly have more discretionary thinking time, the ideals of accountability can be lost or simply taken for granted among the demands of other organizational concerns. Quite often the "urgent" overrides the "important" and tactical considerations supersede strategic planning and management.

The leader's job is to focus (and perhaps refocus) whatever discretionary thinking time exists on the priorities he or she deems most important.

Who Must Assume Leadership for Institutional Accountability?

Leadership for accountability must begin at the very top of the organization and work its way down through supervisory levels to the individual worker. As Horton (1992) says, "Beyond intellectual capacity and interpersonal skills, [leadership] requires the desire to be held accountable" (p. xiv). In government organizations, this means that accountability begins with the elected governing body. Similarly, in private nonprofit organizations, accountability begins with the board of trustees.

Leadership by the Governing Body

With respect to accountability, the governing body of the organization must focus on two fundamental questions: To whom is the governing body itself accountable? and, For what is the governing body accountable?

Carver, in his book *Boards That Make a Difference* (1990, pp. 130–148), addresses both these questions. With respect to the first, Carver states emphatically that the governing body of any organization—public or private—is primarily accountable to what he calls the "moral owners" of the organization. The moral owners are "those *on whose behalf* the board is accountable to others" (p. 131). While the stakeholders of any organization—clients, donors, peer agencies, and others—often overlap, Carver isolates moral owners as a special class distinct from direct beneficiaries and other stakeholders. Thus, using his examples, the moral ownership of a school system is the population of the school district; the direct beneficiaries are the students. The moral ownership of a community mental health center is the community at large; the beneficiaries are a subset of that community. Carver is very clear regarding his convictions on the supremacy of moral ownership: "'Moral' rather than legal ownership is to be the basis on which a board determines its accountability. In cases where state law requires a nonprofit organization to have a membership (a legal ownership), the board must determine whether the moral ownership is a larger body, far beyond the bounds of the formal ownership. . . . Ownership is not merely paying the bills, although this may be a consideration. . . . The test of ownership is not with whom the board makes a deal, but whom the board has no moral right *not* to recognize" (pp. 131–132).

Carver says that the board's accountability to the moral owners "supersedes its relationship with staff" (p. 132). In fact, one of the primary themes of his book is that governing boards too often engage in activities that duplicate those of staff, thereby losing sight of their primary accountability to the moral owners. Board committees, for example, typically are organized along lines that duplicate staff functions like planning, personnel, finance, development, facilities, and so on.

With respect to the second question (For what is the governing body accountable?), Carver says that the governing board is accountable for three core products: linkage to the moral owners of the organization; explicit governing policies reflecting the values and philosophies of the organization; and assurance of executive performance, that is, holding the staff accountable to performance criteria set by the board. Carver stresses that these are products, not activities. They emphasize the board's accountability for outcomes (ends) rather than tasks (means).

On the whole, Carver believes that governing boards should be far more concerned with their accountability to the stated objectives of the organization than with how those objectives are achieved. Consequently, he recommends job descriptions for both the board and the staff that stress products or outcomes rather than activities or tasks. Carver's recommended job descriptions typically allow for substantial discretionary judgment by the professional staff within broad accountability parameters (limitations) outlined by the board.

But, as we have seen in Chapter Seven, discretionary judgment is susceptible to abuse, especially in areas where the governing board may lack the incentives or expertise for close oversight. To protect against abuse of discretionary authority, Burke suggests, "Political authorities should establish rules governing service delivery if professional practice is likely to conflict with the desires and interests of the public or its representatives" (1986, p. 148). Thus, the governing body must be willing to candidly address these key questions:

- In what aspects of the organization are professional discretion and autonomy of the staff most likely to conflict with the interests of the public?

- How can the governing board protect the public interest without completely stifling the judgment and creativity of the professional staff?

Carver's answer to these questions is for the governing board to draft a set of "executive limitations" that spell out prohibited activities in areas like resource management, communication with the board, and executive succession. The limitations may refer to legal, ethical, or managerial norms that executives pledge not to violate. But they are given substantial latitude regarding the means they use to operate within these limitations. By specifying *proscribed* behaviors rather than *prescribed* tasks, the board gives professionals discretionary authority but still holds them accountable to its operating values and philosophies. Carver's approach is an innovative response to concerns about abuse of discretionary authority. His model represents a fundamental departure from traditional board structures and, as such, requires a substantial and sustained commitment from many people. Nor is his model essential for all nonprofit boards to follow. Many nonprofit organizations have boards that operate effectively, efficiently, and accountably without resorting to a fundamental redesign of their structures and procedures as recommended by the Carver model (Murray, 1994). A slightly more technical (and financial) approach to board accountability is provided by Herzlinger (1994), with special reference to private nonprofit organizations. In her view, "The board must ensure that the nonprofit's mission is appropriate to its charitable orientation and that it accomplishes that mission efficiently. In the absence of concrete measures and market signals about mission, quality, and efficiency, that is no easy task. Consequently, the board must devise its own system of measurement and control" (p. 53).

Herzlinger's proposed system of measurement and control is based on four questions and financial indicators associated with each:

- *Are the organization's goals consistent with its financial resources?* Many organizations have goals that are too modest considering their substantial financial reserves, while the goals of other organizations may be too ambitious to support with existing resources. Financial indicators such as liquidity and the ratio between service revenues and total assets can be useful indicators of whether the organization is aiming too high or too low (p. 55).

- *Is the organization practicing intergenerational equity?* Organizations should not sacrifice present clients for the benefit of future ones or vice versa. An inflation-adjusted fund balance may indicate from year to year if the organization is maintaining a balance between current and future users (p. 57).

- *Are sources and uses of funds appropriately matched?* Fixed expenses should be funded primarily by fixed revenues whereas variable expenses should be matched with variable revenues (p. 57).

- *Is the organization sustainable?* Strategic planning for new initiatives must be accompanied by financial and budgetary analysis. Also, resources and investments should be dispersed in a way that spreads risk (p. 58).

Herzlinger's approach is, of course, more specific than Carver's in that it focuses substantial attention on indicators of financial health and long-term viability. But both authors agree that the governing board is primarily accountable to the public, not to the professional staff.

Staff Leadership: The Chief Executive and Middle Management

The professional staff of the organization, along with the governing board, must exercise leadership of and responsibility for institutional accountability. To a greater extent than the board, however, the staff must be concerned with the details of accountability and its management on a day-to-day basis. Also to a greater extent than the governing body, the professional staff must be concerned with managing downward to subordinates as well as outward to the moral ownership. That is, they must make accountability an overarching priority for employees and focus at least some of their discretionary attention on the imperative of serving the public trust.

In some respects, the challenge of leadership for the executive staff is even greater than for the board because the executive must capture and hold the attention of subordinates whose discretionary thinking time is relatively limited. Thus, while it might be relatively easy for the governing board to focus the attention of the chief executive on issues of accountability, the executive in turn may have greater difficulty focusing the attention of subordinates.

Nonetheless, here are some suggested leadership strategies drawn from the literature and from personal experience.

Capturing Attention Through Images and Examples

With regard to focusing organizational attention on the notion of accountability, leaders might begin with a kind of storytelling exercise rather than launching immediately into motivational exhortations, detailed policy initiatives, or strategic planning activities like those described in this book (Kouzes and Posner, 1993, pp. 197–199).

It is a fact of human nature that our discretionary attention is riveted by stories and vivid images rather than by abstract words, concepts, or ideals. This natural tendency is tapped (and perhaps exploited) by marketing professionals, entertainers, and even politicians, who have become increasingly adept at creating sound-bite images with examples and metaphors rather than substantive explanations of policy issues and choices. Perhaps we are even more inclined to pay attention to powerful images because our society bombards us with raw data and synthesized information from a growing array of sources, drowning out all but the most compelling (and perhaps the simplest) messages (Ries and Trout, 1981).

It is easy to feel cynical—perhaps even guilty—about our selective appetite for form over substance, until we remember that form and substance are and always have been inseparable components of communication. Any scholar of history, anthropology, or theology can attest that storytelling and imagery—even when based on little more than myth—are important building blocks for cultural norms, mores, and values. Leaders from all walks of life—politics, business, and religion—have always used stories to convey their message. The Parables, for example, are stories designed to convey a compelling moral lesson. And great orators throughout history have conveyed their ideas as much through images as through words and concepts.

With respect to storytelling about accountability, one approach is to compile a file of news stories, journal articles, and case studies that concern selected aspects of accountability in similar or at least comparable organizations. These could be positive examples of organizations that have taken steps to enhance their accountability as well as negative examples of controversies, scandals, and the like.

The leader might circulate these stories to staff members, inviting their comments and perhaps even assigning someone to gather more information and lead a discussion at an upcoming staff meeting. The process should not be a one-shot effort; rather, there should repeated communiqués over several weeks or months to gradually penetrate the consciousness of employees. At first, the staff may question the leader's motives, objectives, or mental stability ("What's the boss up to now?") but this curiosity (and even initial skepticism) is a sign that their attention is being captured. Over time, this process will sensitize the staff to the many facets of accountability and the consequences of losing sight of it in the rush of daily activities. Also, a general and wide-ranging discussion of accountability issues and the experiences of other organizations will prepare the staff for more focused dialogue on policies and procedures.

Formalizing Commitment

With people sensitized to the notion of accountability, the process of focusing their attention continues by making a formal and explicit commitment to accountability in the organization's mission statement, operating philosophies, and strategic vision statement. When my employer, the Graduate School of Public and International Affairs at the University of Pittsburgh, redrafted its mission statement, we inserted the following phrase just before the listing of the School's activities and degree programs: We provide the following programs and services and *stand accountable* for relevant outcomes and performance criteria associated with each. Another nonprofit organization with which I have consulted chose to address issues of accountability in several places throughout its statement of operating philosophies and values. Involvement of employees, especially midlevel managers and supervisors, in this process will help build ownership of the ideas and how they are expressed.

The writing of the mission statement is relatively easy. The difficult part is building commitment to the mission and transforming it from words on paper to a blueprint for action. Following my own advice in the section above, here is a story about how one executive breathed new life and meaning into his organization's mission statement.

During a recent seminar for health care executives, I asked the participants to generate ideas on how to build employee commitment to missions. After developing a long list of rather typical approaches (for example, soliciting employee input) the discussion was beginning to wane and I silently wondered how to pull the various ideas together into something of value. Then one of the participants who had been rather quiet throughout the discussion offered the most compelling idea. His organization, like many, gave an award to the "employee of the month" based on typical criteria like exemplary customer service, unbroken attendance, suggestions for a cost-saving, and so forth. But recently this executive announced a change in the criteria for the award—henceforth the employee of the month would be the person whose actions best exemplified the mission of the organization. Almost immediately, copies of the mission statement were circulated by the employees throughout all levels of the organization and, for the first time, they began to read the statement, interpreting its meaning and application to their jobs. The executive admitted that he too was forced to become more familiar with the mission statement, sometimes learning from his own mistakes. "Last week," he said, "A junior employee came to my office, mission statement in hand, and pointed out how one of my recent decisions was not consistent with our mission. It was a humbling experience."

The executive had been reluctant to offer this idea earlier in the discussion because he feared it was too simple or gimmicky. All management strategies should be this simple!

Put Your Resources Where Your Mouth Is

Actions often speak louder than words, and employees pay attention to what leaders do as well as what they say. They will quickly become cynical about accountability initiatives if they perceive that the leader is not willing to devote resources to support the effort, including time and information as well as money.

The investment must be more than a single infusion of resources, announced with fanfare at the start of the initiative. There must be a sustained (even if modest) investment to demonstrate the leader's long-term commitment. People who have studied innovation and planned organizational change have long recognized the difference between the initial adoption of a new tool or procedure and its long-term institutionalization in the routines and culture of the organization (Rogers, 1962; Zaltman, Duncan, and Holbeck, 1973). A critical factor in moving from adoption to institutionalization is a sustained and consistent level of tangible support (resources) from the organization's leaders (Yin, 1979; see also Kanter, 1983, pp. 82–84). For example, in a longitudinal study of productivity programs, Goodman (1982) cites examples where initiatives like quality circles, labor-management committees, and organizational development efforts have enjoyed initial success only to wither and fade over time as leaders turned their attention to more pressing concerns or the latest management fad. It seems we are seeing the same phenomenon more recently with the rapid adoption and subsequent fading of Total Quality Management initiatives; there is evidence that the vast majority of TQM initiatives are not sustained for more than a few years (Brown, 1993; Brown, Hitchcock, and Willard, 1994). Goodman's research suggests that successful institutionalization of new initiatives requires not only initial commitment but periodic recommitment from the organization's leaders.

Thus, with respect to nurturing a climate of accountability, leaders should not assume that their job is finished after they have captured the attention of employees and launched a formal initiative. They should look for opportunities to express their long-term commitment again and again. Can the notion of accountability be built into employee recruitment, selection, and orientation strategies? What types of ongoing training and professional development will be necessary to give employees the tools they need to manage in a dynamic accountability environment? How can accountability best be incorporated in the performance appraisal and reward systems? What types of information will employees need to support an accountability strategy? How can the leader continuously reinforce the ethos of accountability within the organization's culture?

Recognize the Importance of Symbols

The leader's commitment to accountability can be expressed in intangible or symbolic ways as well as with infusion of tangible resources. For example, Gardner notes that effective leadership inevitably involves effective teaching. "People want to know what the problem is, why they are being asked to do certain things, how they relate to the larger picture" (1986, p. 18). Gardner also says that the problems and circumstances of most organizations rarely remain constant over time and that leaders must be prepared to renew the organization by keeping abreast of changing needs and mobilizing resources accordingly (Gardner, 1988a). The two symbolic activities of teaching and renewing often go hand-in-hand as employees rely on leaders to be the boundary-spanners in the organization—to monitor emerging trends outside the organization and to report back by teaching organizational members how to respond to these challenges and opportunities.

Finally, it is important for leaders to remember that they convey important messages about accountability when they lead by example. Employees look to leaders to set the tone and the climate in the organization with their own behavior. Thus, it would be difficult for leaders to have credibility if there are no rigorous mechanisms for holding them accountable for their performance. Leaders must also hold their immediate staff accountable if they want to convey that the same standards apply to everyone in the organization. For example, President Jimmy Carter lost some of his credibility among White House staff when he failed to hold some of his senior advisers to the same high standards of performance and integrity that he so effectively demanded of others and even himself (Fallows, 1979a, 1979b).

Leadership Skills

There are other strategies of leadership, too numerous to discuss in detail. The three discussed here—capturing attention, making a formal commitment, and continuous recommitment—seem especially germane to the topic of serving the public trust and ensuring accountability.

What skills are needed to implement these approaches? To answer this question, let us return to the accountability framework presented earlier in this book.

Compliance

As noted in Chapter Four, compliance with legal and regulatory requirements is essentially a stimulus-response activity catalyzed by the imposition of formal accountability standards. But compliance is rarely a passive or mechanical activity. Thus, the following leadership skills are essential for compliance with mandates imposed by oversight organizations:

- Interpreting formal accountability standards in terms of both the letter and the spirit of the mandate
- Foreseeing the implications of the mandate in terms of its systemic effects on the organization's resources, its processes, its desired outcomes, and its relationships with other organizations
- Designing and implementing structural and procedural mechanisms to ensure compliance with the mandate
- Educating and motivating employees regarding the intent of formal mandates, their implications for the organization's mission, and the imperatives of compliance

Recall from Chapter Four that compliance refers to bureaucratic rules and procedures generated inside the organization as well as to mandates imposed from outside. Thus, leaders not only must mobilize their organization for compliance with external mandates, they also are the principal architects (or at least supervisors) of the organization's own internal accountability infrastructure. The following attributes and skills are important for leaders as they contemplate the imposition of accountability standards within their organization:

- Understanding when internal standards of compliance are critical to the mission and goals of the organization and when they detract from goal accomplishment
- Understanding that formal policies and procedures for compliance are tangible representations of the organization's (and the leader's) espoused values and operating philosophies, and that they will be interpreted as such by workers
- Understanding that subordinates often know their job much better than their leaders and therefore can be a valuable source of advice on the design and implementation of the organization's accountability infrastructure
- Understanding the accountability infrastructure as a system, and recognizing how it can inadvertently reinforce artificial

boundaries between subunits of the organization or between the organization and its strategic environment

Negotiation

The concept of negotiated accountability imposes substantial demands on leaders and requires a special blend of attributes and skills:

- Detecting and interpreting the demands of outside constituencies and other stakeholders, with empathy for their legitimate concerns as well as the organization's own interests and objectives
- Assessing the distribution of power among relevant individuals and coalitions and identifying points of leverage for the organization
- Diagnosing problems and distinguishing causes from symptoms and assessing the range of feasible alternative solutions
- Using negotiating strategies and tactics that focus on the underlying interests of the parties as well as their bargaining positions
- Building lasting trust before, during, and after the negotiations

Discretionary Authority and Entrepreneurship

In a relatively unregulated environment, leaders must take personal responsibility for the discretionary actions of their subordinates. The following leadership skills are essential:

- Reaffirming the core values of the organization and the omnipresence of accountability even in an unregulated environment
- Perceiving when the organization must be protected against itself by implementing self-imposed checks and balances
- Applying a clear sense of mission and vision to detect when discretionary or entrepreneurial ventures are leading the organization astray from its core purpose
- Keeping abreast of the accountability strategies employed by competing or comparable organizations
- Applying the concepts of strategic planning and management to position the organization for emerging trends in the accountability environment

Anticipation and Advocacy

When organizations attempt either to prepare themselves for compliance with anticipated accountability standards or to participate in the policy process that produces those standards, they will be well-served by leaders who have the following attributes and skills:

- Detecting emerging legal and regulatory trends and interpreting them in terms of the needs of the organization and its constituents
- Advocating effectively on behalf of the organization and its constituencies
- Working effectively with legislators, regulators, and other outside stakeholders
- Maintaining credibility as sources of information and advice for legislators, regulators, and others

Certainly, there are many other attributes and skills that leaders can bring to bear on issues of accountability in their organization. But the lists in this chapter represent a good place to start.

Concluding Remarks

It is tempting to conclude a book like this with words of inspiration and encouragement. But, as I stated in the Preface, I believe there is relatively little to be gained by motivational exhortations for public and nonprofit organizations to serve the public trust. First, most of the professionals I know in these two sectors already are committed to the concept of accountability. Second, those who are less committed are not likely to be persuaded by a motivational speech.

I undertook this project to explore for myself and for others the strategic dimension of accountability, somewhat distinct from the intellectual approaches found in the writings of political theorists, organizational behaviorists, and ethicists. While the motivational value of such a pragmatic approach may be limited, I do hope this book inspires readers to reconceptualize accountability as not only a legal and moral imperative but also as a strategic organizational resource to be protected, nourished, and enhanced. Also, I hope the book has provided some useful tools for monitoring the accountability environment and mobilizing resources to address opportunities and challenges proactively as well as reactively. Finally, I hope the book stimulates some creative and critical thinking among both scholars and professional managers regarding conceptual definitions of accountability and strategies for serving the public trust in a variety of organizational contexts.

The world around us grows more complex with every passing day. But the fundamental challenge remains the same: To manage public and nonprofit organizations in a way that is consistent with our implied promise to our constituencies and responsive to their ever-changing standards of performance and accountability.

Special Resource Section: Accountability Worksheets

The worksheets in this section provide a distilled summary of the key questions decision makers should ask as they attempt to implement the approach suggested in this book. The questions and suggested approaches are organized according to the components of the strategic management process outlined in Chapter Three and elaborated on in Chapters Four, Five, and Six.

I hope these worksheets will be especially useful as a step-by-step guide to help decision makers and other participants find their way through the process. But I want to emphasize again that users of this approach should freely adapt the process to fit their own needs.

Worksheet 1

Looking Backward: The Organization's Mandate

The organization's mandate is found in its legal charter, authorizing legislation, by-laws, binding contracts, and any other documents that dictate formal duties and obligations within the interorganizational chain of command and authority. A review of these documents should, at minimum, address the following questions:

1. What does the mandate require in terms of:

a. Scope of service and beneficiaries: _____

_____

_____

_____

b. Internal operating procedures: _____

_____

_____

_____

c. Governance structures and procedures: _____

_____

_____

_____

d. Outcomes and reporting mechanisms: _____

_____

_____

_____

2. What limits or constraints does the mandate place upon the organization? Does it explicitly or implicitly forbid certain activities, programs, or procedures? Is the organization engaged in any of these forbidden activities, programs, or procedures? _____

_____

_____

3. What degrees of freedom, if any, are presented by the mandate? To what extent is the organization engaged in activities, programs, or procedures that are not explicitly addressed in the mandate? _____

_____

_____

_____

4. What reporting relationships and channels of accountability are specified by the mandate? _____

_____

_____

_____

5. Would a reasonable person conclude that the organization's existing programs and procedures are consistent with and supportive of the mandate? _____

_____

_____

_____

Worksheet 2

Looking Forward: Mission and Values

In any organization, the mission statement is the public account-ability document. It represents how decision makers have inter-preted their legal mandate. The mission statement should be widely distributed both internally and externally.

When drafting the mission statement, decision makers should solicit input from internal and external stakeholders in answering the following questions:

1. What business are we in? What business does the public think we are in? What business should we be in? _____

    _____

    _____

    _____

2. What are our core products and services? _____

    _____

    _____

    _____

3. What societal needs are filled by these products and services? How do we assess these needs and account for whether or not they have been met by our products and services? _____

    _____

    _____

    _____

4. Who are our primary clients or beneficiaries and what are their expectations of us? How do they judge our accountability to their expectations? _____

_____

_____

_____

5. Beyond clients and beneficiaries, who else has a stake in what we do and how do they judge our accountability to their interests? _____

_____

_____

_____

6. What values and operating philosophies do we espouse? How are these translated into policies, procedures, and budgetary priorities? Do we follow these values and operating philosophies, or are they merely public relations rhetoric?

_____

_____

_____

7. What are our aspirations and priorities for the future? How will we judge success and failure? _____

_____

_____

_____

The product of these deliberations should be a concise statement that includes the following:

- The purpose of the organization expressed in terms of products, services, targeted customers, and needs filled

- The operating philosophies and values expressed in terms of the organization's self-image, how it perceives its niche or distinctive characteristics in the marketplace, how it makes decisions and manages resources to preserve or enhance its accountability
- The aspirations for the future, expressed in terms of broad strategic goals and priorities

Worksheet 3

Looking Outward: The Accountability Environment

Chapter Four presented a conceptual framework for dividing the accountability environment into four segments for closer scrutiny of opportunities and threats. If decision makers find this process too rigorous for their needs, or beyond their limited resources, they should at minimum ask the following questions about their accountability environment:

1. What external events and trends could affect how accountability is defined and perceived by the organization's constituents and other stakeholders? _____

_____

_____

_____

2. What external events and trends could threaten the ability of the organization to continue serving the public interest and preserving the public trust? _____

_____

_____

_____

3. What external events and trends could damage the credibility of the organization in the eyes of the public? _____

_____

_____

_____

4. What types of accountability challenges and controversies have arisen for other similar organizations? What is the history and context of these controversies? Are there any parallels to our own organization? _____

_____

_____

_____

5. What external events and trends pose the most significant threats to the organization's accountability? _____

_____

_____

_____

6. What external events and trends offer the most promising opportunities for the organization to enhance its accountability?

_____

_____

_____

For decision makers who are convinced that they must segment the accountability environment in order to understand its complexity, here is a cell-by-cell summary of questions presented in the conceptual framework.

Legal Accountability (Cell 1)

1. What are the legal, regulatory, and bureaucratic standards to which the organization is held accountable? _____

_____

_____

_____

2. Who enforces these standards? Who is the higher authority in the accountability chain? _____

_____

_____

_____

3. Over the past five years, what significant changes have taken place in the legal and regulatory environment of the organization? _____

_____

_____

_____

4. Are there any political, economic, social, or technological forces likely to affect the legal and regulatory environment over the next five years? _____

_____

_____

_____

5. Have peer organizations encountered significant problems regarding their compliance with laws and regulations?

_____

_____

_____

6. Does the legal and regulatory environment provide opportunities to enhance the organization's performance in serving the public trust? What strengths and weaknesses will affect our ability to respond to these opportunities? _____

_____

_____

_____

7. Conversely, does the legal and regulatory environment
   pose any threats that will hinder the organization's efforts
   to be accountable to the public trust? What strengths
   and weaknesses will affect our ability to respond to these
   threats? _____

   _____

   _____

   _____

   Participants in the scanning process will be greatly assisted if
they have at their disposal the following information:

- A complete listing of oversight agencies to which the organization is generally accountable or which have jurisdiction
  over selected portions of the organization's mandate and
  mission
- A compilation and analysis of the legal or regulatory standards
  of accountability to which the organization is bound by its
  mandate, charter, authorizing legislation, and contractual
  arrangements with other organizations
- Assessments of how well the organization has performed in
  meeting these standards
- Assessments of compliance with the spirit and the letter of
  the law
- Demonstrated efforts to provide full disclosure of the
  organization's performance in both the spirit and the letter
  of the law

Negotiated Accountability (Cell 2)

1. What are the implicit (nonbinding, nonlegal) standards of
   accountability by which the organization is judged?

   _____

   _____

   _____

2. Over the past five years, have there been significant changes in these implicit standards? _____

_____

_____

_____

3. Are there external stakeholders who are particularly interested in the enforcement of these standards? _____

_____

_____

_____

4. Is the pressure exerted by these stakeholders sufficiently strong to require an immediate tactical response? Are they widely viewed as legitimate representatives of broader interests or other stakeholders? Who is the higher authority in the accountability chain? _____

_____

_____

_____

5. Are any of these accountability standards negotiable? Is the reporting mechanism negotiable? _____

_____

_____

_____

6. What accountability issues currently are being negotiated by similar organizations? What are the likely outcomes of these negotiations? Who have been the most active and influential stakeholders in these negotiations? _____

_____

_____

_____

7. Would it be in the organization's best interest to negotiate now or later? _____

_____

_____

_____

8. On what philosophical or legal grounds should the organization negotiate? _____

_____

_____

_____

9. Does this portion of the accountability environment provide any opportunities for the organization? What strengths and weaknesses will affect our ability to respond to these opportunities? _____

_____

_____

_____

10. Does this portion of the accountability environment pose any threats to the organization? What strengths and weaknesses will affect our ability to respond to these threats? _____

_____

_____

_____

When searching for opportunities to negotiate accountability standards and mechanisms, participants should be guided by several philosophical principles and overriding objectives:

- To clarify the multiple and perhaps conflicting interpretations of the public interest and accountability
- To clarify which (if any) accountability issues in a specific programmatic domain are negotiable and distinguish them from those that are nonnegotiable

- To clarify the respective objectives and interests of various policy stakeholders and separate these objectives and interests from specific proposals or programs to achieve them
- To clarify and agree on reasonable standards of compliance or performance to which an organization or an individual should be held accountable
- To reach agreement on reasonable measures, behaviors, processes, or outcomes with which to assess organizational or personal accountability
- To reach agreement on whether there are uncontrollable factors and contingencies that may affect the accountability relationship to ensure, in advance, that actors are not held responsible for events beyond their control
- To reach agreement on what resources and investments are needed to maintain given levels of accountability and the marginal costs and benefits of incrementally greater (or lesser) degrees of control
- To build trust among the participants in the negotiation process

Discretionary Accountability (Cell 3)

1. In what types of activities is the organization free to exercise substantial discretion, flexibility, and autonomy? _____

   _____

   _____

   _____

2. Within these domains of activity, are there any implicit performance standards that are defined by the competitive marketplace or by professional norms of practice? While formal chains of accountability may not exist, are there any stakeholders who have particular interest in promulgating higher standards of voluntary accountability?

   _____

   _____

   _____

3. Over the past five years, has there been any change in the legal or regulatory environment that allows for greater discretion, flexibility, and autonomy in serving the public trust?

_____

_____

_____

4. Over the past five years, have new management or governance tools emerged that are related to voluntarily serving the public trust? Are these tools becoming widely accepted on a voluntary basis among comparable organizations?

_____

_____

_____

5. Are there any external stakeholders, like watchdog organizations, who are particularly interested in monitoring the organization's exercise of its discretion, flexibility, and autonomy?

_____

_____

_____

6. Can the organization take proactive steps to improve its accountability? _____

_____

_____

7. Have other comparable organizations encountered significant accountability crises due to the inappropriate exercise of discretionary authority or as the result of an entrepreneurial venture? _____

_____

_____

_____

8. Does this portion of the accountability environment present any opportunities for the organization to maintain or enhance its accountability? What strengths and weaknesses will affect our ability to respond to these opportunities?

_____

_____

_____

9. Does this portion of the accountability environment pose any threats that may hinder the organization's efforts to be accountable? What strengths and weaknesses will affect our ability to respond to these threats? _____

_____

_____

_____

When considering discretionary or entrepreneurial ventures, decision makers should consider the following principles:

- Above all, discretionary actions or entrepreneurial ventures must be consistent with the legal mandate and authority of the organization.
- Such actions or ventures should be mission focused and value driven, guided by an explicit and publicly stated set of goals, operating philosophies, and measures of success.
- All participants must take professional responsibility to obtain full information on the risks as well as the potential benefits and to fully understand the detailed mechanics of the proposed initiative—how it works as well as what it is designed to achieve.
- Discretionary programs, especially entrepreneurial ventures, should have an internal (preferably formal) system of checks and balances with which to monitor and assess progress toward objectives as well as the procedural means of achieving those objectives.
- Participants should foster an organizational culture or climate wherein dissenting opinions among participants

and stakeholders not only are tolerated but are encouraged and facilitated.

- Discretionary initiatives, especially entrepreneurial ventures, should be informed by a formal process of scenario construction wherein the participants examine probabilities of various chains of events (however improbable), and consequences of those events, leading to best-case, worst-case, and most-likely scenarios.
- In the absence of meaningful citizen or client input, participants in discretionary ventures should engage in a "rehearsal of defenses" (Cooper, 1990, p. 23) by asking How and to whom would we defend our actions if called upon to do so?
- In the absence of citizen or client input, there should be a mechanism for periodic disclosure of how well the initiative has performed in meeting objectives.
- The disclosure document should be prepared by an independent body.
- Discretionary initiatives, especially entrepreneurial ventures, must have a contingency plan that allows the organization to withdraw or otherwise adjust its commitment if the public interest becomes threatened by unforeseen or uncontrollable events.
- Discretionary investments should be overseen by a review body, with prohibitions against single-bet, winner-take-all investment strategies.

Anticipatory Accountability (Cell 4)

1. What legislative or regulatory actions—pending or emerging—are likely to have the greatest strategic importance for the organization? _____

_____

_____

_____

2. Can the organization influence the outcome or participate in deliberations on these issues? _____

_____

_____

_____

3. Should the organization propose formal standards or reporting channels of accountability to fill a void in the current system? _____

_____

_____

_____

4. Does this portion of the accountability environment present any opportunities for the organization? What strengths and weaknesses will affect our ability to respond to these opportunities? _____

_____

_____

_____

5. Does this portion of the accountability environment pose any threats? What strengths and weaknesses will affect our ability to respond to these threats? _____

_____

_____

_____

Worksheet 4

Looking Inward: Accountability Audit

Chapter Five presented a method for doing an accountability audit that focused on seven organizational variables. If decision makers find this process too rigorous for their needs or beyond their capabilities, they should at least ask the following questions:

1. How well has the organization performed in meeting explicit and implicit accountability standards? Has the organization demonstrated that it is especially effective in meeting certain kinds of accountability standards and, perhaps, less effective in meeting other standards? _____

   _____

   _____

2. Does the organization have appropriate accountability controls and are they working properly? What components of the organization's accountability infrastructure are especially strong? Are any components vulnerable to criticism? _____

   _____

   _____

3. Is the organization devoting sufficient resources to maintaining and enhancing its accountability? If there is need for additional investment of resources, where would these best be spent? _____

   _____

   _____

4. Is the organization positioned to respond effectively to new or emerging performance standards or reporting requirements arising from shifts in the accountability environment? _____

_____

_____

_____

5. What is the organization's current image among key stakeholders? How is the organization currently perceived by key audiences? _____

_____

_____

_____

6. Are there gaps between what the organization wants its constituencies to believe and what they actually believe? If so, what are the probable causes of those gaps? _____

_____

_____

_____

If decision makers want to conduct a more thorough accountability audit, they should carefully examine the following organizational variables:

Financial Resources

1. There is evidence that the organization is regularly audited by an independent professional, in accordance with generally accepted accounting principles, and that problems or shortcomings raised in management letters from the auditor are promptly addressed by the administrators and the governing board. _____

_____

_____

2. There is evidence that individual services and program
    categories also are audited as required by statutory or contrac-
    tual agreement. _____

    _____

    _____

    _____

3. There is evidence that the organization uses its budgeting and
    accounting procedures to assess the relative cost-effectiveness
    of its programs, not just a line-item listing of expenditures
    and revenues. _____

    _____

    _____

    _____

4. There is evidence that the organization manages its finances
    in accordance with generally accepted accounting principles
    and legal requirements. _____

    _____

    _____

    _____

5. There is evidence that the organization follows internal pro-
    cedures, with appropriate checks and balances, to minimize
    the risk of fraud, waste, and abuse in managing its financial
    resources. _____

    _____

    _____

    _____

6. The organization plans its resource development activities
    with a view to ensuring its long-term solvency. _____

    _____

    _____

    _____

7. There is evidence that the majority of the organization's income is spent on programs and activities directly related to the mandate and mission. _____

_____

_____

_____

Human Resources

1. There is evidence that the organization employs personnel who are competent, ethical, and qualified to contribute to the mission. _____

_____

_____

_____

2. There is evidence that the organization follows personnel policies and procedures that promote effective and accountable performance. _____

_____

_____

_____

3. There is evidence that employees are trained to follow internal and external chains of accountability. _____

_____

_____

_____

4. There is evidence that the organization applies appropriate standards of accountability to its volunteers and has volunteer recruitment and management policies to promote effective and accountable performance. _____

_____

_____

Information Resources

1. There is evidence that the organization's information system is designed to provide readily accessible proof of compliance with accountability standards. _____

_____

_____

_____

2. There is evidence that the organization's information system is designed to provide documented program outputs, outcomes, and impacts. _____

_____

_____

_____

3. There is evidence that information on program outputs, outcomes, and impacts is used by decision makers to improve efficiency, effectiveness, and accountability. _____

_____

_____

_____

4. There is evidence that information on performance, outcomes, and finances is regularly shared with relevant stakeholders inside and outside the organization. _____

_____

_____

_____

5. There is evidence that the organization regularly reports its performance to stakeholders inside and outside in annual reports, audited financial statements, and program evaluation reports. _____

_____

_____

6. Where appropriate, the organization has taken steps to ensure confidentiality and security of its information system.

_____

_____

_____

Legal Mandate

1. There is evidence that appropriate documentation establishing the organization's legal authority is in place and up to date.

_____

_____

_____

2. There is evidence that appropriate documentation regarding policies and procedures is in place and followed by the organization. _____

_____

_____

_____

3. There is evidence that the organization is in compliance with relevant legal and regulatory requirements. _____

_____

_____

_____

4. There is evidence that the organization is in compliance with all contractual arrangements with internal and external stakeholders. _____

_____

_____

_____

Networks

1. There is evidence that the organization maintains contact with relevant professional associations to keep abreast of standards of professional practice. _____

   _____

   _____

   _____

2. There is evidence that the organization regularly utilizes formal methods and procedures to monitor the needs of current and prospective clients. _____

   _____

   _____

   _____

3. Where appropriate, the organization seeks ways to work in collaboration with other organizations to achieve its mission.

   _____

   _____

   _____

Image

1. The organization regularly communicates its mission, its goals, its strategies, and its actual performance to relevant constituencies. _____

   _____

   _____

   _____

   _____

2. There is evidence of ongoing two-way communication between the organization and relevant constituencies.

_____

_____

_____

Procedures

1. The organization's mission and operating philosophies demonstrate a commitment to quality and accountability.

_____

_____

_____

2. There is evidence that the pursuit of accountability permeates all levels of the organization. _____

_____

_____

_____

3. The organization and its governing body are structured to achieve the mission, and these structures are consistent with the expressed operating philosophies. _____

_____

_____

_____

4. Program goals are clearly defined, with observable outputs, outcomes, and impacts. _____

_____

_____

_____

5. There is evidence that resources are allocated and managed so as to achieve goals and desired outputs, outcomes, and impacts. _____

_____

_____

_____

6. There is evidence that responsiveness to explicit and implicit standards of accountability is a focus of the organization and is reflected in all of its management and governance procedures. _____

_____

_____

_____

Worksheet 5

Thinking Strategically: Clarifying Strategic Issues

Chapter Six presented a framework for integrating and synthesizing the scans of the external accountability environment and the scan of the internal strengths and weaknesses. If decision makers decide that this synthesizing framework is not appropriate for their needs, they should at least ask the following questions:

1. What key opportunities and threats were uncovered in the scan of the accountability environment? _____

   _____

   _____

   _____

2. Is the organization's accountability strategy in line with these opportunities and threats? Is the strategy appropriate for the type of accountability environment in which the organization operates? _____

   _____

   _____

   _____

3. If the environment provides the organization with substantial discretion to set its own accountability standards, have appropriate steps been taken to ensure that discretionary decision making is not abused? _____

   _____

   _____

4. Conversely, if the accountability environment is primarily rule driven and dominated by regulatory controls, have proper internal procedures and reporting routines been implemented to comply with these requirements?

_____

_____

_____

5. What key strengths and weaknesses were uncovered in the accountability audit? _____

_____

_____

_____

6. Is the organization's accountability strategy well matched to its mission, goals, objectives, and tasks? _____

_____

_____

_____

7. Is the organization's accountability strategy consistent with its professional culture, its values, and its historical evolution?

_____

_____

_____

8. Does the accountability strategy play to the organization's strengths or to its weaknesses? _____

_____

_____

_____

_____

A more thorough effort to identify strategic issues will require reflection on the following issue areas:

Comparative Advantage Issues

1. Does the organization have any accountability strengths that are particularly germane to specific opportunities in the accountability environment? _____

   _____

   _____

   _____

2. What are the organization's comparative advantages with respect to serving the public interest and preserving the public trust? _____

   _____

   _____

   _____

3. What strategies are appropriate to nurture and protect these comparative advantages? _____

   _____

   _____

   _____

Mobilization Issues

1. Does the organization have any accountability strengths that can help it respond effectively to emerging threats in the accountability environment? _____

   _____

   _____

   _____

2. What mobilization strategies should be pursued to ensure that these strengths help the organization avoid or minimize the negative impacts of the threats? _____

_____

_____

_____

Investment Issues

1. Is the organization constrained in its efforts to take advantage of certain accountability opportunities because of internal limitations or weaknesses? _____

_____

_____

_____

2. Can these weaknesses be overcome with a reasonable investment of resources? _____

_____

_____

_____

3. If not, is it desirable for the organization to divest these weaknesses by, for example, shedding weak programs or altering its mission to focus on strengths, not weaknesses? _____

_____

_____

_____

4. Is it possible to address these weaknesses through some type of formal or informal collaboration or partnership with another organization? _____

_____

_____

Damage Control Issues

1. In what ways is the organization especially vulnerable to accountability challenges and threats? How do its weaknesses play into threats in the external environment? _____

_____

_____

_____

2. Is it possible to develop a damage control strategy in advance?

_____

_____

_____

3. Following an accountability crisis, how can the credibility and focus of the organization be restored? _____

_____

_____

_____

References

Ackoff, R. *Redesigning the Future: A Systems Approach to Societal Problems.* New York: Wiley, 1974.

Allison, G. T. "Public and Private Management: Are They Fundamentally Alike in All Unimportant Respects?" In R. J. Stillman (ed.), *Public Administration: Concepts and Cases.* (4th ed.) Boston: Houghton Mifflin, 1988.

Anthony, R. *Management Control in Nonprofit Organizations.* Homewood, Ill.: Dow Jones-Irwin, 1988.

Baily, S. K. "Ethics and the Public Service." In R. J. Stillman (ed.), *Public Administration: Concepts and Cases.* (4th ed.) Boston: Houghton Mifflin, 1988.

Barry, B. W. *Strategic Planning Workbook for Nonprofit Organizations.* St. Paul, Minn.: Wilder Foundation, 1986.

Barry, D. D., and Whitcomb, H. R. *The Legal Foundations of Public Administration.* St. Paul, Minn.: West, 1981.

Beck, S. A., Meadowcroft, P., and Kiely, E. S. "Multi-Agency Outcome Evaluation of Children's Services: A Case Study." *Journal of Mental Health Administration,* forthcoming.

Bellone, C. J., and Goerl, G. F. "Reconciling Public Entrepreneurship and Democracy," *Public Administration Review.* 1992, *52*(2), 130–134.

Bennett, J. T. *Unfair Competition: The Profits of Nonprofits.* Lanham, Md.: Hamilton Press, 1989.

Bennett, J. T., and DiLorenzo, T. J. *Unhealthy Charities.* New York: Basic Books, 1994.

Bennis, W. *Why Leaders Can't Lead: The Unconscious Conspiracy Continues.* San Francisco: Jossey-Bass, 1989.

Bennis, W., and Nanus, B. *Leaders: The Strategies for Taking Charge.* New York: HarperCollins, 1985.

Bookman, M. *Protecting Your Organization's Tax Exempt Status: A Guide for Nonprofit Managers.* San Francisco: Jossey-Bass, 1992.

Bowman, J. S. (ed.). *Ethical Frontiers in Public Management: Seeking New Strategies for Resolving Ethical Dilemmas.* San Francisco: Jossey-Bass, 1991.

231

Bremner, R. H. *Giving: Charity and Philanthropy in History.* New Brunswick, N.J.: Transaction Press, 1994.

Brown, M. G. "Why Does Total Quality Fail in Two Out of Three Tries?" *The Journal for Quality and Participation,* Mar. 1993, *16*(2), 80–89.

Brown, M. G., Hitchcock, D. E., and Willard, M. L. *Why TQM Fails and What to Do About It.* Burr Ridge, Ill.: Irwin Professional, 1994.

Bryson, J. M. *Strategic Planning for Public and Nonprofit Organizations: A Guide to Strengthening and Sustaining Organizational Achievement.* San Francisco: Jossey-Bass, 1988.

Buckholdt, D. R., and Gubrium, J. F. "Practicing Accountability in Human Service Institutions." *Urban Life,* Oct. 1983, *12*(3), 249–268.

Burke, J. *Bureaucratic Responsibility.* Baltimore: Johns Hopkins University Press, 1986.

Carver, J. *Boards That Make a Difference: A New Design for Leadership in Nonprofit and Public Organizations.* San Francisco: Jossey-Bass, 1990.

Certo, S., and Peter, J. P. *Strategic Management: Concepts and Applications.* New York: Random House, 1988.

Chait, R. P., and Taylor, B. E. "Charting the Territory of Nonprofit Boards." *Harvard Business Review,* Jan./Feb. 1989, *67*(1), 44–54.

Clark, J. "The Greensburg YMCA." Unpublished paper, 1991.

Cooper, T. *The Responsible Administrator: An Approach to Ethics for the Administrative Role.* San Francisco: Jossey-Bass, 1990.

Council of Better Business Bureaus. *Standards for Charitable Solicitations.* Arlington, Va.: Council of Better Business Bureaus, 1982.

Cyert, R. M. "How Managers Can Be Leaders." *Pittsburgh Post-Gazette,* February 12, 1995, p. E-1.

Davis, T.R.V., and Patrick, M. S. "Benchmarking at the Sun Health Alliance." *Planning Review,* Jan./Feb. 1993, *21*(1), 28–31.

Day, G. S. "Diagnosing The Product Portfolio." *Journal of Marketing,* Apr. 1977, *41*(2), 29–38.

Dayton, K. N. *Governance is Governance.* Occasional Paper Series, Washington, D.C.: Independent Sector, 1987.

Drucker, P. F. "What Business Can Learn from Nonprofits." *Harvard Business Review,* July/Aug. 1989, *67*(4), 88–93.

Drucker, P. F. "Judge Nonprofits by Their Performance, Not Only by Their Good Intentions." *Chronicle of Philanthropy,* Oct. 2, 1990, *2*(24), 32.

Dunn, W. N. *Public Policy Analysis.* Englewood Cliffs, N.J.: Prentice-Hall, 1994.

Egol, M. "Information for Public Advantage: A New Concept of Government Accountability." *Vital Speeches of the Day,* Dec. 15, 1988, *55*(5), 149–152.

Espy, S. *Handbook of Strategic Planning for Nonprofit Organizations.* New York: Praeger, 1986.

Espy, S. *Marketing Strategies for Nonprofit Organizations.* Chicago: Lyceum, 1993.

Estes, C., Binney, E. A., and Bergthold, L. "How the Legitimacy of the Sector Has Eroded." In V. A. Hodgkinson, R. W. Lyman, and Associates (eds.), *The Future of the Nonprofit Sector: Challenges, Changes, and Policy Considerations.* San Francisco: Jossey-Bass, 1989.

Fallows, J. "The Passionless Presidency: The Trouble with Jimmy Carter's Administration (Part I)." *Atlantic Monthly,* May 1979a, *243*(6), 33–48.

Fallows, J. "The Passionless Presidency: The Trouble with Jimmy Carter's Administration (Part II)." *Atlantic Monthly,* June 1979b, *243*(7), 75–81.

Finer, H. "Administrative Responsibility in Democratic Government." *Public Administration Review,* Summer 1941, *1*(4), 335–350.

Fisher, R., and Ury, W. *Getting to Yes: Negotiating Agreement Without Giving In.* New York: Penguin, 1981.

Ford, S. "The Oakland Library Consortium." Unpublished paper, 1991.

Freedman, N., and Van Ham, K. "Strategic Planning in Philips." In B. Taylor and D. Hussey (eds.), *The Realities of Planning.* Elmsford, N.J.: Pergamon Press, 1982.

Fremont-Smith, M. R. "Trends in Accountability and Regulation of Nonprofits." In V. A. Hodgkinson, R. W. Lyman, and Associates (eds.), *The Future of the Nonprofit Sector: Challenges, Changes, and Policy Considerations.* San Francisco: Jossey-Bass, 1989.

French, R., and Howey, B. "Mental Health Facility's Priorities Draw Fire." *Fort Wayne Journal Gazette,* January 10, 1993, p. 1A, 6A.

Friedrich, C. J. "Public Policy and the Nature of Administrative Responsibility." In C. J. Friedrich and E. S. Mason (eds.), *Public Policy.* Cambridge, Mass.: Harvard University Press, 1940.

Gardner, J. "The Tasks of Leadership." *Leadership Series #2.* Washington, D.C.: Independent Sector, 1986.

Gardner, J. "Renewing: The Leader's Creative Task." *Leadership Series #10.* Washington, D.C.: Independent Sector, 1988a.

Gardner, J. "The Changing Nature of Leadership." *Leadership Series #11.* Washington, D.C.: Independent Sector, 1988b.

Gaul, G., and Borowski, N. *Free Ride: The Tax-Exempt Economy.* Kansas City, Mo.: Andrews and McMeel, 1993a.

Gaul, G., and Borowski, N. "Nonprofits: America's Growth Industry." *Philadelphia Inquirer,* Apr. 18, 1993b, p. 1, 10–12.

Geneen, H., with Moscow, A. *Managing.* New York: Avon, 1984.

Glaser, J. *The United Way Scandal: An Insider's Account of What Went Wrong and Why.* New York: Wiley, 1993.

Goldberg, D. "Letter to the Editor." *Pittsburgh Post-Gazette,* Apr. 14, 1994, p. B-2.

Goldin, H. J. "How Orange County Can Dig Out of Its Hole." *Wall Street Journal,* Dec. 14, 1994, p. A12.

Goodman, P. S. "Why Productivity Programs Fail: Reasons and Solutions." *National Productivity Review,* Autumn 1982, *1*(4), 369–380.

Goodsell, C. T. *The Case for Bureaucracy: A Public Administration Polemic.* (2nd ed.) Chatham, N.J.: Chatham House, 1985.

Gordon, T. J., and Hayward, H. "Initial Experiments with the Cross-Impact Matrix Method of Forecasting." *Futures,* 1968, *1*(2), 101.

Gore, A. *From Red Tape to Results: Creating a Government That Works Better and Costs Less.* Washington, D.C.: National Performance Review, 1993.

Gortner, H. F. *Ethics for Public Managers.* New York: Greenwood Press, 1991.

Gortner, H. F., Mahler, J., and Nicholson, J. B. *Organization Theory: A Public Perspective.* Chicago: Dorsey Press, 1987.

Grant, J. H., and King, W. R. *The Logic of Strategic Planning.* Boston: Little, Brown, 1982.

Gross, M. *Financial and Accounting Guide for Not-for-Profit Organizations.* New York: Wiley, 1991.

Gruber, J. E. *Controlling Bureaucracies: Dilemmas in Democratic Governance.* Berkeley: University of California Press, 1987.

Hall, P. D. "A Historical Overview of the Private Nonprofit Sector." In W. W. Powell (ed.), *The Nonprofit Sector: A Research Handbook.* New Haven, Conn.: Yale University Press, 1987a.

Hall, P. D. "Abandoning the Rhetoric of Independence: Reflections on the Nonprofit Sector in the Post-Liberal Era." In S. A. Ostrander, S. Langston, and J. Van Til (eds.), *Shifting the Debate: Public/Private Sector Relations in the Modern Welfare State.* New Brunswick, N.J.: Transaction Books, 1987b.

Hammer, M., and Champy, J. *Reengineering the Corporation: A Manifesto for Business Revolution.* New York: HarperCollins, 1993.

Hart, S. L. "An Integrative Framework for Strategy-Making Processes." *Academy of Management Review,* Apr. 1992, *17*(2), 327–351.

Hayllar, B. "Charity Begins at City Hall," *Pittsburgh Post-Gazette,* Dec. 12, 1990, p. 7.

Hedley, B. "Strategy and the Business Portfolio." *Long Range Planning,* Feb. 1977, *10*(1), 9–15.

Henson, H. H. *The Analysis of Leadership.* London: Oxford University Press, 1934.

Herman, R. D., and Heimovics, R. D. *Executive Leadership in Nonprofit Organizations: New Strategies for Shaping Executive-Board Dynamics.* San Francisco: Jossey-Bass, 1991.

Herman, T., and Lambert, W. "Filing Spotlights Murky Corner of Finance." *Wall Street Journal,* Dec. 8, 1994, p. A9.

Hersey, P., and Blanchard, K. *Management of Organizational Behavior.* (4th ed.) Englewood Cliffs, N.J.: Prentice–Hall, 1982.

Herzlinger, R. E. "Effective Oversight: A Guide for Nonprofit Directors." *Harvard Business Review,* July/Aug. 1994, *72*(4), 52–59.

Herzlinger, R. E., and Krasker, W. S. "Who Profits from Nonprofits?" *Harvard Business Review,* Jan./Feb. 1987, *65*(1), 93–106.

Hirschman, A. *Exit, Voice and Loyalty.* Cambridge, Mass.: Harvard University Press, 1970.

Hofmeister, S. "A Strategy's Creator Also Drafted the Law." *New York Times,* Dec. 8, 1994, p. C16.

Hopkins, B. *The Law of Tax Exempt Organizations.* New York: Wiley, 1992.

Hopkins, B. *A Legal Guide to Starting and Managing a Nonprofit Organization.* New York: Wiley, 1993.

Horton, T. R. *The CEO Paradox: The Privilege and Accountability of Leadership.* New York: American Management Association, 1992.

Independent Sector. *Ethics and the Nation's Voluntary and Philanthropic Community: Obedience to the Unenforceable.* Washington, D.C.: Independent Sector, 1991.

Isenberg, D. "How Senior Managers Think." *Harvard Business Review,* Nov./Dec. 1984, *84*(6), 81–90.

Jones, D. R. "Crisis Management: When Bad Things Happen to Good Organizations." *Nonprofit Times,* November 1992, pp. 1, 54–55.

Kahn, R. "How Much is Too Much in Nonprofit Compensation?" *Nonprofit Times,* Apr. 1992, p. 18.

Kanter, D. L., and Mirvis, P. H. *The Cynical Americans: Living and Working in an Age of Discontent and Disillusion.* San Francisco: Jossey-Bass, 1989.

Kanter, R. M. *The Change Masters.* New York: Simon & Schuster, 1983.

Kanter, R. M., and Summers, D. "Doing Well While Doing Good: Dilemmas of Performance Management in Nonprofit Organizations and the Need for a Multiple-Constituency Approach." In W. W. Powell (ed.), *The Nonprofit Sector: A Research Handbook.* New Haven, Conn.: Yale University Press, 1987.

Kearns, K. P. "From Comparative Advantage to Damage Control: Clarifying Strategic Issues Using SWOT Analysis." *Nonprofit Management and Leadership,* 1992, *3*(1), 3–22.

Kearns, K. P. "The Strategic Management of Accountability in Nonprofit Organizations: An Analytic Framework." *Public Administration Review,* 1994, *54*(2), 185–192.

Kearns, K. P., Krasman, R. J., and Meyer, W. J. "Why Nonprofit Organizations Are Ripe for Total Quality Management." *Nonprofit Management and Leadership,* 1994, *4*(4), 447–460.

King, W. R., and Cleland, D. I. *Strategic Planning and Policy.* New York: Petrochelli/Charter, 1978.

Kingsley, J. D. *Representative Bureaucracy.* Yellow Springs, Ohio: Antioch University Press, 1944.

Knecht, G. B. "Merrill Lynch's Role as Broker to the Fund May Expose It to Liability, Lawyers Say." *Wall Street Journal,* Dec. 8, 1994, p. A9.

Koteen, J. *Strategic Management in Public and Nonprofit Organizations.* New York: Praeger, 1989.

Kotler, P. *Marketing for Nonprofit Organizations.* (2nd ed.) Englewood Cliffs, N.J.: Prentice-Hall, 1982.

Kouzes, J. M., and Posner, B. Z. *Credibility: How Leaders Gain It and Lose It.* San Francisco: Jossey-Bass, 1993.

Krislov, S., and Rosenbloom, D. H. *Representative Bureaucracy and the American Political System.* New York: Praeger, 1981.

Lederman, L. L. "Foresight Activities in the U.S.A.: Time for a Reassessment?" *Long-Range Planning,* June 1984, *17*(3), 41–50.

Levine, C. H., Peters, B. G., and Thompson, F. J. *Public Administration: Challenges, Choices, Consequences.* Glenview, Ill.: Scott, Foresman, 1990.

Levis, W. C. "Taking IRS Form 990 Seriously." *Philanthropy Monthly,* Mar. 1992, *25*(14) p. 1.

Lewis, C. W. *The Ethics Challenge in Public Service: A Problem-Solving Guide.* San Francisco: Jossey-Bass, 1991.

Lorentzen, P. B. "Organizational Evil: Concepts and Practices." In C. Bellavita (ed.), *How Public Organizations Work: Learning From Experience.* New York: Praeger, 1990.

MacMillan, I. C. "Competitive Strategies for Not-for-Profit Agencies." In R. Lamb (ed.), *Advances in Strategic Management.* Vol. I. Greenwich, Conn.: JAI Press, 1983.

Madison, J. "Federalist Paper #57." In A. Hamilton, J. Madison, and J. Jay, *The Federalist Papers.* New York: New American Library, 1961. (Originally published 1788.)

Madsen, P., and Shafritz, J. M. (eds.). *Essentials of Government Ethics.* New York: Meridian, 1992.

Mansfield, H. "Accountability and Congressional Oversight." In B.L.R. Smith and J. Carroll (eds.), *Improving the Accountability and Performance of Government.* Washington, D.C.: Brookings Institution, 1982.

Mehegan, S. "Local Watchdogs Step Up Charity Monitoring." *Nonprofit Times,* Feb. 1995, pp. 1, 5, 10.

Meyers, G. C. *When It Hits the Fan: Managing the Nine Crises of Business.* New York: Penguin, 1986.

Millar, B. "United Way in Florida Battles Group's National Leaders." *Chronicle of Philanthropy,* Mar. 10, 1992, *4*(10), 32.

Mintzberg, H. "The Fall and Rise of Strategic Planning." *Harvard Business Review,* Jan./Feb. 1994a, *72*(1), 107–114.

Mintzberg, H. *The Rise and Fall of Strategic Planning.* New York: Free Press, 1994b.

Mitroff, I., and Emshoff, J. "On Strategic Assumption-Making: A Dialectical Approach to Policy and Planning." *Academy of Management Review,* 1979, *4*(1), 1–12.

Moe, R. C. "The 'Reinventing Government' Exercise: Misinterpreting the Problem, Misjudging the Consequences." *Public Administration Review,* 1994, *54*(2), 111–122.

Moore, J. "Peggy Charren's Closing ACT." *Chronicle of Philanthropy,* July 28, 1992, *4*(20), 1, 25–26.

Moore, J. "Non-Profit Advocates' Latest Tool: Technology." *Chronicle of Philanthropy,* Oct. 4, 1994, *6*(25), 1, 40–42.

Moore, J., Rocque, A., and Williams, G. "A Debacle for Charities' Credibility." *Chronicle of Philanthropy,* June 1, 1995, *7*(16), 1, 24, 29.

Murray, V. "Is Carver's Model Really the One Best Way?" *Front and Centre,* Sept. 1994, *1*(5).

Mydans, S. "Shock and Confusion In Offices and Streets." *New York Times,* Dec. 8, 1994, p. C16.

National Commission on State and Local Public Service. *Hard Truths/ Tough Choices: An Agenda for State and Local Reform.* (Winter Commission Report.) Albany, N.Y.: Nelson A. Rockefeller Institute of Government, 1993.

"New Era Scandal: A Chronology of Legal Actions Taken Thus Far." *Chronicle of Philanthropy,* 1995, (7), 27.

Nielsen, W. A. "Reporters, Not Trustees, Make the Best Watchdogs." *Chronicle of Philanthropy,* Mar. 24, 1992, *4*(11), 41–42.

Nutt, P. C., and Backoff, R. W. *Strategic Management of Public and Third Sector Organizations: A Handbook for Leaders.* San Francisco: Jossey-Bass, 1992.

O'Connell, B. *Evaluating Results.* Occasional Papers in Nonprofit Management, no. 9. Washington, D.C.: Independent Sector, 1988.

Olenick, A., and Olenick, P. *A Nonprofit Organization Operating Manual.* New York: Foundation Center, 1991.

Osborne, D., and Gaebler, T. *Reinventing Government.* Reading, Mass.: Addison-Wesley, 1992.

Paul, S. *Strengthening Public Service Accountability: A Conceptual Framework.* Discussion Paper Series, no. 136. Washington, D.C.: World Bank, 1991.

Paul, S. "Accountability in Public Services: Exit, Voice, and Control." *World Development,* 1992, *20*(7), 1047–1059.

Pearce, J. A., Freeman, E. A., and Robinson, R. B. "The Tenuous Link Between Formal Strategic Planning and Financial Performance." *Academy of Management Review,* Oct. 1987, *12*(4), 658–675.

Petersen, J. E. "It's Better Not To Belly-up." *Governing,* Feb. 1995, *8*(5), 56.

Porter, M. *Competitive Advantage: Creating and Sustaining Superior Performance.* New York: Free Press, 1985.

Pratt, J. "Nonprofit Accountability: Internal Scrutiny Needed to Keep Public Trust." Minnesota Council of Nonprofits, Working Paper, Aug. 14, 1992.

Pressley Ridge Schools. *Follow-up Project: 1993 Report.* Pittsburgh, Pa.: Pressley Ridge Schools, 1994.

Pressley Ridge Schools. *SumOne for Kids Sample Management Reports.* Pittsburgh, Pa.: Pressley Ridge Schools, 1995a.

Pressley Ridge Schools. *SumOne for Kids Self-Instructional Guide.* Pittsburgh, Pa.: Pressley Ridge Schools, 1995b.

"Public Finance Chiefs Are Often Very Boring; That's the Good News." *Wall Street Journal,* Dec. 8, 1994, p. 1.

Raiffa, H. *Decision Analysis.* Reading, Mass.: Addison-Wesley, 1968.

Rhyne, L. C. "The Relationship Of Strategic Planning to Financial Performance." *Strategic Management Journal,* Sept./Oct. 1986, *7*(5), 423–436.

Ries, A., and Trout, J. *Positioning: The Battle For Your Mind.* New York: Warner Books, 1981.

Rogers, E. M. *Diffusion of Innovations.* New York: Free Press, 1962.

Rohr, J. *To Run a Constitution: The Legitimacy of the Administrative State.* Lawrence: University of Kansas Press, 1986.

Rohr, J. *Ethics for Bureaucrats: An Essay on Law and Values.* (2nd ed.) New York: Dekker, 1989.

Romzek, B., and Dubnick, M. J. "Accountability in the Public Sector: Lessons from the *Challenger* Tragedy." *Public Administration Review,* 1987, *47*(3), 227–38.

Rosen, B. *Holding Government Bureaucracies Accountable.* (2nd ed.) New York: Praeger, 1989.

Rosenbloom, D. H. *The Federal Service and the Constitution: The Development of the Public Employment Relationship.* Ithaca, N.Y.: Cornell University Press, 1971.

Rosenbloom, D. H., and Carroll, J. D. *Toward Constitutional Competence: A Casebook for Public Administrators.* Englewood Cliffs, N.J.: Prentice-Hall, 1990.

Rotstein, G. "Domestic Disillusionment: Crawford Square's New Tenants Report Series of Problems." *Pittsburgh Post-Gazette,* Mar. 10, 1994, p. B-5.

Rubin, H. "Dimensions of Institutional Ethics: A Framework for Interpreting the Ethical Context of the Nonprofit Sector." In D. L. Gies, J. S. Ott, and J. M. Shafritz (eds.), *The Nonprofit Organization: Essential Readings.* Pacific Grove, Calif.: Brooks/Cole, 1990.

Saaty, T. L. *The Analytic Hierarchy Process.* New York: McGraw-Hill, 1980.

Saaty, T. L., and Kearns, K. P. *Analytical Planning: The Organization of Systems.* Elmsford, N.Y.: Pergamon Press, 1985.

Salamon, L. *America's Nonprofit Sector: A Primer.* New York: Foundation Center, 1992.

Schaffir, W. B., and Lobe, T. J. "Strategic Planning: The Impact at Five Companies." *Planning Review,* Mar. 1984, *12*(2), 39–41.

Scrivner, G. "100 Years of Tax Policy Changes Affecting Charitable Organizations." In D. L Gies, J. S. Ott, and J. M. Shafritz (eds.), *The Nonprofit Organization: Essential Readings.* Pacific Grove, Calif.: Brooks/Cole, 1990.

Sennot, C. *Broken Covenant.* New York: Simon & Schuster, 1992.

Shafritz, J. M. *The HarperCollins Dictionary of American Government and Politics.* New York: HarperCollins, 1992.

Sheridan, J. H. "Where Benchmarkers Go Wrong." *Industry Week,* Mar. 15, 1993, *24*(6), 28–34.

Simon, J. G. "The Tax Treatment of Nonprofit Organizations: A Review of Federal and State Policies." In W. W. Powell (ed.), *The Nonprofit Sector: A Research Handbook.* New Haven, Conn.: Yale University Press, 1987.

Smith, B.L.R. "Accountability and Independence in the Contract State." In B.L.R. Smith and D. C. Hague (eds.), *The Dilemma of Accountability in Modern Government: Independence Versus Control.* New York: St. Martin's Press, 1971.

Staats, E. "Governmental Performance in Perspective: Achievements and Challenges." In B.L.R. Smith and J. Carroll (eds.), *Improving the Accountability and Performance of Government.* Washington, D.C.: Brookings Institution, 1982.

Starling, G. *Managing the Public Sector.* (3rd ed.) Chicago: Dorsey Press, 1986.

Stecklow, S. "A Big Charity Faces Tough Questions About Its Financing." *Wall Street Journal,* May 15, 1995, pp. 1, A8.

Steinberg, R. "Nonprofit Organizations and the Market." In W. W. Powell (ed.), *The Nonprofit Sector: A Research Handbook.* New Haven, Conn.: Yale University Press, 1987.

Tead, O. *The Art of Leadership.* New York: McGraw-Hill, 1935.

Terry, L. D. "Why We Should Abandon the Misconceived Quest to Reconcile Public Entrepreneurship with Democracy." *Public Administration Review,* 1993, *53*(4), 393–395.

Thompson, A., and Strickland, A. J. *Strategic Management: Concepts and Cases.* (6th ed.) Homewood, Ill.: Dow Jones-Irwin, 1992.

Thompson, D. F. *Political Ethics and Public Office.* Cambridge, Mass.: Harvard University Press, 1987.

United Way of Allegheny County. "Allocation Decision Criteria and Program Evaluation Instrument." Pittsburgh, Pa.: United Way of Allegheny County, 1995.

VanDenBerg, J., Beck, S, and Howarth, D. "What Pennsylvanians Want From Children's Services: Summary of the Social Validation Survey." Pittsburgh, Pa.: Center for Research and Public Policy, Pressley Ridge Schools, 1992.

Wayne, L. "The Search for Municipal 'Cowboys.'" *New York Times,* Dec. 8, 1994, p. C1.

Weber, M. "Bureaucracy." In J. M. Shafritz and A. C. Hyde (eds.), *Classics of Public Administration.* Chicago: Dorsey, 1987. (Originally published 1922.)

Wensley, R. "Strategic Marketing: Betas, Boxes, or Basics?" *Journal of Marketing,* Summer 1981, *45*(3), 173–182.

Wheelen, T., and Hunger, J. D. *Strategic Management.* (3rd ed.) Reading, Mass.: Addison-Wesley, 1990.

White, L. *Introduction to the Study of Public Administration.* New York: Macmillan, 1926.

Williams, G. "End of New Era Sparks Renewed Debate Over the State of Charity Regulation." *Chronicle of Philanthropy,* June 1, 1995, *7*(16), 30.

Wilson, W. "The Study of Administration." In J. M. Shafritz and A. C. Hyde (eds.), *Classics of Public Administration.* Chicago: Dorsey, 1987. (Originally published 1887.)

Yin, R. K. *Changing Urban Bureaucracies: How New Practices Become Routine.* Lexington, Mass.: Lexington Press, 1979.

Young, D. *Profit-Making by Nonprofits.* Cleveland: Mandel Center for Nonprofit Organizations, 1988.

Zaltman, G. R., Duncan, R., and Holbeck, J. *Innovations and Organizations.* New York: Wiley, 1973.

Zartman, I. W., and Berman, M. *The Practical Negotiator.* New Haven, Conn.: Yale University Press, 1982.

Index

Note: *Italic* page numbers reference worksheets, diagrams, and tables.